WELLINGTON'S
RIFLES

WELLINGTON'S
RIFLES

THE BRITISH LIGHT INFANTRY AND RIFLE REGIMENTS, 1758–1815

RAY CUSICK

FOREWORD BY IAN FLETCHER

Contents

Acknowledgements

Shortly after he had completed the manuscript of this book, Ray Cusick's health, which had not been good for some time, began to deteriorate further. Sadly, he died before he could see his book in print. As a consequence he was unable to thank those people who had helped him in the preparation of *Wellington's Rifles*.

Though I do not know all those who assisted and supported Ray, I do know that Ray, a former Rifleman, received considerable guidance from the Royal Green Jackets (Rifles) Museum at Winchester. Ray also benefited from the encouragement of historian Ian Fletcher who, in addition, provided the Foreword to this book. Though Ian may not remember, it was originally his idea that Ray should write a book on the development of the British rifle regiments, which ultimately led to *Wellington's Rifles*.

Many thanks must also be given to Richard Doherty who diligently edited the manuscript. His kind patience and consideration, combined with his great depth of knowledge, proved absolutely vital in editing Ray's manuscript.

Ray had provided detailed footnotes to accompany the text of the book but these still had to be finalized before he passed away. Rather than include incomplete notes, Richard and I have decided to omit them.

I was the one who eventually persuaded Ray to write this book. He had published so much material detailing the battles and skirmishes that the likes of the 5/60th and the 95th Rifles had been involved in that he was the natural choice to write a book of this nature.

Though the study of the early days of the rifle regiments of the British Army will be much the poorer for his passing, *Wellington's Rifles* will be a lasting legacy that will benefit us all.

John Grehan
Assistant Editor
Britain at War Magazine
March 2013

Foreword

When Sir Arthur Wellesley sailed to the Iberian Peninsula in the summer of 1808 he had a fairly good idea of the tactics he would use to defeat Napoleon's all-conquering legions. During the previous three years the French had defeated the very best that the Austrians, Russians and Prussians could throw at them at such battles as Austerlitz, Jena, Friedland and Eylau. The British army, on the other hand, sailed to the Peninsula on the back of embarrassing reverses in Egypt and South America, both of which had occurred in 1807. So how, it may be asked, did Wellesley think he would be able to achieve what the armies of various other nations had failed to do? Well, for a start he was not up against Napoleon himself – that would have to wait until 1815, when he duly defeated him, with the help of the Prussians – but he was, nevertheless, up against some of the emperor's best marshals. Indeed, a succession of those marshals of France, Soult, Mortier, Ney, Marmont, Victor, Jourdan and Masséna, would in turn be defeated by Wellesley, who would become Wellington in 1809. So, just how did he intend to defeat the French? Well, apart from having great belief in his own abilities he always thought steady troops, in line, were capable of overcoming French armies, which habitually fought in column. Of course, there was much more to it than this simple expedient. Indeed, from the very first defensive battle that Wellesley fought, at Vimeiro on 21 August 1808, he demonstrated his use of the ground, of a heavy skirmish line, his judicious use of artillery and, of course, his deployment of infantry in line. The tactics worked a treat and, indeed, had it not been for the misadventures of the 20th Light Dragoons his victory at Vimeiro was almost a total success, tactics-wise.

The Battle of Vimeiro has, however, given rise to a myth, that of Wellington habitually deploying his troops on a reverse slope, out of sight of the French, using his lines to defeat the French wherever and whenever. However, when one examines the battles Wellington fought in the Peninsula we find few examples of the use of such tactics. Indeed, Wellington has suffered much over the years from what might be termed 'the Waterloo factor'. The most enduring images of Waterloo are of Allied troops, out of sight on a reverse slope, forming squares to face cavalry and, finally, forming line to defeat the Guard at the climax of the battle. As Waterloo was his most famous victory this image is understandable. But between Vimeiro and Waterloo there are surprisingly few examples of Wellington employing these sorts of mythical tactics against the French. Busaco is perhaps the classic example, whilst Sorauren qualifies also.

But there were no reverse slopes at Talavera, Fuentes de Oñoro, the Nive or Salamanca, whilst Vitoria, the Nivelle, Orthes, and Toulouse were all offensive actions, as were the great sieges. Thus, Wellington suffers from what might be called 'the Waterloo factor', for the popular image of his armies being deployed on a reverse slope, and fighting in line at all of his battles is a false one.

There is no doubt, however, that when his lines were employed against French columns they rarely failed to deliver him victory. It was, in some ways, a simple mathematical equation that the French never really came to appreciate in the Peninsula; that a column of, for example, 1,200 men, with a frontage of thirty men and a depth of forty, may well outnumber a line of, say, 600 by two to one. However, in terms of firepower, the 600-strong line outgunned the 1,200-strong column by ten to one, simply because the column had locked its firepower carefully away in the depths of its formation. There was, of course, more to it than this; as stated above, the use of ground and artillery played an important part, but steady troops in line, covered initially by a heavy screen of light troops, were always and did always emerge victorious in the Peninsula. Indeed, only once, at Sorauren on 28 July 1813, did French columns break an Allied line, and only then very briefly.

The use of linear tactics was nothing new in the British army, however, and was certainly not an expedient that Wellington introduced. He simply took what was on offer, tailored it to his own specifications and took it from there. This 'tailoring' involved the use of a heavy screen of light troops who would operate in front of his main battle line, countering the French skirmishers whose job it was to shield their main attacking columns from Allied fire until the final moment, at which point they would move aside and allow the column to engage the Allies. The problem for the French was, however, that Wellington's own skirmish line was often so effective that the main attacking columns were often employed against it, let alone against the main Allied line. Indeed, by the end of the Peninsular War Wellington's light troops – and in particular his Light Division – had become one of the most important elements in his army. This did not happen overnight, however. Indeed, it took some time for his light troops to achieve the extremely high standard they had reached by 1814.

Wellington's light infantry regiments were amongst the finest in his army but by far the most famous was the 95th Regiment of Foot which, after 1815, became the Rifle Brigade, with the number '95' being given to the Derbyshire Regiment when it formed in 1823. The 95th was distinguished by its green uniform, as was the only other rifle battalion in the British army during the Peninsular War, the 5/60th. But it was their weapon that really set them apart from the rest of Wellington's infantry, being the famous Baker Rifle. This weapon, slower to load than an ordinary smoothbore musket but far more accurate, was indeed a deadly one in the hands of a trained rifleman. It was also a weapon that Napoleon scorned, much to his cost, considering it too slow to load. The 95th always claimed to be 'first in the field, and last out of it', and indeed, their fame has been increased enormously since the *Sharpe* novels of Bernard Cornwell (as has the value of Baker Rifles!). However, there is little doubt that the 95th would not have achieved their great status without their comrades of the 43rd and 52nd Light Infantry regiments, not to mention two battalions of Portuguese *caçadores*, all of which formed the Light Division in the Peninsula. Indeed, one of the most famous riflemen of them all, John Kincaid, said, 'A regiment of riflemen were never in the hands of such supporters.' Between them, the regiments of the Light Division blazed a trail of glory across the Peninsula and enjoyed some great successes. They also endured their share of setbacks. The 5/60th, on the other hand, could never achieve the same status as the 95th. Composed largely of Germans, the 5/60th was split into companies and scattered throughout Wellington's army, with single companies being attached to brigades. Thus, the battalion served at virtually every battle in the Peninsula, albeit being represented sometimes by a company or two. Nevertheless, armed with the Baker Rifle the 5/60th provided great service for King and Country and emerged at the end of the Peninsular War with a very distinguished service record.

Ray Cusick's book is not just about the use of Wellington's light infantry, for a great deal of theory and practice had gone into the training and development of light infantry and the use of rifles in the British army before Wellington came along, as this book will demonstrate. The experiences and pain of the French and Indian Wars in the mid-eighteenth century and of the War of American Independence are examined in order to show the lessons that were handed out to the British, especially by the colonists, lessons that men like Sir John Moore took notice of. Indeed, *Wellington's Rifles* will show how Moore trained light infantry at Shorncliffe in Kent, and how he laid the foundations for the light infantry which Wellington would employ to such great effect in the Peninsula and, to an extent, at Waterloo. By focusing on a few choice actions involving the Light Division and, in particular, the 95th, *Wellington's Rifles* shows how this training was put to good use. Barba del Puerco, Sabugal and Fuentes de Oñoro are perfect examples, although it is a pity this book does not show them at work in the complicated battlefields of the Pyrenees and southern France, where once again the Light Division was perfectly at home. Nevertheless, *Wellington's Rifles* is a long overdue account of the development and use of light infantry and riflemen in the British army. Enjoy it.

Ian Fletcher,
Rochester, 2012.

Chapter 1

Firepower: Fire and Shock Linear Warfare in Europe in the Eighteenth Century

By the beginning of the nineteenth century firepower still dominated the battle-field as it had done since Marlborough, who had developed tactics to make full use of the concentration of musket-fire, thereby creating the firing line.

By 1740 France, still the most powerful military nation in Europe, was exerting her power in the War of the Austrian Succession (1740–48) by sending a large force of 80,000 men under Marshal Saxe to invade the Austrian Netherlands.

It was at Fontenoy on 11 May 1745, that the third son of King George II, the Duke of Cumberland, showing great courage and leadership, led the Coldstream Guards as if on the parade ground onto the field by the river Scheldt and wheeled them to face the French Guards. When the troops were in a continuous line separated from the French only by a few hundred yards, the latter were acknowledged by the British officers with a flourish as they raised their hats as if to invite the French to fire first. The French officers raised their hats like-wise, offering the British the opportunity to fire first. This was a show of gentlemanly bravura, not one of a foolhardy behaviour, as they knew full well the weapon they faced, the flintlock musket, and its limitations.

As Maurice Comte de Saxe stated earlier in 1732:

> It was unnecessary for the battalion to interrupt its advance to trade volleys with the enemy. The firearm is not so terrible as one thinks; few men are killed in action by the fire from the front. I have seen volleys that did not hit four men and neither I nor anyone else saw an effect sufficient to have prevented us from continuing our advance and revenging ourselves with bayonets and pursuing fire.

Some 200 years later Colonel Fuller made the same observation when he pointed out the main drawback of the flintlock musket. He referred to army surgeon Robert Jackson who said in 1804:

> The flintlock musket is an instrument of a missile force. It is obvious that the force, which the missile ought to be directed with aim,

otherwise it will strike only by accident. It is evident that a person cannot take aim with any correctness unless he be free, independent and clear of surrounding encumbrances; and, for this reason, there can be little dependence on the effect of fire that is given by platoon or volleys, and by word of command. Such explosions may intimidate by their noise; it is mere chance if they destroy by their impression. History furnishes proof that battle is rarely gained by the use of the musket; noise intimidates; platoon firing strikes only at random; the charge with the bayonet decides the question.

But at Fontenoy the superior firepower of the British troops won them great glory, culminating in a magnificent charge with bayonets fixed only to be checked by, of all men, the Irish Brigade, (the sons of the 'Wild Geese') who were in the pay of the French. Despite the great efforts and the Duke of Cumberland distinguishing himself the French finally won the battle. The British troops had to be hurriedly withdrawn from the Netherlands to be sent to Scotland to suppress the sudden Jacobite rebellion with the appearance of the Young Pretender. The overall command was given to the Duke of Cumberland with James Wolfe as a senior officer.

The Weapon – The Firelock

'As random as the common musket' – Ezekiel Baker
The universal infantry weapon of the European armies during the eighteenth century and into the nineteenth was the smoothbore flintlock musket, with each country producing its own models. It was a well-tried design that was relatively cheap to produce and required little practice for recruits to master its use. The main fault of the musket was its inaccuracy, which gave it limited range, especially in the hands of young nervous soldiers in the noise and smoke of battle. The weapon's drawbacks determined the way it was used, which governed tactics that were designed to compensate its deficiencies.

The musket used by the British Army was the Land Pattern, considered to be the best of its type, and was known commonly as 'Brown Bess', a name thought to have derived from the browned barrel with the added affectionate name of Bess; it is also thought to be a corruption of the German *Brawn Buss*, or strong gun, the name applied to various types in use. Named the Land Pattern to distinguish it from the Sea Service musket, the barrel was 46 inches long and the calibre was .75 inches; there was also the Short Land Pattern with a 42-inch barrel. The various models were in use for 116 years, from 1722 to 1838. The musket fired a spherical lead ball, almost an ounce in weight, and was able to take a triangular-sectioned bayonet. Injuries inflicted by the lead ball were bone-crushingly horrendous, far more so than the modern bullet. Ammunition, of ball cartridge, was sixty rounds per man and was issued in the form of a greased paper cartridge, which contained the lead ball and sufficient powder for a single shot. In a battle situation extra ammunition was carried in the knapsacks.

There were problems at the beginning of the eighteenth century with providing adequate supplies of good muskets. Many were purchased from other parts of Europe, the best being of Dutch make as the Dutch were proficient gunsmiths with many immigrant Dutch in the Colonies producing, mainly, hunting weapons including the Pennsylvania long rifle, which British troops would soon confront in the French and Indian War. Many muskets purchased from abroad were of poor quality but in the latter part of the eighteenth century a much improved method of supply was arranged when the East India Company was requested by the government to transfer its arsenal, originally intended for use by the Company's own troops in India, to the Board of Ordnance. A transfer of 30,000 firelocks was made and the East India Pattern musket was found to be superior to the Short Land Pattern; consequently the Ordnance was ordered to produce only the India pattern muskets. These were of a simpler design with a 39-inch barrel and proved much quicker to produce. By the turn of the century, and throughout the war against Napoleon, it was the standard infantry weapon. There were further patterns, the New Land Service Pattern with a 42-inch barrel and the 39-inch version, made especially for use by the new light infantry regiments, which was of superior manufacture and fitted with a rear and a foresight.

Board of Ordnance

The problems concerning the musket's inaccuracy were due to several factors other than poor skill at arms. There was the quality of the blackpowder, which was variable, although English powder was considered superior to French powder. But foremost was the quality of the muskets which at the early part of the eighteenth century was well known to be defective or, as it was termed, 'bad'. It all stemmed from the haphazard way the Board of Ordnance conducted their acquisition and maintenance of the stands of arms. In total, a mixed bag of purchases was made from various sources, including Prussia, well known for exporting, or offloading, sub-standard weapons.

Common practice in the early part of the eighteenth century was the case of colonels (proprietors), of regiments deciding not to take arms offered by the Ordnance but to take the equivalent value in money and then purchase their muskets from agents or dealers who could offer cheaper and usually inferior pieces. The colonels would then pocket the balance as their perquisite.

Consequently, the quality and standard of firelocks varied considerably, which ultimately accounted for their variable reliability and effectiveness.

So incompetent was the Board of Ordnance in overseeing the quality of muskets that it became necessary to re-equip a regiment if it was about to go on campaign, exchanging their unreliable and sometimes dangerous pieces with more reliable ones and hoping they would do well in battle. Some units were so concerned about the reliability of their muskets that they were reluctant to fire them at practice firing, or even fire a volley in a *feu de joie* as it was too dangerous.

The continuous conflicts in Europe before the Treaty of Utrecht, which, for Britain, included Marlborough's campaigns, saw heavy demands and competition for the procurement of weapons. This gave opportunities to less scrupulous dealers in arms to off load sub-standard muskets at inflated prices. But in 1715 the Board of Ordnance, prompted by the Treasury, regulated the system by adopting an 'Ordnance system of manufacture', whereby all component parts, locks, stocks, barrels and brass furnishings were contracted out to individual manufacturers and the parts were then sent to the Tower of London and Dublin Castle where they were kept until firelocks were required. When needed the parts were sent to several reliable gunsmiths for 'rough stocking', setting up and assembly. Even so, in critical situations, large numbers of muskets were imported.

An interesting comment related to the muskets' effectiveness is found in the journal of Nicholas Cresswell, who was serving in the Colonies on 22 June 1777. He relates:

> A party of our men were met by about the same number of rebels. When they were about 100 yards from each other both parties fired, but I did not see any fall. They still advanced to the distance of 40 yards or less, and fired again. I then saw a great number fall on both sides – I never before saw such a shocking scene.

Most of the rebels were armed with muskets (ex-militia) and some hunting rifles. The idea that all of the rebels were experts at using the rifle is not true, as many rebels were from the towns and had never handled weapons before.

'You may as well fire at the moon'

Perhaps the final word ought to come from Colonel George Hanger who was known to be good at firing at marks and was an expert 'marksman'. He was also known as an eccentric, with strong views on military matters. Hanger published a book, *Reflections on the Menaced Invasion*, in which he expressed his views on 'the great terror', or expected invasion by the French. In his book *To all Sportsmen* (1814), he expressed his ideas on the worth of the musket.

A soldier's musket, if not exceedingly ill-bored (as many are), will strike the figure of a man at 80 yards; it may even at a hundred, but a soldier must be very unfortunate indeed who shall be wounded by a common musket at 150 yards, provided his antagonist aims at him; and as to firing at a man at 200 yards with a common musket, you may as well fire at the moon and have the same hope of hitting your object. I do maintain and will prove that no man was ever killed at 200 yards, by a common musket, by the person who aimed at him.

Concerns at the ineffectiveness of the musket in the Prussian Army caused them to carry out a series of tests with muskets, firing at a target six feet high by one hundred feet wide, representing a line of a hundred six-foot-tall grenadiers. At 150 yards from the target a marksman would miss the group every time. At seventy-five yards the number of hits would be less than fifty per cent. The result of this was that the 'danger zone' was extremely shallow and could be travelled in quick time. In other words, if the opposing force started at 400 yards and advanced, they could cover the first 325 yards probably not suffering any casualties from musket fire. At seventy-five yards the risk of casualties would be less than fifty per cent. The result of this was that the 'danger zone', those last seventy-five yards, could see a rapid charge with fixed bayonets. The results confirmed the view that muskets, to be effective, should be packed together so that, when fired, they released a wall of lead shot to ensure that at least some would find a target. Prussian soldiers spent plenty of time loading at speed with little time spent on the ranges firing at marks. Marksmanship was not considered important. It took extra time to take aim and as the test proved you just have to point the musket at the enemy and the bullet would be bound to find a target. The Prussians expected to fire up to three volleys per minute. But constant drill raised the rate to four volleys per minute; in 1740 they replaced the wooden ramrod with a double-ended metal rod which eliminated the need to reverse the ramrod, thus saving time. This was all based on Frederick the Great's policy that battles are decided by superiority of fire. Scharnhorst summed it up when he remarked after Prussia's disastrous war with France at Jena in 1806, 'Before the war we taught the men to load quickly, but not well, to fire quickly without aiming. This was ill considered.'

The British Army also carried out tests when it was accepted that the extreme range of the musket was 400 yards. The musket could not be relied upon to hit a mark at 100 yards. When fired the ball was liable to fly anywhere at random within a variable arc but, if massed together and fired at an enemy from fifty to 100 yards, who would also be in massed ranks, the missiles of fourteen one-ounce balls to the pound would, with sufficient force and direction, hit men, but not necessarily those aimed at. At 150 yards a marksman would miss a six-foot-square target practically every time. Consequently firing practice was limited to perfecting loading and pointing the piece in the direction of the enemy rather than aiming. The inaccuracy of the musket was, in a sense, a built-in design fault. By having a loose-fitting ball, which made it easier and quicker to load, allowing the ball to slide easily into the barrel this left a minute clearance, enough to allow an amount of the propellant gases to escape, causing windage and the bullet to lose momentum, speed and direction.

So it was the factor of windage, plus the probable defectiveness of the musket, combined with the clouds of smoke issuing from each discharge blinding every soldier's vision, and the distraction from those close to him when they fired, as well as the noise and fear within the soldier that all made it impossible for the soldier to offer accurate firing.

As any ex-soldier, rifleman or member of a gun club will know from experience of shooting with a rifle, holding the weapon steady in the firing position without wavering is not easy; support of the arms to steady the aim is necessary. In the prone, or basic, position the body and both elbows form a tripod, which gives the rifle a steady mount. 'The blade of the foresight should be in line and in the centre of the U of the rear sight', so the instruction went. In the original training schedule for the 95th Rifles the men were taught to shoot from different positions, standing, prone, kneeling, sitting and supine, all designed to give the steadiest aim and at the same time be able to make full use of cover.

James Wolfe who, on the Heights of Abraham in the battle for Quebec, preferred to carry a musket rather than a sword, cautioned younger officers in 1750:

> There is no necessity for firing fast, a cool and well levelled fire with pieces carefully wadded is much more destructive and formidable than the quickest fire in confusion.

The common practice, when engaged in rapid volleys, of not ramming down the bullet but banging the butt of the piece on the ground hoping the ball would slide down and then firing caused the discharge to lack full propellant force.

Fire and Shock

By the beginning of the eighteenth century there appeared to be two approaches to fire tactics for infantry; one stressed firepower, the other shock, the charge with the bayonet. The first method was a case of controlled volleying, in either battalion or company form, or by alternate ranks, three at a time, with the aim of reducing the enemy's numbers. The purpose of the firepower tactic was to batter the opponents' will to stand their ground or crush their attempt to attack by launching a continuous fusillade of fire by each of the three ranks firing in turn. By the nineteenth century the firing line became two ranks.

The three ranks of the British Army during the early part of the eighteenth century would 'lock up' the files in the ranks for firing. The front rank would kneel down, the second rank would move slightly to its right and the third rank would move half a pace to its right making each file in echelon with the fire-locks of the two rear ranks levelled through the file intervals.

On the command 'make ready' (present your firelocks), then (give) 'fire' the firing would be continuous with each rank firing in turn, setting up a constant fusillade of fire. A battalion could divide its fire by firing volleys from each company or division in turn, with those who had fired having time to reload.

The second method was considered the most economical: firing one volley and then, with bayonets fixed, charging the enemy in a rapid advance to put fear into them and cause them to panic and flee, thus winning the ground. Battles were in the end a case of winning ground and holding it. This second method was the basis of Frederick the Great's tactic of 'Fire and Shock'. Infantry shock tactics were planned to put fear into the enemy. It was intended that it should not end in a hand-to-hand, bayonet-to-bayonet melee. It was not meant to end in actual contact but to crush the defenders' resolve to stand their ground and induce them to break their ranks and retreat in panic before the attackers got too close. But there was a case where there was fierce contact and that was at the Battle of Culloden where James Wolfe instructed his men on how they should, with bayonets, repel the fearsome clansmen as they hurled themselves in their Highland charge. The clansmen carried a *targe*, or shield, in their left hand covering mainly the left part of their chest. Their broadswords were held aloft in their right hands, leaving the right side of the chest exposed. So he told the men to thrust their bayonets not at the man to the front but at the man to *his* right, who was partly exposed.

The master exponent of warfare in Europe in the eighteenth century was Frederick the Great, King of Prussia or, as known by his troops, 'der Alte Fritz (Old Fritz)'. In 1748 he argued that the advance was likely to stall if attacking infantry stopped to fire. This was fatal as Frederick the Great said, 'It is not the number of enemies we kill which gives the victory but the ground which we gain. To win a battle you must advance proudly and in good order claiming ground all the time.'

Frederick II (The Great), King of Prussia, formed a small but very successful army and created the Kingdom of Prussia out of the small state of Brandenburg. He did this in a series of battles with the basic principal of winning territory economically and holding it without incurring too many casualties and without causing unnecessary damage; he did not want to take territory that was ruined. The battles were fought for the most part on the great plain of northern Europe, which at that time was less encumbered and ideal for wide sweeping manoeuvres. The Prussian tactics were successful until they confronted the Revolutionary Army of the new French Republic.

With all the musket's faults exposed it was Frederick who created his tactics of 'fire and shock'. The general practice in the latter part of the seventeenth century into the eighteenth was for the attacking force to start by preparing a plan of attack. Bearing in mind the limited means of communication during this period, which was left almost entirely to the services of aides de camp, once battle started it had its own momentum and it would be very difficult to change the plan during the course of the battle. However, it is known that Napoleon had with him on campaign a mobile version of semaphore apparatus.

But Frederick realized that, if he could train his troops to react quickly to new orders during a battle, he could with judicious moves outmanoeuvre the enemy. For this reason constant drill was carried out and by the introduction of cadence marching in the early eighteenth century he could parade them onto the battlefield doing the 'lock step', better known as the goose step.

The system of fire and shock as developed by Frederick's infantry precluded the major use of light troops such as the *Feldjäger* Corps, but after Frederick's defeat at Kolin he saw the necessity for skirmishers and raised a company of jägers. After the Battle of Mollwitz he also realized the need for light troops. By the Second Silesian War he was able to meet the Austrians with their Grenz troops. As Scharnhorst said, 'The present war against the French Republic reminded us of the principal that one should always try to regulate one's disposition according to the enemy's methods.' Jägers were of little practical use in Frederick's tactics, so they amounted to few in number and, because they were armed with rifles that took longer to load, they could not contribute to the overall system of rapid fire. As the short rifle could not be fitted with a bayonet the jägers carried short swords for personal protection. When Ezekiel Baker designed his rifle, based on a German design, he adapted the sword, or spadroon, to be fitted as a long bayonet giving the Baker rifle the same length as a musket with a fixed bayonet. In the Rifle regiments the bayonet is still referred to as a sword, with the order to fix swords.

The key to Frederick's system was its harsh iron discipline and drill practised on the drill fields of Potsdam to make the men totally obedient so that every soldier behaved as one man. It was to instil into his troops or, one could say, programme them, to react to orders with speed and without question to perform their complicated evolutions and bring to bear as many muskets as possible on the enemy and deliver a wall of lead shot in the form of rolling volleys, all at great speed. Their will and steadfastness would eventually crush the weaker will of the enemy. These complicated evolutions were executed automatically in the din of battle to the sound of the drum when commands were smothered by the crescendo of cannon fire and everyone disappeared in clouds of smoke. When asked if he would prefer his soldiers to be thinking soldiers, Frederick said 'If my soldiers began to think, not one would remain in the ranks.'

So long as both sides adhered to the established formations and manoeuvres of the eighteenth century there was no practical need for arms of greater precision. The rifle was expensive to manufacture, required greater training and had the disadvantage that it took longer to load. It was for these reasons that Napoleon banned the use of rifles. He was himself a poor shot with a hunting rifle, injuring a marshal when out hunting. It was accepted that you took your chance in battle; the ritual of the system was that some considered it against the accepted tenets and rules of warfare to deliberately pick off individuals which was seen as ungentlemanly.

Most European armies were impressed by the show of powder, pomp and pipe-clay, and the successes of Frederick's regiments; many followed his system, hoping that it would also give them victories. One firm believer in all that was Prussian was David Dundas, the Adjutant General, who made visits to Potsdam, to witness training, and to Silesia to watch the manoeuvres of Frederick's troops. He was impressed at the Prussian troops executing their manual drills and manoeuvres, impressive in their massed ranks, resplendent in their uniforms, marching dutifully, or robotically, into position with the balance step or lock step. But behind the spectacle of parades, bands, colours and pomp was a military structure that was harsh, brutal and dehumanising. He was also very critical of the concept, and use, of light infantry as it went against all the rules of Fredrician tactics, the proof being that the army of Prussia was the most successful in Europe, or had been up to 1806.

In 1788 Dundas produced his drill manual *The Principles of military Movements*, a modified version reduced to eighteen movements, based on the Fredrician tactics of the Prussian General von Salden's *Elements of Tactics*. Dundas emphasized the importance of the pivot man; in all the wheeling and counter wheeling, the pivot man became vital to the smoothness of the operation, and consequently Dundas had the cognomen of 'Old Pivot'.

Controlled Firing

Once the battalion had been deployed into the firing line a system of close fire control was applied. It was imperative that fire discipline was observed. It was the repetitive manual drills that embedded into the men the automatic response to fire orders. The premature firing off induced by tension and fear could encourage others to follow and destroy the controlled fire pattern. There were two different systems. At the beginning of the eighteenth century it was known as 'platoon firing', or firing by 'chequer', which was much used by Marlborough's regiments and was in common use until the 1750s. This was replaced by a system known as 'alternate firing', which continued until the turn of the nineteenth century and was easier to execute than 'platoon fire'; but both required intensive training before they could function in any action. 'Alternate fire' consisted of fire given by companies, platoons, or other divisions going from right and left alternatively towards the centre of the battalion line; 'platoon fire' consisted of fire given by platoons grouped into three 'firings', all the platoons in each shooting together according to a prearranged sequence.

'Alternate fire' was officially adopted with the publication of the new Regulations in 1764, although those battalions who were well trained were already practising it. Such a regiment was the 20th Foot, whose commanding officer was Lieutenant Colonel James Wolfe.

Wolfe was a first-class officer who trained his troops well according to the current regulations, but at the same time he thought 'alternate fire' far more practical than the current regulation 'platoon fire', the 'impracticable chequer' as he described it and so he taught both in the 20th.

Wolfe issued a regimental order in January 1755 which stated:

> As the alternative fire by platoon or devisions [sic], or by companies is the most simple, plain and easy, and used by the best disciplined troops in Europe (i.e. the Prussians), we are at all times to imitate them in that respect . . . (and otherwise) to conform to the established discipline, and to practise all those things that are required at the reviews, to which the knowledge of other matters be no hindrance.

Not all commanding officers were as thorough as James Wolfe. Many did not observe the contemporary practices and follow the standard drill manual, which was rarely referred to, so drill was left very much to the fancy of each commanding officer. It was not always possible to assemble three regiments together to form a brigade for a field day or a mock battle; these could not take place until the commanding officers agreed beforehand to a common form of drill, as each regiment could be practising its own version.

Wolfe pointed out that officers should inform the soldiers of their platoons, before the action begins, where they were to direct their fire; and they were to take good aim to destroy their adversaries. Furthermore, 'There is no necessity for firing very fast; a cool well levelled fire, with pieces carefully loaded, is much more destructive and formidable than the quickest fire in confusion.' There were some particulars in relation to firearms that soldiers should know:

> One is, the quantity of powder that throws a ball out of a musket in the truest direction to the mark, and to the greatest distance; a matter

of experience and practice will best discover; soldiers are apt to imagine that a great quantity of powder has the best effect, which is a capital error. The size of the cartridge with ball is another material consideration, because when the musket grows hot with repeated firing, a ball too near the calibre of the musket will not go down without great force, and the danger of firing the piece when the ball is not rammed well home is well known (i.e. the musket will blow up); the soldiers should be informed that no other force in ramming down a charge is necessary than to collect the powder and place the ball close upon it. If the ball is rammed too hard upon the powder, a great part of it will not take fire and consequently the shot will be of so much less force.

Eighteenth-century drill books illustrated the positions of the soldiers in the manual drills. None of the illustrations of the soldiers at the 'present' and 'fire' positions show them actually taking aim along the barrel; the soldier is usually shown with his head held erect. Also, none of the front rank men in the kneeling position are shown supporting the weight of the musket to steady the aim by placing the elbow on the knee. None of the Land Pattern muskets were fitted with sights except the light infantry musket. They could use the bayonet lug as a guide, but this would be obscured if the bayonet were fitted. It was probably thought that taking aim after the first discharge was unnecessary as all would be shrouded in clouds of powder smoke and would be unable to see a thing.

As the eighteenth century progressed the British Army was gaining confidence in its standing as an army built on Marlborough's successes during the War of the Spanish Succession against the forces of Louis XIV, confident in its prowess to bear arms and face all known enemies; proud of its reputation as a master of the delivery of firepower equal to all in Europe, especially the French. But the French were once again contesting Britain's interests, although not in Europe. In 1754 disturbing despatches from Lieutenant Governor Robert Dinwiddie of Virginia had reached King George II.

Chapter 2

The French and Indian War: Fire and Move

The opening shots 'I have heard the bullets whistle'

The despatch from Lieutenant Governor Robert Dinwiddie caused great consternation in London as its contents carried reports, intelligence and also included a separate alarming despatch from a certain young major in the Virginia Militia in which he reported: 'I have spent some time in viewing the rivers, the Monongahela and Allegheny and the land in the fork, which I think extremely well situated for a fort as it has absolute command of both rivers.'

King George II read the young major's alarming despatch in which the officer had reported, 'I have heard the bullets whistle, believe me there is something charming in the sound.' But, more importantly, it included the news of a strong French military presence about to make its appearance down the Ohio valley on land that was immediate to the eastern seaboard colonies, including Pennsylvania and Virginia, whose settlements stretched no more than 200 miles inland without a marked western boundary where it became open to the vast Indian territory of the Shawnee and Delaware. The land beyond was earmarked for further penetration and settlement; ranging parties were already infiltrating this virgin land assessing the possible occupation of flat land suitable for farming and settlements for the expanding population.

What had prompted the young major in the Virginia Militia to view the rivers? Dinwiddie had received a despatch from the King during October 1753. The acting governor's instructions from the King were direct and to the point.

Whereas we have received information of a number of Europeans not our subjects, being assembled in a hostile manner, upon the river Ohio, intending by force of arms to erect certain forts, within our territory on the said river, contrary to our peace and to the dignity of our Crown, we do hereby strictly enjoin you to make diligent enquiry into the truth of this information and if you shall find that any number of persons whether Indians or Europeans shall presume to erect any fort within the limits of our province of Virginia you are first to require them peacefully to depart and not persist in such unlawful proceedings. And if not withstanding your admonition, they do still endeavour to carry on such unlawful and unjustifiable designs, we do strictly charge and command you to drive out by force of arms.

George R.

The Treaty of Aix-la-Chapelle in 1748, signed by both the British and French, failed to define clearly the boundaries between the British (the Colonies), and the French (New France and Louisiana) in the New World. The Hudson Bay area containing the trading settlements and forts was the province of the British Hudson Bay Company.

Traders and trappers from the colonies had been active in the Ohio valley area, reaching it by using the Potomac, Monongahela and Susquehanna rivers and crossing the Allegheny Mountains. Dinwiddie had heard reports from traders that the French were building a series of forts along the Ohio river from Montreal to Fort Rivière au Boeuf by Lake Erie, making a claim that the Ohio Valley was French territory. The French had their reasons, which was part of a grandiose plan which was to link New France to Louisiana on the Gulf of Mexico by using the Ohio river as a corridor, which would give them access to the ocean when the St Lawrence river was frozen during the winter months.

Dinwiddie was very much aware of Virginia's importance and standing in the thirteen colonies. It had a motto which would have been inscribed on Washington's gorget in Latin, *En Dat Virginia Quartum*, or 'Behold! Virginia Yields the Fourth' meaning, somewhat inaccurately, that Virginia was the fourth kingdom of the British Empire after the United Kingdom, England, Scotland, Ireland and France (Calais); Ireland had yet to join the United Kingdom. Although Dinwiddie was making a stand against French incursions he represented the view of the Virginia Assembly only. Whereas the French were governed by the decision of the governor of New France, the thirteen colonies were all independent entities. They were governed separately by each colony's own assembly and did not always act in concert.

Dinwiddie was alarmed at the French military presence and encroachment on land adjacent to the Colonies which he saw as a hostile act. He decided to send a representative to meet the French, not to negotiate but to deliver a request for the French to return to New France. And the person he chose to deliver the request was a twenty-one-year-old major in the Virginia Militia, George Washington who was delighted at being chosen for this important duty, and desperate to prove himself and impress Dinwiddie, even though he was aware of the arduous nature and dangers involved.

On 21 June 1752 a French raiding party including Indians allied to the French, Ottawas and Chippewas, attacked an English trading mission at Pickawillany in the Ohio country; they killed or captured the half-dozen English merchants present. They made an example of the Indian chief who traded with the English, who was known to the Anglo-Americans as 'Old Britain': they boiled and ate him. The warlike Ottawas acted as shock troops for the French.

Washington needed a guide to lead him through the vast trackless forest that was the wilderness, where the canopy of trees was so thick that it was possible to travel for days without seeing the sky. He was to meet an Englishman Christopher Gist, a trader and entrepreneur who knew the trappers' trails and was as equally at ease in the backwoods as in polite society. Also included in the venture was a Dutchman named Van Bramm, who would act as French interpreter as well as Davison, a trader who would be the Indian interpreter, and four woodsmen who were general helpers.

They travelled over 800 miles from Williamsburg and back, from the coast to fort Rivière au Boeuf by Lake Erie, a perilous journey through blizzards and raging torrents with the constant threat of ambush by the Indians. When they eventually arrived at the French fort Washington presented the letter to the French commander; the letter asked, 'By whose authority have the French invaded the King of Great Britain's territories? It becomes my duty to require your peaceable departure.'

The French commander had received Washington with all the courtesies and gave his polite reply, 'As to the summons you send me to retire, I do not think myself obliged to obey.'

Washington, Gist and party returned to Williamsburg with the French reply, but also with interesting information and intelligence. Washington had a keen eye and a sharp ear; he had observed by the fort fifty large birch-bark canoes and 170 pine-built bateaux drawn up on the banks awaiting the spring thaw to bring large numbers of troops down the Ohio river. Whilst at the fort he had been invited to dine with the French garrison officers who, with the drink and conversation flowing and tongues suitably loosened, unwittingly gave Washington plenty of indications of their future intentions.

The frozen river by the French fort underlined the strong predicament that faced the French in New France. The rivers were their lifelines, the only way they could traverse through the wilderness of trackless forest was by using the rivers and adopting the Indian canoe and, with portage, they could cover long distances.

Washington kept a journal in which he noted that the confluence of the Ohio, Allegheny and Monongahela rivers at these forks would be 'extremely well situated for a fort'.

When Washington returned to Williamsburg on 16 January 1754 he reported immediately to Dinwiddie to relay the French answer to the request to quit the Ohio valley; he also gave an account of the discoveries he had observed and heard at the French fort. Dinwiddie was shocked at the French refusal to comply and thought their response and actions were threatening the colonies. He decided to send an urgent despatch to England by the next ship.

Dinwiddie made plans to capture the forks of the Ohio and commissioned William Trent, a trader from Pennsylvania and western agent for the Ohio Company, as a captain in the Virginia Regiment. Trent raised a company of 100 men and set out with Ensign Ward to skirt the Monongahela river and erect a fort at the river juncture. They began work on 17 February 1754, and named it Fort Prince George.

The governor decided to organize an expedition to reinforce this outpost and the Virginia Assembly made a reluctant decision to vote £10,000 for the expedition; at the same time the French force of 500 men in 300 canoes and sixty bateaux, under the command of Captain Pierre de Contrecoeur, was moving swiftly down river from Rivière au Boeuf.

A large detachment of Virginia Militia, which included Major Washington, together with a company of King's troops from South Carolina, made up the force of some 300 men. They had orders to further fortify the outpost at the Forks of the Ohio and destroy all persons who should impede their mission. Command of this detachment was given to Lieutenant Colonel Joshua Fry, Colonel of the Virginia Regiment, an Englishman originally from Oxford who, at the last minute, suffered a fatal fall when he was thrown from his horse. So Washington took over command, with the brevet rank of lieutenant colonel. It was unusual for a militia officer to be given command over regular king's troops. Governor Dinwiddie granted Washington's rank as a Militia officer. It was not given by a commission from the King, as colonial militia officers could not normally command regular troops. This loss of authority and status always rankled with Washington.

Dinwiddie ensured that they were well supplied, including arms and ten 4-pounder cannon. The force left Alexandria in the north of Virginia and trekked overland to Winchester and Wills Creek, a tributary of the Potomac river, in western Maryland. Then, proceeding westwards, they followed an old Indian trail over the mountains.

Washington's warning of the probable intentions of the French had proved correct as, with the spring thaw of April 1754, the French armada of 360 canoes and bateaux arrived at the forks of the Ohio to claim the valley for the French. The French force, which numbered several hundred men, ordered, with civility, Edward Ward, in Trent's absence, and his party of forty Virginians, to leave and return to Virginia. They surrendered and marched back to Wills Creek Station

(Fort Cumberland). The French then set about enlarging the fortifications with palisades and earthworks. Square with bastions projecting at the corners, it was named Fort Duquesne, after the Governor General, Ange Duquesne de Menneville.

Whilst still on the march and at Wills Creek Washington learned that the French had arrived at the forks of the Ohio and, in Trent's absence, dislodged Ward and his party. So there now had to be a change of plan and Washington decided to march to the mouth of Redstone Creek and await reinforcements. They spent April and May cutting their way through the wilderness towards Redstone Creek and were still waiting for the promised supplies and reinforcements, including the Indian allies. By 28 May they arrived at a large clearing called the Great Meadows, forty-five miles south east of Fort Duquesne, and at the same time renewed contact with Christopher Gist. They fed and tended the horses and set up camp and waited for the supplies, when, out of the woods appeared an Iroquois chief named Tanacharison, also known as the 'Half King' who was wearing his tricorne hat, red coat, with a gorget from King George, trade blanket. Apparently he had a Union Jack on his canoe; he was proudly pro-British, a man of strange appearance but who carried himself with dignity. He held a high position in the Six Nations and exerted some authority but the British never understood his status. He had arrived with news that a force of thirty-five French soldiers from Fort Duquesne was encamped only seven miles away on the east side of Chestnut Ridge.

Washington decided that immediate action was necessary and with forty soldiers and the Half King and eight Indians they left that night hoping to make a dawn attack. They crept up on the French camp in the morning light, a shot was fired, probably by a French picquet, and a brisk fire-fight of no more than fifteen minutes followed and then the Virginians charged in with the bayonet. Ten Frenchmen were killed, including Ensign Joseph Coulon de Villiers and, importantly, Sieur (Lord) de Jumonville. A legend that has some substance tells how the Half King descended on the wounded Jumonville, split open his skull with his tomahawk, scooped out his brains and 'washed his hands' in them, a pagan Indian ritual that horrified Washington and his men. The barbaric practices and customs of the Indians were well known and alarmed the colonists, and were often retold to frighten unsuspecting people. The attackers took twenty-one French as prisoners, but not before one managed to escape and rush back to Fort Duquesne with the alarm. One Virginian was killed. The young Washington was pleased with his military achievements; he boasted of it and thought he had done well, not realizing the consequences of this rather rash act.

There was outrage among the French at Washington's attack on what they said was a group of peaceful emissaries who were only there to request the Virginians to withdraw. This was plausible, as so far the French had behaved impeccably. The French were furious, especially at the 'assassination' of Jumonville, who was the half-brother of Captain Louis Coulon de Villiers, a senior French officer at Fort Duquesne. They considered that this attack was against the rules of war. When news eventually reached Paris and London there was incredulity all round at the shock and it sent waves of indignation through the royal courts and seats of government. With much table thumping it had all the signs of an international incident. Washington had unwittingly lit a fuse that would ignite yet another conflict between Britain and France to become the French and Indian War, or the opening phase of the Seven Years war.

The belligerent action by the Virginians was causing Dinwiddie to rethink his response and play down the whole unfortunate affair. His report to London called the incident a 'little skirmish' that was really the work of the Half King and the Indians; 'we were auxiliaries to them.' Dinwiddie's assessment was supported by John Davison, the Indian interpreter who witnessed the action. Davison stated, 'there were but eight Indians who did most of the execution that was done.' It seems that the Indians acted independently, ignoring Colonel Washington's orders. They separated and hid in a hollow and, when the firing started, rushed at the French with their tomahawks to take scalps. It was their custom to prove the warrior status.

When Coulon de Villiers was told of the Virginians' attack and the death of his half-brother he was enraged. On 28 June Contrecoeur, the commander of Fort Duquesne, ordered Coulon de Villiers to 'avenge the attack against Jumonville's detachment and chase the English out of the territory claimed by France, (the valley of the Ohio)'. A force of 600 French and Indians set out to evict Washington who, in the meantime, had ordered his detachments to fall back to Great Meadows in anticipation of a French reaction. In two days they constructed a circular palisade with entrenchments as a rough and ready fort and mounted seven swivel guns. At the centre of the fort was a small cabin as a storehouse for supplies and powder. When finished, the Virginians, or English as the French called them, and the South Carolina regulars waited for the expected attack.

On 2 July the French came down from the north and invested the fort. Rather than make a frontal assault they took up positions among the trees and set up a continuous fire. The firing continued all day with the Virginians' returning fire to the extent that they began to run out of ammunition. Then it began to rain heavily, soaking the men and their powder. Washington's militia became dispirited, discipline became lax, they broke into the cabin and took a cask of rum and were getting drunk on spirits of another kind. Rum was used to bribe the Indians but they preferred brandy from the French.

The majority of the weapons used by the Virginians and the French were smoothbore muskets. Some individuals would use their personal hunting rifles, non-military weapons with a small bore firing a small ball, large enough to bring down their prey without causing too much damage to the pelt and which could not take a bayonet.

Then, fortunately, the French called for a ceasefire and a parley. At midnight, by spluttering candlelight in the cabin, they agreed terms with Captain Jacob Van Bramm, a fencing master and teacher of languages acting as interpreter as he was the only one in Washington's party who understood French, albeit not very well. The terms were finally agreed and the French were very magnanimous and surprisingly generous, considering the provocative actions of the Virginians. The swivel guns were to be spiked and abandoned, the cattle to be handed over to the French, but the surrender was with all honours; the officers were paroled not to take up arms again for one year. Van Bramm and another officer, Robert Stobo, were to remain as hostages. Washington signed a document, which acknowledged the 'assassination' of Jumonville and an admission that he accepted full responsibility for the incident. The disclosure of the document caused a diplomatic row.

On the following day, 4 July, Washington, attempting to put a brave face on, led his force of Virginians and South Carolina regulars out of Fort Necessity with colours flying and drums beating. Unfortunately, in his haste to leave, he left the colour of the Virginia Militia behind which the French seized as a trophy of war.

Despite protests from the French, the Indians allied to the French harassed Washington's motley body of wet, muddy and crestfallen troops. The Indians could not understand how the defeated were permitted to leave without the victors claiming scalps.

Washington's force returned to Williamsburg in disgrace, having failed in their mission and been evicted from the Ohio Valley, losing the colour of the Virginia Militia in the process. They had committed a military blunder by provoking an attack on supposedly peaceful French emissaries which, in turn, created a diplomatic row. Washington, due to his lack of knowledge of French, signed a document that was a full admission of responsibility for the aggressive action and the casualties. There were recriminations with the Half King blaming Washington's lack of experience, saying that Washington was only twenty-one and ignored the Half King's advice; the latter said, 'the French acted like cowards and the English like fools.' Washington's military future was in doubt due to his ineptitude and failure to carry out the mission while causing a diplomatic incident. This was all brought to the notice of King George II whose reaction was, 'I do not think he has heard many if he thinks that the bullets whistle sounds charming.'

Dinwiddie's plan to scotch the French attempt to establish a foothold in the Ohio valley had set in motion a military reaction to the French ambitions and a

British plan to seize the opportunity to extend their sphere of influence and dominion.

The Plan

On 24 September 1754 a number of carriages rattled down Whitehall and arrived at Horse Guards, the new headquarters of the British Army only completed the year before. They were bringing the 'big wigs' of the British Army with the last to arrive being the Captain General or Commander-in-Chief of the Army, William Augustus, Duke of Cumberland.

The generals were in serious mood as they gathered round a large table strewn with documents and maps. Prominently placed in the centre was a map of North America. This was the 1754 'Map of the Inhabited Part of Virginia', drawn by Peter Jefferson, father of the future president, and Joshua Fry, Commanding Officer of the Virginia Militia. This was a council of war and there was voluble discussion as a finger traced a line across the map following the Ohio river.

They had read the despatches from Dinwiddie and a certain Major Washington, which confirmed reports of which they had already been made aware of what amounted to a French threat to the colonies' expansion and, importantly, a threat to the lucrative trade with North America.

After the War of the Austrian Succession and the signing of the Treaty of Aix-la-Chappelle there were heavy reductions in troop numbers in the British Army. The government established settlements in Nova Scotia for them and their families, about 4,000, mainly from Scotland. To protect them, companies of rangers or militia were raised. The French resented these settlers and provoked an Indian war against them and began planning to forge a safe route along the Ohio Valley as an outlet for their trade and a link between the French centres of Quebec and Louisiana.

Cumberland came to the table with an established reputation; he had commanded the allied forces in the Low Countries when his father, King George II, the last British king to lead his troops into battle, decided to hand command to his son. Even so, Cumberland had been beaten at Fontenoy. But his recent success in crushing the Jacobite rebellion and his relentless pursuit of the clans after the Battle of Culloden had earned him the epithet the 'Butcher of Culloden'. After the battle his senior officers, who included James Wolfe and a Colonel Braddock, asked for further orders. Cumberland wrote on the back of a playing card, the nine of diamonds, 'no quarter'. Newcastle had reason to call him a militarist. The English on the other hand honoured him and named a flower after him: Sweet William.

Cumberland came with the best qualifications of the military sort. He had known many actions in Europe, and had proved himself in combat. He was a good organizer, a disciplinarian, a reformer in the organization of the army. He created a professional officer corps, standardized uniforms and equipment and established new drills. He was an advocate of light infantry and light horse – was this an influence of Frederick the Great's new jäger corps? He even proposed to form a corps of jägers, of Hanoverian marksmen, both foot and mounted. Overall, he put the Army on a more professional basis. Cumberland had been schooled in the Prussian tradition of Frederick the Great: Prussian discipline, Prussian methods, Prussian tactics, Prussian firepower as it was all played out in the cockpit of Europe, the great flat north European plain. But would this qualify Cumberland to plan and send an expedition based on such regimes into an uncharted wilderness?

Cumberland was there to contribute to the discussion about a proposed expedition to North America, but the overall responsibility was with the politicians; the military were only the instruments of political decision. The politicians were the Secretary of State, Sir Thomas Robinson, for the Southern Department, assisted by The Board of Trade, which administered the affairs of the North American Colonies. Robinson reported to the Prime Minister, the Duke of Newcastle, who, it was said, was ignorant of most matters, particularly the geography of North America.

Newcastle was a political enemy of Cumberland whom he regarded as a dangerous militarist. All politicians have an automatic distrust and dislike of the military; they cost too much money and they abhor the idea of a large standing army. An army had too much power, removed power from the Crown and could harbour republican elements. It was shades of the Commonwealth and the New Model Army.

But, in the end realizing that none could offer worthwhile advice, especially military advice, Newcastle had to consult the Captain General. Once Cumberland realized it was up to him he swiftly took command and began to make plans. He started to set in motion his decisive plan of attack on the French forts along the Ohio. It was later to develop once William Pitt replaced Newcastle and began his policy of 'The Great War for Empire' by driving the French completely out of America and seizing their territory. But neither Cumberland nor any of those who would assist him had ever been to America; all they knew was based on others' reports and hearsay. The British Army had never campaigned in North America; there was no previous experience on which to base the planning. All they knew came from their campaigns in Europe, which could be reached by a short voyage of a few days, whereas America would take almost two uncomfortable months in trying and uncomfortable conditions.

Cumberland established his close group of advisers, which included the king. They worked in secret, behind closed doors, drawing on their own sources of information and excluding all others.

On 14 November 1754 King George II made his speech on the opening of Parliament. He said that trade would improve and, to promote it, he declared in his German accent, 'to protect those possessions which constitute our great source of their wealth a liberal grant would be made for the service of the year'. America was not mentioned but all understood him, including the French, which confirmed their fears.

Dinwiddie's despatch had asked for regular troops to be sent. Was the implication a judgement on his part on the competence of the colonial militias, especially after Washington's mishandling at Great Meadows? Cumberland took the opposite view and thought that all the troops should be from the colonies, which would have meant that they would have to bear the costs. The king disapproved of that plan and in a compromise it was decided to send two regiments of regular troops and raise two more regiments in America from volunteers. This would be the first time that British troops would serve in America.

It was decided to send the 44th Regiment (later, in 1782, it would be known as the 44th East Essex regiment), commanded by Sir Peter Halkett with the second in command the then unknown Lieutenant Colonel Thomas Gage, who would feature in the Revolutionary War. The second regiment was the 48th (in 1782 the Northamptonshire Regiment), commanded by Colonel Thomas Dunbar. Both regiments came without any reputation; the 44th was considered 'one of the most worthless regiments in the British Army'. Both were raised to 500 men, which is half the standard complement of 1,000. Once in the colonies, recruiting a further 200 would augment each regiment, with volunteers bringing both up to a strength of 700. Of the 700 on the muster roll of each regiment six would be 'warrant men', who did not actually exist, but their pay went for allowances for officers' widows, recruiting and clothing lost by deserters. There were deserters and 'more would have done had they foreseen what awaited them'. There were also several 'non effectives' called 'contingent men', who were mustered as armourers; these were older men classified as 'worn out'.

The Crown was also to raise two new regiments in the colonies of 1,000 men each. Americans Sir William Pepperell of Maine and William Shirley, Governor of Massachusetts, would command them. Neither British regiment could meet its basic complement and a hurried call was sent out to other regiments in England and Ireland for drafts. It was on such occasions that colonels of regiments took the opportunity to weed out their undesirables, the drunks, felons, wasters and troublemakers, the stuff of a sergeant major's nightmare. This posting was not of the troops' liking when they found out that they were to serve in North America.

The total would comprise a mixed force of 3,400 British and Colonial troops, plus the Kings Independent Companies in America. Together with the mobilization of all the militia regiments it would make a force of somewhere between 12,000 and 15,000 troops, plus as many Indians that could be persuaded to contribute for arms and scalps.

A Name to Remember – 'Braddock was a brave man'

Then came the decision on who would command the expedition. Would it be someone who had displayed courage and leadership, someone who had proved their military skills in the Low Countries? The choice was unexpected and no doubt a surprise to many including the one chosen; or was it a question that he was chosen from a group of one?

It was the Duke of Cumberland who recommended the preferred choice to the king, a man relatively unknown outside regimental circles and the gaming rooms of Mayfair. His former commander in the Coldstream Guards, the Earl of Albemarle, could have promoted his name. It was said that his actress friend, George Ann Bellamy, had friends in high places, including Henry Fox, Secretary at War. Was he an influence?

The chosen one was Edward Braddock, a fifty-nine-year-old major general, who had not long been promoted after completing two years as commander and acting governor of the garrison on Gibraltar. Cumberland remembered Braddock from service in the Low Countries and at Culloden. Braddock would have been on the fringe of these campaigns, involved in logistical duties without actually being in action. He was usually to be found well behind the lines in a favourable billet, somewhere where good food and company was to be found.

Who was Major General Edward Braddock? On 10 October 1710 his father, also a major general, obtained for him a commission at the age of fifteen as ensign in the Coldstream Guards. In 1736, after twenty-six years of being a 'mister', he was finally promoted to the rank of captain at the age of forty-one. His lacklustre career continued with regimental duties, including guard duties at the palaces of St James and Windsor Castle and the inevitable riot duties. With a large part of the Army, including the Coldstream Guards, on the continent during the War of the Austrian Succession in 1740, Braddock remained for the most part on home duties with the depot company. In 1745 he secured the rank of lieutenant colonel for £5,000, becoming a senior officer and acting brigadier of the Guards Brigade.

He was now a short stocky figure, nose and fingers snuff stained, and became well known in the London social circles. He frequented the coffee houses and gaming rooms of Mayfair and was described as 'a joyous, rollicking soldier of the old fashioned type, rather popular in London as a good companion and a good fellow, who loved his glass'. Braddock frequented the theatre and, more particularly, George Ann Bellamy, a Covent Garden actress more than thirty years his junior.

In 1745 Braddock resigned his commission in the Coldstream Guards and purchased a colonelcy in the 14th Regiment. As a result he was appointed commandant and acting governor of the garrison at Gibraltar. It was his second extended absence from London in forty-three years of service. The outcome was that, at the age of fifty-nine, he was promoted to major general on 2 April 1754. Towards the end of 1754 he was offered 'out of the blue' the supreme command of all His Majesty's troops in America. It seemed a strange choice; his experience in the Army was limited to the parade ground, the orderly room and the officers' mess. He was Cumberland's choice; the duke felt that Braddock was, like himself a disciple of Frederick the Great, where the making of the ideal soldier was based on the German model of drill, more drill and still more drill, total obedience, never thinking or showing initiative. Braddock did not have a glowing *palmares* with accrued and hard-won honours; in fact, he had little or no experience of command in battle. It seems that his only qualifications were that he was of the right rank and was towards the top of the seniority list. His selection was a mystery.

Braddock was on holiday in Italy when the King and the Duke of Cumberland's group decided that he should command the expedition and, at the same time, be given command of all troops, regular and colonial, in America. Major General Braddock was advised to return to England post haste 'as there was business of the greatest consequence to himself'. Braddock had no idea of what the 'consequence' was and he had no intimation of himself or anyone else being considered for an important command. Although Cumberland conducted his close group discussions in secret, word had got out that America was being discussed since the French had 'got wind' of a campaign being planned.

The Duke of Newcastle's preferred original plan was to mount a limited military action to quickly and decisively force the French to negotiate and avoid a full-scale conflict, thereby re-establishing the status quo antebellum. But Cumberland had strengthened the plan into three final stages. It was to be a full scale attack on the French. The first stage was a major thrust of the expedition under Braddock's command with the 44th and 48th Regiments marching against Fort Duquesne and clearing the French from the Ohio. Was this the opportunity to demonstrate that Prussian-style firepower would crush the French? The second stage was for the 50th (Shirley's) and the 51st (Pepperell's) to attack Fort Niagara. Then, later in the season, the four regiments would march together against Crown Point on Lake Champlain, which the French had held for twenty years but which was well within British North America.

With the final plan agreed it was then decided who would be on Braddock's staff. It was 29 November 1754, Braddock's last night in England. He decided to dine with his actress friend, George Ann Belamy, at her house in Brewer

Street; Lieutenant Colonel Ralph Burton and his aide de camp, Captain Robert Orme, accompanied him. Braddock was in a gloomy, thoughtful mood.

Before they parted, George Ann Bellamy recalled:

> the general told me that he should never see me more, for he was going with a handful of men to conquer whole nations and to do this they must cut their way through unknown woods. He produced a map of the country saying at the same time 'Dear Pop we are sent like a sacrifice to the altar'.

A strange presentiment for a man of his steady temper. As he left, Braddock placed a folded document in her hands. It was his last will and testament, made out to ensure that she would be well provided for and so avoid her creditors.

Little of Braddock's past survives. He lived in Arlington Street. The house was locked up and the furniture covered in dust sheets, but it no longer exists as it was bombed during the 1939–45 war. There are a brace of flintlock pistols, a leopardskin saddle pad and his father's red silk officer's sash, twelve feet long and thirty inches wide with tassels at each end. Woven into the sash at each end was a row of standing figures and the date 1709. These are in several American museums.

The Long March

Braddock and the main body set sail from Cork on 13 January 1755 and, after a stormlashed and stomach-churning voyage of fifty-six days, arrived without loss at Hampton Roads on Tuesday 20 February. The first thing they did when put ashore was to accept an invitation to the nearest tavern where a spread was prepared. They dined well on ham and wild turkey with French wines. The general then went to Williamsburg, the capital of Virginia, to meet the governor of the colony, Dinwiddie. His discussions proved to be disappointing and very soon discovered that all was not meeting his expectations. The many demands made on local resources were not forthcoming.

The 44th Regiment (Halkett's), and the 48th (Dunbar's) had to be brought up to strength, which meant recruiting 200 men for each regiment to increase their totals from 500 to 700 men. But the recruits were not volunteering in any numbers. There were few from Pennsylvania, which was being settled by many German and Dutch non-conformist sects who eschewed war. Braddock was not impressed by the quality of the men and their officers. He ordered Lieutenant James Allen to take charge of their general instruction and drill the American recruits to make soldiers of them. They had to learn the basic evolutions and manual exercises and the elements of controlled firing, the Prussian way.

Braddock's command had Lieutenant Colonels Halkett and Dunbar as his two field commanders. Lieutenant Robert Orme was an aide de camp, as was Roger Morris. After Washington's debacle at Fort Necessity he resigned his commission. But when Braddock arrived Washington wrote to him stating that he was eager to join the expedition and would join as a volunteer. A volunteer would have the nominal rank of ensign, without pay, would fight with the men but dine with the officers and await the availability of promotion. Braddock took this as a good sign as there was a lack of enthusiasm elsewhere. Braddock invited him to join with the brevet rank of captain and acting as his third aide de camp, which was a considerate offer in spite of Washington's previous failure. But no doubt Braddock thought that here was one who had actually fought the French and knew the wilderness and so he was a useful person to have on his staff and after all 'he had heard the charming sound of the bullets whistle'. Washington came with three companies of Virginia Militia and in personal command of a troop of Virginia light horse, or mounted infantry.

The English soldiers called the Virginian Militia 'Bobtails' due to their short blue jackets, which were more practical in the American terrain. The Virginians used to tell tales to frighten the English soldiers, with bloodcurdling stories of Indian savagery. They did this particularly when they were on the march in the dense forest. To stir up interest and enthusiasm, Braddock tried to impress the Virginians with grand marches, with colours flying, and displays of powder, pomp and pipe clay with drums beating and fifes playing the 'British Grenadiers'.

Deputy Quartermaster General Sir John St Clair had gone ahead to America to pave the way for Braddock's arrival. He was to seek sources of supply, the availability of wagons, wagoners and their horses, packhorses for hire, large quantities of food and fodder supplies. Many horses were needed to pull the artillery pieces and packhorses to carry the food supplies. A large quantity of fodder was required as there was a lack of grazing in the wilderness. St Clair had to scout to find the best routes and the possibility of using the rivers. He found gorges to be deep cut roaring channels choked with yellow ice floes and trunks of fallen trees cast down from upriver. To move one large cannon and its ammunition for one day overland required nearly forty horses with all their fodder. To move the same cannon by water required only two bateaux, no fodder and fewer men.

The French had built their forts with impunity, considering that it would be impossible for the English to strike through the wilderness and conquer New France, or Canada; their task would be impossible, a job of mammoth proportions.

Braddock had been given assurances that his many needs to mount his siege train would be available when he and his men arrived. All St Clair and

Dinwiddie could offer were their apologies. It appears that the Virginians had very little they could offer. There was a total lack of wagons and horses in Virginia.

It was Benjamin Franklin, as Deputy Post-Master General of the American colonies, who came to discuss with Braddock a series of postal relays for Braddock's reports and the Army's post. He listened to Braddock's tale of troubles and warned Braddock that his column would stretch out nearly four miles long, caused by the 'road' being only wide enough for a single wagon making it vulnerable to ambush, 'to be cut like thread into several pieces'. Braddock smiled at Franklin's 'ignorance' and replied that 'These savages may indeed be a formidable enemy to your raw American militias but upon the King's regular disciplined troops, Sir, it is impossible they should make any impression'.

After a march of 120 miles from Alexandria, the column or siege train reached Fort Cumberland, the new fort and barracks complex on the Maryland bank of the Potomac, where they assembled ready to face the final march to Fort Duquesne, another 112 miles of 'road' no wider than twelve feet through the wilderness. Daniel Boone, a wagoner arrived, as did Captain Horatio Gates with his New York Independents and Captain Dobbs with the North Carolina Rangers.

Braddock was on the point of cancelling the expedition due to the lack of the promised wagons, carts and the horses plus all the supplies of food and fodder. It was then that a group of Quakers arrived with the wagons and cart-loads of supplies, which had all been arranged by Benjamin Franklin who also arranged for food parcels for the officers from the good people of Pennsylvania. The officers found the prices in America were so high that they could not afford purchases to supplement their rations – or was it a case of prices being temporarily high whilst they were there?, as Braddock had noticed. Braddock was a good organizer. It was the basis of his army career. He became busy seeing that stores were checked, recruits were drilled and the camp women, of sixty per regiment, were medically examined 'to see who was clean and proper'.

William Johnson, Superintendent of Indian Affairs, had arranged for Indian chiefs of the Delawares, Shawnees and Mingos to meet Braddock. When they asked what he intended to do with the land, he replied that the English should inherit and inhabit the land; 'no savage should inherit the land'. In short this caused all the Indians to leave and eventually side with the French, leaving Braddock with little or no support from the Indians. Braddock, in his blunt and self-assured 'blimpish' way, was too naïve to understand the tensions of Indian-White relations. To him they were troublesome exotics.

When the column set off Braddock ordered the men to travel light and leave their shoulder and waistbelts behind as well as their hangers; officers were to leave their spontoons and the sergeants their pikes. It was also decided to leave the four 12-pounder naval cannon, but the hundred seamen would continue the march.

Captain Washington led the troop of Virginia Light Horse to escort Braddock; mounted troops were at a disadvantage in the close confines of the forest. It was also at Fort Cumberland that they met their first friendly Indians, one seaman noting that they were very dexterous and armed with rifled-barrelled guns (which they would meet in earnest later). They also had tomahawks 'which they threw with great certainty'.

Braddock decided that, to speed up the progress, he would divide the column and create a faster moving flying column. He sent Sir John St Clair ahead with 400 men, two companies of Virginia Rangers, the Indian scouts and two 6-pounders. They would act as a vanguard, but in a European situation the light cavalry would be well ahead with vedettes on the flanks to give ample warning. Braddock would follow with the two senior grenadier companies of 550 men from the 44th and 48th Regiments, as well as the sailors and the Virginia Light Horse as his escort. Also included in his column were four howitzers with fifty rounds each, three coehorn mortars and thirteen wagons which carried the ammunition, although one carried presents for the Indians. Colonel Dunbar would follow with the remainder of the troops and artillery, which included the baggage and the pack horses carrying thirty-five days of provisions and victuals. As Franklin had warned he was splitting the column.

As the march continued they found a camp used, it seems, by about 150 braves. They had stripped the trees and painted many threats and brave expressions in French. As they continued the march they were aware of movements of Indians in the depths and shadows of the forest. A number of wagoners who tended their horses in the forest were killed and scalped. They were visited by so-called 'friendly' Mohawks who were obviously sent as spies. Ottawas, whom the French used as their shock troops led by Chief Pontiac, made many of the raids on the column. Braddock issued new marching orders to all officers with the outer detachments that they should always keep one of the men within sight of the line of march and that these parties be no closer than a hundred yards with the detachments of officers, sergeants and corporals to be no closer to their officers than fifty yards. To lift the men's spirits he offered £5 for any Indian scalp taken. This is a strange reversal of his earlier order when he tried to force his friendly Indians to stop scalping.

The closer they got to Fort Duquesne the more aware they became of the presence of Indians in the forest. At first they were shadowy figures moving swiftly through the undergrowth. The column reached Great Meadows, the site of the abandoned Fort Necessity, the scene of Washington's defeat where the swivel guns lay discarded in the ditch and a British officer recorded that 'There are many human bones all around ye spott.'

They passed Jumonville Glen where, the year before, Washington and the Half King started what developed into the French and Indian War, the first stage of The Seven Years' War. They also discovered a recently abandoned Indian camp; again the trees were stripped of their bark and painted red with signs and shapes of the scalps taken the day before; the fires were still burning. They crossed the Youghiogheny river which, at that point, was one hundred yards wide but fordable. The men were getting nervous and some were firing off their muskets at shadows, creating false alarms. The signs were proving that they were entering threatening country.

Braddock now faced a situation that he instinctively felt spelt ambush. They were entering the sphere of 'bush fighting'. The British Army was not trained in the technique of bush warfare against regulars or irregulars; in fact such warfare was not even acknowledged. The British Army, as disciplined troops, were trained in their evolutions to manoeuvre to present to the enemy mass firepower. It was expected that their adversary would also present its force in a similar manner – in Europe.

The nature of the terrain in the American wilderness, the thick forest that closed in all round like wooden walls, forced the column to squeeze into a thin line that stretched back several miles. The commander was placed at the head but his control was limited to those in his immediate vicinity or as far as his or his officers' orders would carry. As Franklin had warned, the column could be severed at several places creating disorder and disunity. With Braddock's troops massed in several areas he had lost the impact of the Fredrician effect of total firepower, whereas the French and Indians were operating under a system of 'Fire and Move', shooting accurately from behind cover, not remaining there to present a target, but moving to further cover, finding a target and shooting accurately with their rifles. The French would have no problem with parity of numbers as they could attack the column piecemeal.

Ambush is a problem that had faced disciplined armies before where difficult terrain forced troops from open country into defiles, valleys and thick forest. If Braddock had read his histories he would have discovered how the Roman legions had faced this problem from the barbarians in the forests of Germania and Gaul. It is thought that the famous IX Legion was destroyed by the Picts in the dense forests of Caledonia. There was no formal training for the British Army in such situations. British troops in America had to make changes to adjust to bush fighting, even creating new regiments solely to operate in such extreme circumstances.

On 9 July 1755 Braddock and the flying column had advanced sixty miles ahead of Dunbar and the main force. They had forded the Monongahela River but all were suffering from sickness, dysentery or, as they called it, 'the flux', including captain Washington who was laid low with haemorrhoids the pain of which caused him to strap cushions on his saddle. Hunger was now a problem as they were out of food, which was behind in the main column. But their morale was high as they had very few encounters with the French Indians, were only ten miles from Fort Duquesne and expected to surprise and attack them the following day.

Leading the vanguard were George Crogan and seven Indians, behind them were 300 grenadiers keeping formation. The grenadiers functioned in a light infantry role; they were led by Colonel Thomas Gage, the future Governor of Massachusetts, and a future exponent of light infantry.

The main body of the flying column followed about a hundred yards behind, moving cautiously with flankers scouting ahead and along the flanks. They were all on a nervous edge, eyes scanning possible areas for ambush, seeing shapes they thought were Indians everywhere. The French commander at Fort Duquesne, Contrecoeur, had 1,600 French regular marines, Canadian militia and Indians under his command. The small fort could hold about 200 and his concern was that his Indians would not fight to defend the fort, as they had no concept of fighting to defend ground. They fought to capture trophies and slaves; to them that was profit. Otherwise, they would kill and take scalps as proof of their warrior status. Other captives would be tortured or butchered, so that all could share in the victory.

The best plan was to attack the column and disrupt its advance whilst it was on the move. Contrecoeur had the advantages of surprise and his force's knowledge of how to fight in the forest, using stealth, cover and keeping on the move. An attack group was formed with half the men at the fort, thirty-six officers, seventy-two regulars of the *troupes de la marine*, 146 Canadian militia-men, (Canadians were French settlers, trappers, traders and backwoodsmen), 637 Indians made up from a few Mingos, Delawares, a large group of Shawnees and some Hurons, with the majority being Ottawas, a total force of 841. They were well armed, the regulars with their Charleville muskets, the others with hunting rifles while the Indians also had rifles but their favoured weapon for close-quarter fighting was the hatchet or tomahawk. Otherwise, they were unencumbered with equipment; the Indians were semi-naked except for breach clouts and were painted with red, blue and black warpaint. Captain Daniel Liénard de Beaujeu commanded them; he was also stripped to the waist with just his gorget round his neck.

It was just after noon when Crogan with the Indian scouts spotted the French attack party just a few hundred yards to their front. Colonel Gage acted correctly, as they had been trained. He raised the alarm and wheeled the grenadiers into line, then, on the order 'Look to your front – form three ranks', the front rank knelt, followed by the order 'present' and 'give fire', then the cry 'huzza!'. They fired three quick volleys. Even though it was at the maximum range Captain Beaujeu, who was at the front, was shot in the third volley. At this crushing blast of lead and with their commander shot the Canadians scattered in all directions in a panic. The grenadiers moved forward shouting 'God save the King!' But where was the front, who to shoot at, because all the French war party had dispersed. They knew exactly what to do, this was their country, they had gone to ground seeking cover. From the protection of the trees they set up a fast rate of fire and began to decimate the grenadiers. The Indians ran either side of the column finding cover and keeping up a continuous fire, they were just fleeting shapes hidden in the shadows of the undergrowth and felled the hapless grenadiers who had no notion of who opposed them or where the fire was coming from, apart from movements in the forest and the screeching yells of the Indians. It was known that the engineers in the vanguard were armed with twelve rifles but it is not known of what type as all were lost in the first crushing attack.

It was the colonials who, reacting from experience to the Indian threat, had scattered, taken cover and began to return fire. After the initial volleys the grenadiers were in confusion. The officers were mounted and were obvious targets and began to fall rapidly. Without any orders the grenadiers began to fall back. Braddock ordered up troops from the rear with the colours. He was attempting to rally the troops to their colours but, as they began to form up, they attracted fire and were struck down. At this point it was Colonel Halkett who took command. There was total confusion as those fleeing, including the pioneers, clashed with those trying to advance. Within the first ten minutes of the French attack fifteen of the eighteen officers in Gage's advance group had been killed or wounded. There was utter confusion and all semblance of discipline and order had collapsed in the panic-driven scramble. All the time there were the terrifying screams and yells of the Indians as they flailed about with their tomahawks. Small groups of grenadiers formed and began firing at anything, shadows, shapes and, unfortunately, some of the colonials in the woods whom they mistook for the French; a large number were killed in a 'friendly fire' situation. Braddock was trying to restore some semblance of order in what was total chaos. Surrounded by frightened men desperate to reload and fire, all about them were the wounded, desperate for help, the dying, the massacred. Washington, ill and ineffectual, managed to ride back to the main group to summon help. St Clair was badly wounded, as was Orme. One British officer noted that the enemy fire made a popping sound 'with a little explosion' and 'only a kind of whizzing noise; (which is proof the enemy's arms were rifle barrels)'.

The rifles used by the French proved deadly; they were accurate over a lengthy range, whereas the regulars and colonials armed with Short Land Pattern muskets 'might as well have been firing at the moon'. As a British officer noted, this was probably the first time that the British Army had encountered rifle fire and they found it devastating. At one point Washington asked Braddock if he could post men behind the trees to continue the fight. Braddock's servant later recalled hearing him curse and respond with 'I've a mind to run you through the body! We'll sup today in Fort Duquesne or else in hell!' Late in the fighting Braddock was shot into the arm and chest. With help Washington managed to carry him away to a two-wheeled tumbrel and took him away. There was a claim made by a Pennsylvanian, Tom Fausett, who said that he had shot Braddock to avenge the death of his brother whom Braddock caught cowering behind a tree and ran him through with his sword. Fausett persisted in his claim for many years but it was never proved. In the panic-driven excitable state they were in, it is possible that some extreme measures were taken.

Realizing that all was lost, the wagoners had unhitched their horses and ridden away, including Captain Dobbs and the self-proclaimed heroes Daniel Boone and Daniel Morgan. Then, at about five o'clock, 'as if by the beat of Drumm' the entire army 'turned to ye right about & made a most precipitate retreat everyone trying to be first'.

Washington, with Captain Stewart and Robert Orme, brought Braddock back in the two-wheeled tumbrel, but Braddock's wound was fatal and he eventually expired once across the Monongahela river. His last words were, 'Who would have thought it – we shall better know how to deal with them another time.' It seems that, belatedly, he recognized that war against the French and Indians was a different kind of war. He was buried in the middle of the road so that the column could pass over it to disguise it; the French never did find the grave.

The estimates of the overall British losses were, of a total force of 1,466 British and Americans present in the flying column, 456 were killed and butchered, including eighty officers, which not only proved their bravery but showed that they made themselves obvious in all respects as targets. Nearly all the medical staff were killed. The wagoners who fled at the beginning with their horses all managed to survive. The non-combatants were lost, including the women, most being carried off. Of the others, 421 were seriously wounded, a total of 877 out of 1,466, or about sixty per cent, were casualties. The French casualties were slight, with eleven killed and twenty-nine wounded from a force of 841. The French never did find the pay chest, which contained £25,000 in gold coin.

Outside the sphere of military history very few would recognize the name of Major General Edward Braddock, but his name is well established in the annals of Anglo–American history, and particularly in those of the Coldstream Guards.

As Benjamin Franklin has said, 'This general was I think a brave man, and might probably have made a good figure in some European war. But he had too much confidence, too high opinion of the validity of regular troops and too mean a one of both Americans and Indians!'

The Greeks believed that if a man's name was remembered he would become immortal.

Chapter 3

The Introduction of Light Infantry

When the news of the disaster to Braddock's expedition reached Horse Guards in London it was met with incredulity, dismay and disbelief. How could such a strong force of British regiments and American militias, all well-armed, be routed with so many casualties by a weaker mixed force of French, Canadians and, worst of all, 'savage Indians'? Also, what was unsettling news was that many of the French and Indians were armed with rifles, which was responsible for much of the destruction. The defeat of Braddock's column was a serious reverse to the ambitions of Pitt, and the government's plan to wrest Canada from the French as part of Pitt's grand plan for the expansion of empire.

Braddock's expedition had been seen as a strong force which, with the addition of the 50th (Shirley's) and the 51st (Pepperell's), would make the combined Anglo-American force superior to that of the French. It had been seen as more than adequate to destroy the French forts on the Ohio and, ultimately with additional troops, to capture Quebec and Montreal and cause the French to surrender control over New France.

The 44th and the 48th Regiments had responded to the attack in the way they had been trained to face an enemy on the drill grounds of rural England, or on the pastoral plain of northern Europe. They were not trained to react to the form of bush fighting in the immense wilderness that covered North America. Braddock was a fully competent officer who planned assiduously the details of the expedition and had ensured that the protection of the column was arranged according to the current system in the manual. Any other commander would have done exactly the same, all according to Fredrician practice.

The entire approach to planning, methods and training was based on what those in Horse Guards had experienced in past campaigns in Europe and refined in the tactics of Frederick the Great. But the situation in North America was unforeseen and, therefore, totally unexpected. The Army learnt from it and began to implement many changes to training, tactics and equipment; they had not only to match, but to better the French and Indians. It was realized that to defeat them special bodies of troops must be formed to function in the woods; it would mean less drill-orientated movements, less executing moves by numbers but more attention to flexibility and adapting to the conditions found in North America. It was an alien land without the social structure of connected villages, roads and paths and with no familiar points of reference. Using rivers as roads the French and Indians travelled over long distances by bark canoes and, with portage, crossed impenetrable forest on foot to make close-quarter assaults using rifles and hatchets. To quote Colonel Bouquet of the 1/60th, describing the tactics of the Indians: 'The first of their maxims is to surround their enemy. The second, that they fight scattered, and never in a compact body. The third, that they never stand their ground when attacked, but immediately give way and return to the charge.'

Unlike the western plains Indians who used the horse, introduced by the Spanish, to fight as light cavalry, this was a war of stealth, guerrilla war or *Petite Guerre*, which the Indians had perfected, never offering battle unless they thought they could win. European tactics did not relate to the unfamiliar conditions found in North America.

The massed volley-fire by bodies of highly-trained and disciplined troops 'might as well be firing at the moon' when the enemy did not conform or appear in a mass formation but fought in dispersed groups and often independently in a fire and move mode. They used the terrain to their advantage, blending in with the surroundings and making full use of cover, never exposing themselves as targets and always suitably dressed in clothes that were practical for service in the woods. Thus it was necessary for the Army to adjust the uniform and dispense with some of the accoutrements for soldiers to allow them to function unimpeded in the woods. When Lieutenant Alexander Baille of the Royal Americans worked out the weight of the average soldier's accoutrements and necessaries required on the march the total came to over sixty-three pounds.

General Braddock had previously said that he had 'lighten'd them as much as possible, and have left in store their swords and the greatest part of heavy accoutrements'. Swords were left behind and, in 1759, an order from head-quarters in America instructed sergeants to carry firelocks, instead of halberds, with cartouche box and bayonet instead of sword, the soldier 'no sword (hangers) nor sword belt, if they can take their bayonet securely without them'.

Many officers exchanged their spontoons for muskets; James Wolfe carried a musket at Quebec. It was quickly seen that the rifle was a far better weapon to use when fighting the Indians in the woods, where accuracy was more important than speed of loading. Twelve rifles, with bullet moulds, were issued to the 44th and 48th Regiments in 1758; '10 Rifled Barrelled Guns were delivered out to each regiment to be put in the hands of the best marksmen.' These were probably sent from England and were of German make, short heavy rifles firing a large ball.

There was a single occasion when European tactics were successful and that was when Major General Wolfe's troops finally faced Montcalm and his troops on the Heights of Abraham in Quebec in 1759. The French lost the fight because they were not fully trained to fight in a disciplined line and obey firing orders. Wolfe had six regiments, standing in three ranks. Facing them across the Heights were the French in line, they moved swiftly almost at the double and, when they were about 130 yards from the British line, they stopped and fired a volley. They reloaded and pressed on until they were less than fifty yards from the British, who had been standing steady and at the ready with shouldered arms. Then on the command the British poised, cocked firelocks, presented and gave fire. The French line disappeared, crushed by that single volley. It was thought that Wolfe was shot by an Indian sniping from the flanks.

In contrast to the tactics of bush fighting, there were periods of siege warfare when artillery was dominant and it became a question of storming the French forts when all soldiers took on the role of the grenadier to form assault companies.

The American Rangers

The forerunners of the designation 'light infantrymen' in the British service were those who answered an advertisement in the *Boston Weekly Newsletter* of 4th October 1750:

> All Gentlemen Volunteers and Others that have a mind to serve His Majesty King GEORGE the second for a limited time in the Independent Companies of Rangers now in Nova Scotia, may apply to Lieutenant *Alexander Callender* at Mr Jonas Leonard's at the sign of the *Lamb* at the South End of Boston, where they shall be kindly entertained, enter into present pay, and have good quarters, and when they join their respective companies in Halifax, shall be completely clothed in blue broadcloth, receive Arms, Accoutrements, Provisions and all other things necessary for a gentleman ranger.

The rangers were raised to protect the new settlers and veterans from Scotland in Nova Scotia from attacks by Indians that were being encouraged by the French. They appeared in the Army Lists as North American Rangers. The French in Canada believed that by encouraging Indian violence against the settlers it would drive them back from advancing into new territory. The colonial governors' attention was concentrated on this factor and how best to deal with it; but William Pitt was more concerned about the total conquest of Canada. He sent instructions to Lord Loudoun:

> His Majesty doubts not but (that) . . . your Lordship will find yourself in a condition . . . to effectorate some great essential impressions on the enemy. The King is of the opinion that the taking of Louisbourg and Quebec can alone prove decisive; but as the success of both these

enterprises may depend on circumstances not to be known here, His Majesty is pleased to leave some latitude to your Lordship's discretion and judgement.

The rangers fought a constant guerrilla war during the years between the Treaty of Aix-la-Chapelle and the beginning of the Seven Years' War along the Canadian frontier. The first company organized was led by John Goreham and recruited from woodsmen who considered themselves regulars serving the King. The company performed well at Louisbourg. Wolfe took six ranger companies with him to Quebec. Captain Knox noted that they wore regular issue uniforms cut short, as well as leather caps, and carried powder horns in place of cartridge boxes.

His Majesty's Independent Companies of American Rangers

A Major Rogers approached the Commander-in-Chief and offered to raise several companies of backwoodsmen and Indian fighters to serve as civilian scouts and forest rangers. They were known generally as Rogers's Rangers and would supply their own equipment and their own fire-arms; most had the long Pennsylvanian hunting rifle. These men would act as scouts and infiltrate deep into the forests and Indian lands, going where the regular soldier could not or dared not go. They would gather information on French and Indian movements and activities and organize raids and aggressive attacks. They would not be subject to military orders and King's Regulations and discipline, with which many officers disagreed, although a number, including Lord Howe, did venture out with the rangers to learn how to survive in the wilderness.

Major Robert Rogers's company was neither regular nor provincial, although Rogers did try to get it placed on the regular establishment. He had five companies, each consisting of one captain, two lieutenants, one ensign, four sergeants and 100 privates. The men wore good warm clothing as uniform as possible in each company. Rogers tried to get the government to supply them with uniforms but to no avail. Two companies wore grey duffle coats and greatcoats while others wore green jackets or hunting shirts. Plain buckskin shirts were also worn.

Rogers's men were 'all their own men', individuals who were hard to discipline, so Rogers issued to each a set of Rangers' Rules. It is interesting to note that when the modern American Rangers were formed during the Second World War each ranger was reminded of Rogers and issued with the same set of rules.

One of the most feared Indian nations was the Abenakis, whose territory was above New Hampshire. They were encouraged to attack the settlers' farms and cause devastation by the Jesuit priests, who after converting them (the Abenakis were known as the praying Indians), would tell them to kill the Protestant settlers and hang the scalps from their crucifixes. Rogers carried out a daring raid on their settlements deep in the forest. They set off in bateaux up the Saint Francis River, hid the boats and trekked through the forest. However, as they were about to attack, the men who had been left to guard the boats suddenly arrived and told Rogers that some Indians had discovered the boats and destroyed them. Nevertheless Rogers went ahead and made a surprise attack on the settlement, sparing few and razing the village to the ground. They had a perilous journey back, taking a different route. Although they were meant to rendezvous with a support group with supplies this failed to arrive. Most managed to get back after suffering near starvation.

Rogers's Rules

- Don't forget nothing. Have your musket clean as a whistle, tomahawk scoured, sixty rounds, powder and ball, and be ready to march at a moment's notice. When you are on the march act the way you would if you were sneaking up on a deer, see the enemy first.
- Tell the truth about what you see and what you do. There is an army depending on us for correct information. You can lie all you please when you tell others about the Rangers, but don't lie to a ranger or an officer.
- Don't never take a chance you don't have to. When on the march single file far enough apart so one shot can't go through two men. If we strike swamps or soft ground, we spread out abreast, so it's hard to track us. When we march we keep moving till dark, so as to give the enemy the least possible chance at us.
- When in camp, half the party stays awake, while the other half sleeps. If we take prisoners we keep 'em separate 'till we have time to examine them so they can't cook up a story between them.
- Don't ever march home the same way. Take a different route so you won't be ambushed. Each party has to keep about 20 yards ahead, 20 yards on each flank and 20 yards in the rear so the main body can't be wiped out. Every night you will be told where to meet if surrounded by a superior force.
- Don't sit down without posting sentries.
- Don't sleep beyond dawn; dawn's when the French and Indians attack.
- Don't cross the river by the regular ford. If somebody is trailing you make a circle, come back on your own tracks and ambush the folks that's aiming to ambush you.

- Don't stand up when the enemy is aiming at you; kneel down, lie down or hide behind a tree. Let the enemy come till he's almost close enough to touch, then let him have it and jump up and finish him off with your tomahawk.

These rules were deliberately written by Rogers in a homespun way in the vernacular so that all would understand their importance.

The informality and lack of discipline, and military behaviour bordering on casual sloppiness, did not satisfy the Captain General of the Army, the Duke of Cumberland, who wrote that: 'till regular officers, with men they can trust, learn to best the woods, and act as *Irregulars,* you will never gain any certain intelligence of the enemy.'

> The rangers were all backwoodsmen, strong characters used to being on their own and surviving in the forest under all conditions, so there was, at times, undisciplined behaviour and clashes of personality. In fact at one time there was a small mutiny when they returned from the raid on an Abenaki village. This caused the Earl of Loudoun, the C–in–C for North America, to take an interest in training regular troops to serve as rangers.

In 1767 the 1/60th Royal Americans were in the area of New York when they heard that Major Rogers had been imprisoned in a debtors' prison in New York. It seemed that he was accused of misappropriating the Rangers' funds; his approach to accounting was as unorthodox as were his methods of fighting. Rogers had adopted some of Colonel Bouquet's tactics on frontier warfare. Major Rogers fought alongside Bouquet throughout Pontiac's uprising and, later, during the revolution. Rogers was well known to the 60th Regiment and some of the men who had served with him broke into the prison, released him and allowed him to escape to Connecticut. Rogers was a loyalist and it was impossible for him to stay in the colonies after the revolution when the rebels were making revenge attacks. It appears that some years later he ended up in London.

The Flankers

On 22 December 1757 Lieutenant Colonel Thomas Gage, of the 44th Regiment, late of Braddock's expedition and with the experiences gained thereby, and supported by Lord Howe, petitioned Lord Loudon to raise at his own expense a light regiment. This regiment was designed for scouting and skirmishing only, and was clothed in dark brown with short skirtless jackets. In May 1759 they were issued with a 'sett of 520 carbines without bayonets', the barrels made blue or brown; they also had knives, hatchets, shot bags and powder horns. The regiment was shown in the Army List styled as light infantry and became the first regiment in the British Army to be designated 'Light', as Gage's Light Arm'd Foot, and numbered the 80th Regiment. Another regiment raised later in the war and styled as light infantry was Colonel Morgan's Regiment, and shown in the Army List from 1760 to 1763 as the 90th Regiment of Irish Light Infantry.

All these regiments were disbanded in 1763 and raised again in 1778 at the time of the Revolution and again disbanded at the end of that war in 1784. In 1794 they were raised for a third time for the second American war. Also raised at that time was the famous 90th Perthshire Volunteers, later the 2nd Battalion (Scottish Rifles) of the Cameronians.

From the many disbandments and re-raisings of these light regiments, it would appear that the Commander-in-Chief did not see light regiments as a permanent part of the structure of the infantry. This illustrates how fixed in the Army's thinking was the influence of the Fredrician principles of mass fire-power, or fire and shock.

Experiences so far in North America had shown that the training and tactics of the line troops did not fit them for service in the woods for what looked like becoming a long campaign against the French and Indians. Line troops had a single purpose, which was to conform to the tactical requirements of the European battlefield as devised by the master Frederick II, King of Prussia. His successful tactics were based on the effect of the delivery of total firepower at the precise time and to finish with shock – the bayonet. This required a trained soldier to be completely obedient and to react instantly, and auto-matically, to commands without question or even thinking. He was trained to carry out all the movements as per the drill manual, in unison with the entire unit all acting as one man with the company or battalion all the time remaining steady. 'Steady' meant that he was to remain in line during the noise of the cycle of volleys and the ensuing clouds of powder smoke, the thundering crash of cannonfire, the never-ending beat of the drums, as shot and shell struck those about him; he had to remain steady as the corporals closed up the gaps in the ranks.

Line infantry react to commands. Given commands, they know how to comply but without commands they are at a total loss; independent action is never considered. So when the vanguard of Braddock's 44th grenadiers was attacked in ambush all semblance of order disappeared, they were confused and leaderless, particularly as most of the officers were amongst the first casualties. This incident had exposed a weakness in the Fredrician system that would have a lasting influence on the future structure of the infantry.

Whereas line troops were to obey every command light troops were expected to show initiative even when commands were not forthcoming. The Scottish Highland regiments were considered to make ideal light troops, the 42nd being an example. Highlanders seemed to have a natural aptitude for functioning in light duties. Weapon handling was important and light troops were expected to be good shots, marksmen; for this they needed a keen eye, good eyesight and had to be very observant. Those who had previously followed country pursuits, woodcutters, poachers, gamekeepers or shepherds, made ideal recruits. They were expected to be lithe and dexterous, bright and alert. Their duties were to act as the eyes and ears of their unit, to protect the main force by covering the flanks, by forming a rearguard and a vanguard when on the march, and when in camp by posting picquets and manning outposts.

All light troops were expected to be familiar with and experienced in the drill and movements and evolutions of line troops and function independently or in small groups. Light troops were expected to be self-reliant and show individual initiative on all occasions and be sure of their ability to make decisions and follow them through. It was Sir John Moore, the founder of light infantry, who set the pattern for light troops. From him they flourished to eventually form the famous Light Division which gave Wellington's Peninsular Army an extra sharp edge.

60th Royal American Regiment

Before Braddock's expedition, Cumberland considered that it might be appropriate to create a separate American establishment, rather than service this sphere of operations from the Irish and English establishments. In 1754, for the protection and security of the Colonies, it was proposed to have British-paid American regiments with a total of several hundred thousand men. The plan was eventually rejected as it was thought that it was too much of a risk since it was considered that these regiments could be untrustworthy regarding loyalty to the Crown. There was, anyway, a major fault with the plan which was recruitment. Large numbers of recruiting parties were sent to every town and village to 'drum up' recruits but they discovered they could not compete with the local militias; for service in the Continental regiments offered large bounties of ten pounds, higher pay, and only seasonal duties as the units all stood down and soldiers went back to their homes during the hard winter months.

It was always a problem raising recruits, particularly in time of war when it was necessary to increase the number of troops rapidly. One recourse was to hire existing regiments from foreign armies. The numerous German states and principalities of the Holy Roman Empire all had armies which were often larger than required, but this was intentional as the excess troops could be hired to other states as a lucrative venture. Many of these regiments were *chasseur* or *jäger* units.

Out of Braddock's dilemma was created one of the most unusual regiments in the British Army and this came about in a most auspicious way. A certain Jacques Prevost was a thirty-year-old Swiss officer acting as a military agent who saw opportunities to make money out of the unsuspecting. With dubious credentials he was not exactly trustworthy. After receiving money to procure recruits, which he did, he then sold them to another party for more money. A wanted and pursued man, in 1755 he decided to make a hurried exit from Europe and head for America.

On board ship was William Lyttleton, who was on his way to become Governor of South Carolina, a colony with a large number of German-speaking settlers. From Lyttleton Jacques Prevost heard much about the problems of security, the French and recruitment of troops in North America. This gave Prevost food for thought. The ship was captured by a French privateer and the passengers soon found themselves being ransomed and, eventually, back in England. The Duke of Cumberland was informed of this incident and of Jacques Prevost and his idea of raising a regiment recruited from German-Americans, Germans and British volunteers. Cumberland, whose sister knew the Prince of Orange and had known the Prevost brothers in Holland, agreed that Prevost's plan was worth trying.

Pitt expressed it clearly in the House of Commons:

> The nation would not have been blessed (with the scheme) if by fortuitous co-currence of circumstances Prevost had not been going as an adventurer to America and had not taken it into his head to have a regiment.

Prevost's providential suggestion to raise a regiment for the American service was to recruit from 'deserters' from the 500-odd regiments in the German states. Part of this plan was to augment the recruits from among the German settlers in Pennsylvania and elsewhere; at this time the number of German settlers in America was considerable. In 1750, out of a population of 270,000, there were no fewer than 90,000 Germans, or a third of the population of Pennsylvania. Prevost's scheme seemed to satisfy King George, to the extent that he provisionally authorized him to recruit Swiss and German officers and engineers.

Prevost's plan was implemented with speed. Braddock had been defeated on 9 July 1755 and, barely six months later, on Christmas Day 1755 (25 December was the traditional day to raise a regiment), Lord Loudoun was appointed Colonel of the new 62nd Royal American Regiment of Foot. This was done on Governor's Island, New York, where there is today a memorial plaque commemorating this and also a regimental colour (battalion uncertain).

In February 1756 a Bill was introduced in the House of Commons:

> To enable His Majesty to grant commissions to a certain number of Foreign Protestants who have served abroad as Officers or Engineers to act and rank as officers or Engineers in America only under certain Restrictions and Qualifications.

The reference to 'Foreign Protestants' was a reminder of the continuing religious quarrel that had marked the accession of George I and the importance that George II's ministers attached to 'extinguishing the hopes of the Preferred Prince of Wales (and) his abettors'. The Stuart uprising of 1745 in Scotland had strengthened religious anxieties.

The regiment was originally designated the 62nd but, after the capture of the 50th and the 51st Regiments at Oswego by the French these were 'broken' and disbanded and so, by dropping two numbers, the 62nd became the 60th.

In April 1756 the French invaded Minorca and, the following day, King George II declared war on France. This gave Pitt the opportunity to develop his plans for empire and, eventually, to conquer Canada. An Act of Parliament was passed (Act 29 Geo II cap 5) to raise His Majesty's Regiment of Infantry to consist of four battalions of 1,000 men or other foreigners who volunteered to serve for the better defence of His Majesty's Colonies in America from the colonies of Massachusetts, New York, Pennsylvania, Maryland and North Carolina.

The actual order to raise the regiment was not issued until 4 March 1756 when the establishment was fixed at four battalions, each of ten companies. Each company was to consist of four sergeants, four corporals, two drummers and 100 private men, making a total strength for the regiment of 4,400 NCOs and men.

Limiting the battalions for service in America was due to the government being nervous about the loyalty of foreign troops and very cautious about having at any time large numbers of them stationed in England. The fear was that they could import republicanism and other undesirable political ideas, such as democracy, which did not have the same meaning as it does today. All drafts of foreign recruits arrived at Lymington in Hampshire for enlistment. The members of the 60th were not permitted to be based on British soil, other than the Isle of Wight and the Channel Islands. Occasionally, recruiting cadres came to England en route to the continent to collect recruits. It does seem strange that a numbered British regiment with 'Royal' in its title was not permitted to set foot on English soil.

Prevost went ahead and succeeded in gathering together from Europe about ninety commissioned and non-commissioned officers. Included among them were some very capable men, such as Henri Bouquet, Frederick Haldimand and Augustin Prevost. Bouquet and Haldimand were both Swiss officers of distinction, then serving in the bodyguard of the Prince of Orange. They were appointed to the lieutenant colonelcies of the first and second battalions respectively. Colonel Haldimand is believed to have been at one time in the Sardinian service and also served at Mollwitz in 1741 under Frederick of Prussia. The command of the third battalion went to Lieutenant Colonel Russel Chapman and the fourth battalion to Lieutenant Colonel John St Clair, who had served with Braddock. The 3/60th and 4/60th were raised and disbanded several times depending on needs. Although a four-battalion regiment, making it of brigade strength, it never served as a brigade. The opposite was more the case as its duties caused it to be dispersed to cover an expansive area, operating at times at half battalion or even company strength. The regiment's duties covered the area of North America, from Canada to the West Indies and Central America. During the Seven Years' War its personnel were about twenty-five per cent American, fifty per cent British (including Irish) and twenty-five per cent miscellaneous German speakers with some Poles and Bohemians.

The battalions varied greatly and they were quick to adapt to conditions in America. The purpose of the Royal Americans was to form a body of regular troops capable of combining the qualities of the scout with the qualities of the trained soldier; to concentrate on the duties of light troops and fit them for service in the woods. Although not named as such, they were trained as light troops and their duties were onerous and ubiquitous, serving in most areas of North America, the West Indies and Central America. Being a royal regiment it had blue facings but, unlike most other regiments, the enlisted men's uniforms were without lace until the end of the French and Indian War in 1763. They wore brown canvas marching gaiters for common wear and white gaiters for full dress. Officers wore silver lace. To make the men less conspicuous the leather accoutrements were not pipe-clayed.

Colonel Bouquet – 'none to surpass, none perhaps to equal'

Colonel Bouquet made the first battalion into a first-class light infantry unit specially trained for forest warfare, combining the qualities of the scout with those of the trained soldier. It became a model light infantry battalion. The soldiers adapted their uniforms for service in the woods, cutting down the cocked hats into caps, adopting the American hunting shirts and Indian leggings and discarding their hangers in favour of hatchets. Bouquet knew the value of marksmanship and indented for sixteen rifled carbines 'for the use of the forces employed on the expedition under General Forbes'. Only ten were sent to Bouquet, six being taken by Brigadier General Stanwix.

The Training Schedule of Colonel Bouquet

The soldiers before being armed must be taught to keep themselves clean and to dress in a soldier like manner. This will raise in them a becoming spirit, give them a favourable opinion of their profession, and preserve their health. The first thing they are to learn to walk well, afterwards to run; and in order to excite emulation small prizes should from time to time be given to those who distinguish themselves. They must then run in ranks in extended order and wheel in that order, at first slowly, then by degrees with increasing speed. This evolution is difficult, but most important in order to fall unexpectedly on the flank of the enemy. The men are to disperse and rally at given signals, and particular colours should be given to each company at rallying points. The men must be trained to leap logs and ditches, and to carry burdens proportionate to their strength.

When perfect in these exercises the young soldiers will receive their arms and follow the above-named evolutions on all kinds of ground. They will be taught to handle their arms with dexterity, and without losing time upon trifles to load and fire quickly standing, kneeling or lying on the ground. They are to fire at a mark without a rest, and are not allowed to be long in taking aim. [This of course is the opposite to the view expressed by Wolfe.] Hunting and the award of small prizes will soon make them expert marksmen.

Apart from the last sentence this would all be very familiar to anyone who has been through military training.

The men should learn to swim, pushing before them on a small raft of their clothes, arms and ammunition; they must also learn to use snow shoes; they must be taught to throw up entrenchments, make fascines and gabions, as well as to fell trees, saw planks, construct canoes, carts, ploughs, barrows, roofs, casks, bateaux and bridges and to build ovens and log-houses.

Great care is to be taken to preserve purity of manners, order, and decency among the men; this will be found much easier in the woods than in the neighbourhood of towns. It would be a good plan to give men only a small portion of their pay in cash; the remainder will be accumulated for them until discharge; then they would receive the balance due to them and 200 acres of land.

The first major engagement involving the 60th was not one of bush fighting but of siege warfare. Montcalm decided to invest Fort William Henry with a strong force of 6,000 French regulars and Canadian militias supported by the largest number of Indian braves ever assembled; they totalled 1,300 from various nations from as far as Hudson Bay and the headwaters of the Mississippi.

The garrison of Fort William Henry numbered approximately 1,100, which included regulars of the 35th Regiment, artillery and American militia, reinforced by an additional 800 militia men and two companies, 200 men, of the 3/60th.

After seven days of solid pounding by French cannon and mortars the fort was forced to surrender. Lieutenant Colonel John Young of the Royal Americans conducted the surrender negotiations. The 3/60th had eighty casualties, either killed or wounded.

Montcalm gave the garrison an honourable surrender and they were allowed to march out with arms and colours. As it was impossible to hold, guard and feed large numbers of prisoners in the forest, the only recourse was to let them march off and fend for themselves.

The Indians could not understand an honourable surrender. Since they were the victors they needed proof of their prowess in battle; they had to take back to their villages plunder and scalps. The Indians attacked the column as they marched out of the fort. In the ensuing massacre, men, women and children were killed and many carried off as prisoners.

William Pitt wanted more activity in North America and asked for a three-pronged assault for the summer of 1758. Louisbourg would be the main target as it was a massive fortress and the military headquarters and depot for New France. Major General Amherst, supported by Major General James Wolfe, would plan the attacks. After Louisbourg there would be an attack on Fort William Henry, then an advance north towards Montreal and Quebec. A third column would attack and capture Fort Duquesne.

James Wolfe was about to call off his assault on Louisbourg because the beach he had chosen was defended by 1,000 entrenched troops with eight cannon. It was then that Wolfe saw that two boats commanded by junior officers of the 60th had got ashore in a cove shielded from the main beach. Wolfe reinforced this initiative, causing the French to withdraw into the fortress. The final assault involved the 2nd and 3rd Battalions of the Royal Americans, with their grenadier companies formed as part of the forlorn hope. The capture of the fortress opened up the St Lawrence River and the way to Montreal and Quebec.

Meanwhile, General Abercrombie was leading a strong force to assault Fort Ticonderoga. His command of 16,000 men consisted of 7,000 regular soldiers, including the 4/60th under the command of Colonel Haldimand and six companies of Bouquet's battalion, the 1/60th.

The French were in a very strong, fortified position; the fort had been very well sited and constructed with cannon-proof breastwork. Abercrombie's reconnaissance had given him misleading intelligence and, rather than blast at the defences with cannonfire to break them down, he ordered a frontal assault,

'Somme' style. This was repelled with heavy losses, the Royal Americans losing four officers and forty-six men killed, while Colonel Haldimand was one of the nineteen officers and 212 men wounded. And a sad loss to the 55th Light Infantry was Lord Howe, who was killed leading from the front. The Highland Regiment lost 314 officers and men killed with 333 wounded. In recognition of this sacrifice the King granted it the designation Royal Highland Regiment. Abercrombie was eventually replaced by General Amherst.

By 1758 the 60th was only two years old and had played a prominent role in the capture of Louisbourg. The regiment made a successful attack on Fort Frontenac and played a leading role in the final assault on Fort Duquesne, which was renamed Fort Pitt after the First Minister and today is Pittsburgh.

Wolfe's attack on Quebec was made possible now that the British fleet had access to the St Lawrence river and was able to make the difficult journey up the river, guided by James Cook as navigator using charts prepared by Joseph Des Barres, an engineer officer in the Royal American Regiment.

Major Augustin Prevost of the 3/60th was wounded badly in the first attack to get ashore. Later there was an attempt up the Montmorenci Falls by the 2/60th and a Highland contingent, but it was beaten back. The Royal Americans won praise from General Wolfe who said they displayed so much alertness and intrepid dignity on all occasions and their spirited conduct that he conferred upon them the motto *Celer et Audax* – Swift and Bold.

It was when Sir William Howe's light infantry got ashore farther upstream, and found a way up the cliff to the Heights above, that Wolfe's ten battalions, including the 2 and 3/60th, followed. Wolfe lined up his force of 4,500 men on the Plains of Abraham. Montcalm decided not to wait for Bougainville and his reinforcements of 2,000 regulars and attacked with desultory volley, advanced and fired a second volley. Then Wolfe ordered his line to fire, Huzza! It was all over.

The old school still believed that massed bodies of disciplined troops was proper soldiering and the only answer against motley bands of irregulars who fought in a clandestine manner. To them the real war against the French was being fought in Europe, in the traditional military way of fire and shock. Pitt would have agreed as he was paying the Hanoverians, Hessians and the Brunswickers, together with 8,000 British led by Prince Ferdinand of Brunswick, a field marshal in the Prussian service, to defeat the French, which they did at the battle of Minden in 1759. As Pitt said, 'we shall win Canada on the banks of the Elbe'. But Canada was won not on the banks of the Elbe but on the Heights of Abraham at Quebec by James Wolfe.

Another important victory in Europe also occurred in 1759, which consolidated the British domination of Canada. It was a naval victory in which Admiral Sir Edward Hawke caught the French fleet in Quiberon Bay near

Brest and destroyed the French Atlantic Squadron, ending any fear that the French would launch an attack on the English coast and leaving the French unable to reinforce the garrison in North America.

In August 1759 an attack was launched on Fort Niagara, the principal French fort west of Montreal. The 4/60th was under the command of Colonel Haldimand but it was Sir William Johnson, the principal British agent for Indian affairs, who brought with him 1,000 Iroquois Indian braves to join the column. He was later able to persuade the Indians supporting the French to disperse and go back to their villages. Eventually the French surrendered.

Tactics had changed since Braddock's disaster in 1755. The 60th had introduced a new command when taken in sudden ambush; it was 'Alarm! Find a tree'. When, in 1760, Colonel Montgomery was attacked in a wooded valley by a much larger force of Indians his men immediately went to ground and found cover. They then thrust into the woods and attacked the Indians whilst the Highlanders got round their flanks to attack them in the rear and threaten their line of retreat. The Indians suffered many casualties before making off.

In 1760, as the thaw set in and the Saint Lawrence river became navigable, troops who had been cut off were receiving supplies and reinforcements. The senior French commander, Chevalier de Levis, decided to launch an attack from Montreal towards Quebec with 7,000 men. General Murray with a reduced force, weakened by scurvy, malnutrition and the diseases that thrive in the unhealthy conditions in which the troops had to live, could only muster 3,000 (the 2/60th and 3/60th were reduced to a combined total of just 500 men) of the fittest to face the French. There was a battle outside Quebec with heavy casualties on both sides. But when de Levis discovered British ships were arriving with fresh troops he decided to retreat, which set off a general desertion by the majority of the Canadian militiamen and the Indians.

The final summer campaign planned by Amherst was to be a three-pronged attack on the capital, Montreal, with a strong force of 11,000 regulars and 6,500 American militiamen. Faced with such a force the French commander sued for peace. This marked the end of French resistance in North America and gave Britain the largest conquest of territory in British military history. Colonel Haldimand became the first Governor of Montreal.

When Louis XV heard of the surrender he passed it off with the words, 'What matters the loss of a few acres of snow.'

The West Indies – the First Phase

In January 1761 William Pitt heard the news of the French surrender. He had won Canada as he had vowed. The French and Indian War was over but the Seven Years' War with France continued in Europe for a further two years and, in the Caribbean, it became a continual state of war from the attack on Martinique in 1762 until the attack on Puerto Rico in 1797.

William Pitt was continuing with his plans to build an empire and make Britain rich and, on hearing of the French surrender, immediately despatched orders to Amherst to send 2,000 regulars to join an expedition to attack the French-held islands of the West Indies. He added that a further 6,000 men would be needed by the end of 1761 for an assault on Martinique. There was to be an all-out attack on the sugar islands. Sugar was like gold. It spelt riches, with such heavy demands for this new sweetener that it made the plantation owners and merchants very rich. Many grand houses in England were built on the proceeds of sugar. Pitt was known to have said that the wealth of the sugar islands was worth more to Britain than the thirteen colonies.

After the capture of Martinique in January 1762, the army prepared for an attack on Cuba. Pitt wanted to declare war on Britain's longstanding enemy, Spain, due to the close relations being built between Spain and France. Although Pitt resigned, his bellicose Spanish policy continued and it was decided to attack Havana.

The British force, including the 3/60th, landed on the coast six miles east of Havana. The port was covered by formidable fortifications but what the army was not expecting were the rampant diseases prevalent on the island. In the first four weeks over 1,000 British soldiers died from malaria, yellow fever, swamp fever and dysentery, or the flux as they called it. Another 3,000 men were so ill with various agues that they were unfit for duty.

On 14 August 1762 Havana surrendered, a quarter of the Spanish fleet was captured as well as £3,000,000 worth of gold and silver. And all Havana's warehouses contained large quantities of sugar and tobacco. By the end of September half the soldiers in the expedition had succumbed to some form of disease.

The Treaty of Paris, signed on 10 February 1763, confirmed British control in Canada and North America and also Florida which was previously Spanish. Martinique and Guadeloupe would be returned to France.

Central America and the West Indies

Today when mention is made of the West Indies the first thoughts are of sun and idyllic holidays but, in the late-eighteenth century, it was the last place on earth that any soldier would wish to be sent. The destination of troops leaving England was kept secret, but if it was hinted that it would be the West Indies many would desert rather than face an uncertain future with the possibility that they might never return.

The climate was exceptionally dangerous and unhealthy. It was hot and humid with dense tropical forests and the weather was subject to violent extremes of heat, wind and rain with tropical storms; the terrain varied from impenetrable forests to mountainous ranges. Conditions on the islands made survival very difficult for Europeans, the French and the English, for whom the constant intolerable heat and endemic diseases made life very difficult and fighting almost impossible.

The British forces faced the same difficulties as the French but decided that this was bush warfare and that the best way of beating the French was to form companies of light troops. They enlisted volunteer slaves from the plantations and formed light infantry regiments, formed as temporary irregular battalions and never included in the official Army List. There were approximately 3,600 mulattos and blacks recruited as skirmishers; by October 1794 the number had risen to 9,000 men.

The light regiments were often named after the British commander, such as Druall's Guadeloupe Rangers, Malcolm's Rangers, or Carolina Rangers. Later official West Indies regiments were formed from the nucleus of these Ranger units. These special light ranger units proved to be very effective; as General John Moore told his father, 'The Black troops are the only troops equal to scour the woods ... the British are unequal to such service.'

Henry Dundas, Secretary for War, noted:

> The English troops are inadequate for any length of time to the fatigue of long marches and other duties of the field, destructive to European constitutions in the West Indies ... whilst on the other hand, the native troops are better adapted to this mode of warfare than for garrison service: the only duty on which the English can be employed to an advantage.

Pontiac's War

After the Treaty of Paris the area that had been New France, from Montreal to Quebec, was occupied. The French citizens, the Canadians, were permitted to stay under British rule. The troops who remained after the war had to occupy all the French forts and keep law and order; many of these duties became the responsibility of the Royal American Regiment.

The 1/60th were taking over the French forts to the west of Montreal. The first fort was Fort Detroit which surrendered to two officers and a platoon of men. The British Army was now overstretched but, due to the post-war economies, the 3rd and 4th battalions of the Royal Americans were disbanded. Colonel Bouquet's 1st Battalion of the Royal Americans was to establish a British military presence in Western Canada. By 1763 they were manning fifteen forts stretching from Fort Bedford near Philadelphia to Fort St Joseph near the site of the future city of Chicago. The size of the garrisons was ludicrously small. The small outposts garrisoned by only handfuls of men represented the Crown and were keepers of the King's Peace.

Until the end of the French and Indian War both sides were eager to recruit the Indians as allies to their cause who were provided with weapons, powder and ammunition. For over a hundred years there had been trade with the Indians; furs were exchanged for rifles, utensils, knives and blankets and they were given brandy by the French and rum by the English; they preferred brandy. They were also given presents and usually the French were more generous than the British.

With the war over the Indians were no longer being recruited, trade had almost ceased and, due to the tense situation, it was considered prudent not to supply them with weapons and powder. The Indians felt that they had not benefited by helping the British and were becoming discontented.

Pontiac, chief of the Ottawas, had fought for the French and was telling the Indians that if the British were left in control they would steal the Indian land west of the Alleghenies. That was already happening as settlers moved farther west in search for land to farm. Colonel Bouquet had already burned houses of British settlers who had begun to farm near Fort Pitt. The colonial officials lacked the will to stop the Europeans moving on to Indian lands which was beginning to inflame the Indians who began to attack the settlers, many of whom were murdered.

Pontiac arrived at Fort Detroit with 300 braves but with no intention of attacking the fort. Indians did not enjoy fighting for possession of a fort, especially if it was well defended. Pontiac suggested a parley. Captain David Campbell of the Royal Americans, and deputy commander of the fort, agreed to go and negotiate. Usually, the Indians respected the parties sent to negotiate but, in this case, Campbell was murdered and his body eaten. In the strange custom of the Indians this was meant as a compliment to his bravery.

At Fort St Joseph, Ensign Schlosser had written that there was bad food and boredom. Eleven Royal Americans were killed by the Indians although Schlosser survived. There were many attacks on the Royal Americas at various forts.

General Amherst's principal aide, Captain James Dalyell, arrived at Fort Detroit with a force of 300 men. He set off to attack Pontiac's camp but was ambushed. Dalyell and twenty-one of his men were killed and fifty were wounded or taken prisoner. After the battle Pontiac invited some local French traders to a victory dinner. After the meal he told his French guests that the 'young beef' they had eaten was one of Dalyell's soldiers.

While Dalyell was being ambushed Colonel Bouquet was advancing towards Fort Pitt with a mixed force of almost 400 men from the 42nd Highlanders and 1st Royal Americans. Fort Pitt was better defended than Fort Detroit with

Captain Simeon Ecuyer, a Swiss Royal American, in command with 300 men. It was June 1763 and there were fewer attacks near Fort Pitt as the Indians moved east to attack Bouquet's force.

Bouquet's advanced guard was attacked a few miles east of where Braddock had been ambushed in 1755. In the first attack about eighty of the British force were killed or wounded but Bouquet immediately formed a defensive circle on top of a hill near a river called Bushey Run. He decided to use an Indian tactic, a ruse they had often used. Since the soldiers could not stay on the hill with the wounded and were also short of water, they had to move. The plan was to make a demonstration of a hurried retreat with the pack horses. As they began to leave the Indians rushed across the open ground to fall into the trap Bouquet had set by placing hidden troops to attack them from the sides. The Indians were encircled, suffering many casualties.

The Indians caused much trouble during this unsettled period and the 60th took the full weight of their attacks. For the Indians it proved fatal as every brave who was killed meant a family had lost its food provider and hunter. The Indians began to lose their keenness to fight when Pontiac was himself murdered by another tribe. The uprising was over and the Indians dispersed.

Colonel Bouquet received much praise from the people of Pennsylvania for his efforts in quelling Pontiac's uprising. In recognition of his brilliant command of troops he was given command of all the British forces in the southern colonies and promoted brigadier general. In 1767 his own battalion, the 1st Royal Americans, went to Jamaica. In 1772 the 2/60th captured Antigua and, at the beginning of the American Revolution in 1776, the 3rd and 4th battalions were re-raised. Recruiting began in England and Hanover and they went to Florida under the command of Augustin Prevost.

Nicaragua

The unfortunate war in America was causing many problems and proving to be inconclusive. But in Jamaica the governor, Major General John Dalling, considered he had an answer to Britain's problems, at least where Spain was concerned. John Dalling, then aged forty-eight, was a former officer in the Royal Americans and led the light companies at Louisbourg and at Quebec. He had been a friend of James Wolfe.

The garrison of Jamaica consisted of two regular regiments, the 1/60th Royal Americans, about two companies, 200 men, and the 79th Foot, The Royal Liverpool Volunteers (The Liverpool Blues), about 300 men.

Dalling had been studying the map of Central America and came to the conclusion that there was an opportunity to take Spanish territory with rich savannah pasture to raise cattle and, at the same time, make a way to the Pacific Ocean and, of course, gain the kudos and make a name for himself. He planned to divide the possessions of Spain by cutting them in half. To do so he would send a force to Nicaragua and build a string of forts from the Gulf of Mexico up the San Juan river across the narrowest part of Nicaragua to the Pacific. His plan was based on scanty intelligence from the local fishermen and by studying his map. It all appeared straight forward and, from the scale of his map, seemed feasible.

Captain Polson of the 60th, with the brevet rank of lieutenant colonel, was the commanding officer of the expedition. There were eight other officers, including Lieutenant Despard of the 79th who was acting as engineer officer. There was also Major Dalrymple's Loyal Irish Corps, who were mostly Irish indentured servants and sailors from Kingston. Also included were Major James Macdonald's Royal Jamaica Volunteers, made up from privateers, sailors and freebooters and 125 men from the Royal Bateaux Corps.

Dalling approached Admiral Parker for troop transport and protection. Parker put young Captain Nelson in command of a frigate, HMS *Hinchinbrooke*, and the flotilla; Nelson's command would cease when they reached Greytown. There were delays lasting a valuable month of the dry season. The expedition arrived at the mouth of the San Juan river and the little port of Greytown forty-nine days after leaving Kingston.

They had problems with handling the boats, so Nelson offered his help and thirty-four seamen, a sergeant and twelve marines who would follow the expedition in the frigate's cutter.

The journey upriver was fraught with problems, intense humid heat during the day and cold at night as well as the constant plague of mosquitoes. Colonel Polson was failing to organize the expedition and it was left to others to make the decisions with Captain Nelson and Edward Despard, who struck up a friendship, beginning to organize matters.

The plan was to navigate up the San Juan river to a vast lake and cross the lake from where it was only a matter of a short distance across the savannah to the Pacific Ocean. Halfway up the river the Spanish had a fort, the Fort of San Juan, which had to be captured. Nelson and Despard went ahead in a 'pit-pan', a native canoe.

The fort was besieged and quickly surrendered and, by the fetid conditions inside the fort and the miserable condition of the Spanish, it would seem they were glad to surrender. However, the expedition eventually collapsed, beaten by the onset of the rainy season, the continual torrents of water, the storms and the complete breakdown of everybody's health with dysentery, malaria and yellow fever; over half the men died.

Those who survived retreated back down the river to Greytown and set sail for Jamaica. Nelson was very ill but refused to go into the hospital and was nursed back to health at the governor's house. Despard had a dispute with John

Dalling over money that was owed to him. He eventually left the Army, became somewhat dispirited and involved with a corresponding group of political malcontents. He joined an idealistic movement inspired by the American Revolution, Thomas Paine's *The Rights of Man* and the ideas of Rousseau. He formed links with a subversive group called the Society of United Irishmen whose leader was Wolfe Tone and was recruiting Irishmen from the 1st and 3rd Battalions of the 1st Foot Guards. He was in a plot to kill the King. Despard was caught and tried for treason. If found guilty, he was to be hanged, drawn and quartered. At his trial he called for Horatio Nelson to come forward to give a character reference for him.

Despard was found guilty but, as a mark of mercy, was hanged and beheaded. He was eventually buried in a church that became part of St Paul's churchyard, only seventy yards from where Nelson was eventually buried.

There was also an uprising in Ireland by Wolfe Tone's United Irishmen. This had two distinct elements to it. A Presbyterian rebellion in Ulster was put down by Catholic soldiers of the Irish militia, whilst a Catholic insurrection in Leinster was suppressed by General John Moore with auxiliary troops and the new 5th Battalion of the Royal American Regiment.

60th Royal American Regiment in the West Indies

1793 March	3rd & 4th Bn	Capture of Tobago
1794 April	3rd & 4th Bn	Second Assault on Martinique
1794 June	3rd & 4th Bn	Capture of St Lucia
1796 June	3rd & 4th Bn	Capture of Guadeloupe
1796 June	3rd & 4th Bn	Capture of St Vincent
1797 June	3rd & 4th Bn	Capture of Trinidad
1797 Dec	3rd & 4th Bn	Capture of Porto Rico

Chapter 4

American Revolution 1776–83
Rebels, Tories, Loyalists and Bloodybacks

With the outbreak of war in North America in 1775 the British Army was again in need of light troops. The 60th Royal Americans had been 'holding the fort' and keeping the peace since the end of the French and Indian War but they had been sent to the West Indies. After the war ended in 1763 many regiments and second battalions had been disbanded or withdrawn. The light companies were neglected and training was discontinued. It was then considered that raising local militia rather than relying on British troops was the cheaper way to govern the colonies. These militias became proficient at the Indian way of making war as it was the unsettled Indians who were now causing problems and a growing number of backwoodsmen became skilled Indian fighters. Lord Dunmore, the Governor of Virginia, led a militia force against the Western Indians, the Delawares and Shawnees, and defeated them in a Battle at Point Pleasant. His force included a bush fighting group of riflemen led by Daniel Morgan, who fought Indian style and was known to have taken twenty scalps.

The British Army in North America was not facing an enemy with an army as such. It was facing a citizens' revolt. Organized and disciplined armies are raised and trained to fight armies that are similarly organized and disciplined, with both having comparable tactics and weaponry. Both wage war to accepted rules of warfare and codes of military conduct. Problems arise if the opposing army is of a different structure, composed of only a few regular troops with the rest a mixed bag of part-time militiamen, volunteers and irregulars using an unusual pattern of tactics. Both could be armed with the standard available weapon, the smooth-bore flintlock musket, but the exception that the irregulars would bring into battle one single weapon that was both accurate and deadly, the Pennsylvanian long hunting rifle.

This was a weapon designed and made by the German and Dutch gunsmiths of Pennsylvania. It had a long, rifled barrel to give it accuracy and a small calibre, firing a small lead ball, large enough to kill without causing too much damage to the pelt or fur. Hunting for furs was a lucrative trade and the reason why most backwoodsmen were in the wilderness and such good shots.

The Continental Army

General George Washington was elected by the Continental Congress to be Commander-in-Chief of the Continental Army in 1777. This was not an army in the accepted military sense but a hurriedly put together force of some regulars, part-time militiamen, many volunteers and irregulars, all to be reinforced at a later date by French and Spanish naval and military forces.

Washington soon realized that although his troops were highly motivated, they were not a trained and disciplined army capable of facing the fire and shock tactics they could expect to confront on the battlefield. As a result, he formed a plan based on bush fighting techniques of hit and run or fire and move tactics, making full use of local knowledge and local methods of making war. It was going to be a war where fast-moving light troops would be prominent. To counter the rebel forces' method of making war the British Army set about raising more light troops.

Such was the situation that the British Army faced when brought to America to suppress rebellion in 1776. The situation in the colonies created a dilemma for the members of the Royal Americans as it became a choice of loyalties. The regiment was raised to protect American colonists from the French and the Indians and many had formed close relationships with the Americans; a considerable number were already Americans having been recruited from the colonies, particularly Pennsylvania and so they had divided loyalties. Inevitably there were desertions by those who decided that America would be their future home.

The 1st Battalion sailed to Jamaica in 1767, not before freeing Major Robert Rogers from prison in New York. The 2nd Battalion was also in New York in 1765 and got caught up in clashes with the townspeople when they were protecting a consignment of stamps to be used to raise revenue under the Stamp Act; this was to be the American contribution to financing the cost of the French and Indian War. But, in 1772, the 2nd Battalion went to Antigua where Jacques Prevost was now governor of the island.

When the rebellion began to erupt in 1775, some members of the 60th joined the rebels, the most prominent of them being Major Horatio Gates who became Commander-in-Chief of the American Northern Army. At this time the 3rd and 4th battalions were re-raised and moved to Florida in 1777 with Augustin Prevost in command.

The deteriorating political situation in North America, with the underlying moves for self-determination, led to a fracturing of relationships between the Colonies' assemblies and Parliament in London, with cries of 'down with the Stamp Act' and 'no taxation without representation'. As tensions rose the political unrest and events in Boston, Massachusetts, in 1774 put General Thomas Gage's command as Governor of Massachusetts in perilous situation.

Several officers, including Sir William Howe were sent to assist Gage and support his command. Howe had a distinguished record during the French and Indian War, training the 4th Battalion of the 60th Royal American Regiment and clearing the Heights of Abraham prior to Wolfe's arrival.

On 18 April 1775, with signs of trouble, General Gage decided to forestall the possible increase of disturbances growing into violence by sending light infantry and grenadier companies from Boston to Concord to seize and destroy some military stores. This was meant to be a secret operation. On reaching Concord the light infantry occupied the bridges and approaches whilst the grenadiers went and destroyed the stores.

The problems arose when the companies began their march back to Lexington. To their surprise they were being shot at by rebels – the minutemen – who were concealed behind walls, hidden in barns and houses and setting up a constant sniping fire all the way back to Lexington. Casualties were very high. The light infantry who should have been prepared and able to deal with this attack were in total disorder. There was surprise that the Americans were lying in wait and that this raid on the stores was known about in advance. Since General Gage had an American wife it was thought at the time that her loyalties might have been tested and that she gave the warning. Sometime later she was sent hurriedly to England.

It was a rather inauspicious beginning to what was to become a bitter conflict. General Gage had had plenty of experience of working with light troops since his first encounter on the Monongahela during General Braddock's expedition. He had raised a battalion of light infantry which he commanded and was at the disaster with Abercrombie and Howe at Ticonderoga.

Two months after Lexington Gage fought a hard battle at Bunker Hill against rebels who were in a prepared position. The rebels were defeated but at unwarranted costs. The first attack was made with extraordinary bravery by the British troops but they were repulsed with heavy casualties. When Gage led the attack by a direct assault against heavy rifle fire the battle was eventually won. The light infantry under the command of General Howe were directed in the frontal attack as line troops. This could have been due to the result of lack of training, since it was not possible for them to function as light troops if they were not familiar with the drills.

It would take Gage a year but, in August 1776, he was able to organize the three light battalions although it would take time for them to perfect their tactics to match the American irregulars.

The rebels were not all rifle-armed sharpshooters. Many were in fact from the towns and unused to handling arms and the musket was the weapon in general use. Those who were armed with rifles made a speciality of shooting those in command, the officers and senior NCOs, knowing that this would leave the troops lost and leaderless. The officers' gorgets made excellent target markers.

In 1771, prior to Howe's arrival in America, Horse Guards had decided (much to the disgust of some of the 'pomp and pipe-clay' brigade) to establish light companies in each foot regiment on the English establishment; the Irish establishment would follow suit in 1772. Much of the training, knowledge and hard-won experience of the earlier light companies had been lost since the end of the French and Indian War in 1763. The light companies were very much below standard with poor training and with many commanders unsure how to use them and they became the refuge of the misfits and the unwanted; young officers were unwilling to serve in what was considered a second-class grenadier company that lacked the cachet of the grenadier companies. It was regarded as socially unacceptable to be known as a 'light bob'.

In 1771 Sir William Howe was known as the foremost light infantry officer and was consulted over new and revised training methods, schedules and equipment to be introduced to all infantry regiments. General Gage understood well the need for proficient light troops in America and had promoted their use, raising his own regiment, fostering training and establishing light companies. Problems arose with the arrival of Sir William Howe, who came with his revised light infantry training schedules. At first there was some confusion with conflicting tactical plans and even words of command. Whereas General Gage's training was based on the role of the flank or light company within the regiment, Howe's training was concerned with the broader role of light troops when combined into composite light, or flank, battalions. To some this was a misuse of the light companies but conditions in North America suited the use of these light battalions.

Previously there had been a lack of training and field exercise and the light companies were neglected. There was virtually little or no attention paid to procedures, tactics and training in the manuals until Major General David Dundas issued *Rules and Regulations for the Formations, Field Exercise and Movements of His Majesty's Forces* in 1792. That document included a very inadequate section. Dundas probably felt he had to include something on the subject after its prominence in the American wars but it was well known that he was of the Frederick the Great school of thought. But there did exist non-official publications, one of which was *Instructions, and Training and Equipping of the New Light Companies* issued by Lord George Townsend when he was Lord Lieutenant of Ireland. This was issued to regiments then on the Irish establishment in Ireland in 1772. There was also Major General Howe's *Manual on light Infantry Drill* of 1774.

Townsend's manual was full of practical and useful advice for those training the light companies and was intended as a guide to young officers who would command these troops. It gave an outline of their duties and responsibilities and the use of fieldcraft training, the specific drills for light troops with details on equipment. Particular reference was made to tactics in the field with guidance on skirmishing, particularly in broken or wooded terrain, all executed in small sections, independently, or in large formations.

Townsend preferred the two-deep firing line at open file intervals as opposed to the recommended three-deep line in the 1764 Regulations. With men sometimes detached in separate small groups communication of orders was difficult and he introduced new command methods to enable officers to maintain control over loosely deployed and scattered troops by the use of whistle signals to indicate moves such as advance, retire, extend or contract the advance. (A similar system was adopted in 1800 by the 95th Rifles, but they used bugle calls.) He also recommended the system of firing in pairs, working closely together so that one man was always loaded. (Again this was a method used by the 95th since rifles took longer to load.)

Major General Howe established his first training camp at Salisbury in 1774. The training was based on his experiences in North America during the French and Indian War and it was intended to train light troops to a uniform system based on a two-deep line with movements executed at a quick pace or at the double in open extended order. The skirmish line would be deployed in loose order in front of the main battle line. As they advanced they would fire upon the enemy, disrupting their line and causing casualties. The advantage of the skirmish line was that it did not present a target sufficiently large enough for the opposing line to fire a volley or, in fact, to direct artillery fire. The first light companies to be trained came from the 3rd, 11th, 21st, 29th, 32nd, 36th and 70th Regiments. On 3 October 1776 an extensive field day or demonstration of light tactics was held for King George III at Richmond Park, near London.

Howe's system of light training was at odds with the then commonly accepted system as used and adopted by Gates. Whereas Gates's and Townsend's systems were based on the practice of the individual light company's support of its regiment, Howe's system was much broader and was designed for using a number of light companies in unison as an ad hoc composite light battalion. This followed the contemporary practice of creating composite grenadier battalions. There was no special emphasis on manual drills, firing practice and marksmanship.

All the field evolutions were based on wings, companies and platoons with movement of troops designed to enable the battalion to change formation and its facing. Howe expected individual companies to detach themselves from the light battalion during the action and to act semi-independently. All Howe's movements were executed at three different paces – slow, quick and run.

Howe's system was not entirely satisfactory. Where it solved one problem it created others. The main fault was that to form the composite light battalion meant detaching all the light or flank companies from their parent units leaving them exposed to enemy infiltration. It was a poor substitute for an established light infantry regiment.

Others took an interest in Howe's new light infantry drill, including John Williamson who included a section on the general's light infantry manoeuvres in his light infantry treatise *Elements*. A simple table listed sixty different manoeuvres (those in which the battalion line deployed into columns of double files from the centre of each manoeuvred division before redeploying into the front, flank or rear), half a dozen of which were expounded as illustrative examples. Williamson's drills were intended for the hat men battalion (i.e. the centre or battalion companies, not the flank companies) divided conventionally into two wings, four grand divisions, eight sub-divisions and sixteen platoons.

Many infantry regiments of the British Army at this period were changing their tactics and making drastic changes to their organization to suit the new methods of fighting that they were experiencing from the rebels. The terrain was in sharp contrast to the European landscape that they had previously experienced and began to determine their new tactics. The country was extensively wooded and broken up with settlements, farms and fences, a type of landscape that did not suit large battle formations of infantry and restricted the deployment of cavalry in significant numbers. These features caused the fielding of the troops in a far thinner extended line with 'loose files and open order' being the adopted light infantry method. The drill manual for use in European theatres ordered three deep, close order (elbow to elbow) lines to create a wall of firepower. The rebels' actions and the nature of the land led to fighting in only two ranks and often in skirmish order, frequently breaking into small groups – there was no threat of American cavalry – fighting piecemeal in a series of independent actions.

It became obvious to some that what was needed were troops trained as the rifle-armed jägers of the German states, 'to take to the woods and fight the Virginian riflemen'. An important advocate for jäger-style units was Lieutenant Colonel Andreas (Andrew) Emmerich, a Brunswicker, who had served as a jäger in Germany during the Seven Years' War and in the American War, where he commanded a unit of light troops. Emmerich wrote that these types of troops were essential:

> In war no army can act without light troops. Its operations and even existence depend on them. Such light troops ought properly to be composed of select chasseurs with rifles, light infantry with bayonets and light dragoons or hussars [the reference to bayonets was probably

due to his understanding that the German jäger rifle could not take a bayonet]. The business of the light troops is to form the advanced guard, to protect the flanks, and provide in every respect possible for the safety of the march . . . It is the particular duty of the light troops to prevent being surprised, or disturbed and alarmed by trifling causes. When the army retreats, the corps of light troops must form the rearguard in order to cover the retreat.

Battle tactics were changing during the eighteenth century and the role of light troops was becoming more important. The French and the Germans were introducing battalions of *chasseurs d'élite*. (As early as 1756 Marshal Count Maurice de Saxe had suggested that a tenth of each infantry regiment should be trained to act as skirmishers.) The British Army had faced the new battle conditions of the American wars but were slow to establish light infantry units or flank companies on a permanent basis as part of the army structure.

Oberstleutnant von Ewald of the Hessen wrote a detailed study of the duties of light troops in the 1780s after extensive service in America with the jäger of Hessen, some of the best skirmishers in Europe. He recommended that units of light troops should become a permanent addition to every regiment in preference to using irregulars on a short-term basis.

The light battalions, together with the jäger and light dragoons, performed the majority of the Army's march security, outpost watch and reconnaissance duties. In the main army, as in Burgoyne's Canadian Army, the flank battalions were considered by all as 'the flower of our army'. Flank company officers were among the youngest, toughest, most dynamic and ambitious young gentlemen in the Army, seeking preferment by embracing the most active, dangerous and demanding line of duty. In 1777 Captain the Honourable Colin Lindsay declined to continue as an aide de camp and instead 'desired to go into the light infantry, which at present is the most active service'.

The Legions

Because of the often dispersed nature of the actions, with random attacks by free-moving rebels, it was considered by some that fast-moving mobile shock groups ought to be formed – legions of light cavalry, dragoons or mounted infantry supported in some instances with mobile, or horse, artillery. Several of these legions were formed. One commanded by Lieutenant Colonel John Simcoe and known as Simcoe's Queen's Rangers proved very successful. Another legion was formed commanded by Lieutenant Colonel Banastre Tarleton. Both legions were free-ranging and raised to attack the rebels' communications and supply convoys, lay ambushes and carry out small-scale raids, often penetrating deep into rebel-held territory.

The Rangers

It was also decided to raise special units of rangers, light troops modelled on the ranger groups used in the French and Indian War. They were usually named after their commanders, such as Butler's Rangers which, by 1779, had over 400 men divided into six companies. There was also Jessup's Loyal Rangers, which consisted of nine companies and numbered nearly 600 men by 1783. A loyalist group, the King's Rangers, was commanded by Major James Rogers, the brother of Robert Rogers; this was a small unit of no more than 200 men. There was another American loyalist group, Ferguson's Sharpshooters, commanded by Captain Patrick Ferguson of the 71st Fraser's Highlanders. He not only raised a corps of riflemen but was the inventor and patentee of the first breechloading rifle used in the British Army. Uniquely, his rifle had an ingenious vertical fine threaded bolt or plug that was fixed to a loose trigger-guard that could swivel and act as a handle so that, when turned, it would wind the threaded bolt into the threaded vertical hole in the lock piece, sealing off the chamber once the ball and charge had been loaded.

In 1776 Major Ferguson came to England to give an exhibition of experimental test firings at Woolwich before His Majesty King George III, Lord Amherst and Lord Townsend, the Master General of the Ordnance. Ferguson fired seven shots a minute and made five bull's-eyes at 100 yards. He fired shots in different positions – supine, prone and standing. The principal of the mechanism worked but, in practical terms, it suffered from constant clogging of the breech by the inferior quality of the powder available. Because the pieces needed constant boiling out and cleaning they were not practical and the rifle could not be accepted. The idea was sound but was let down by the inferior contemporary materials. At the Battle of Brandywine in September 1779, when they got the worst of it, they decided to cease using the rifle. When Ferguson was wounded it was because he had failed to follow advice from Sir William Howe who told him to stop using his breechloading rifle as it was just so unreliable. But it did have one advantage over other arms in that it could be reloaded when lying down or in deep cover. Over the next three years the Sharpshooters regularly fought alongside the legions of Simcoe and Tarleton but it was at the Battle at Kings Mountain, Carolina on 17 October 1780, when Ferguson, in command of 1,100 militiamen on the march to Charlottetown, discovered they were being tracked and eventually pursued by 3,000 backwoodsmen and was forced to find and take a defensive position. The backwoodsmen were all veteran Indian fighters and fought like Indians avoiding anything like personal contact. They divided their force into three groups and outflanked Ferguson and by sheer numbers overwhelmed and surrounded them and all were killed including Ferguson, knowing no honour in battle, and in rebel or Indian fashion their bodies were defiled.

Feldjägercorps

The name jäger or *chasseur* means 'hunter', a descriptive name for their function. The jäger units were hired or mercenary troops from the German states of Hesse and Darmstadt and were specialized bodies of troops who were independent of the main force to which they were attached, whether regiment or division. Their duties were to act as scouts, to forewarn of enemy infiltration, to act as sharpshooters in advance of the skirmishers, cut enemy lines of communication and attack supply and baggage trains. Their methods were based on stealth and they operated separately from the main body, on the periphery of the action, taking no part in the battle line. They were not dressed in the standard issue infantry uniforms of bright colours with lace, but usually wore clothes that would blend in with the natural surroundings, such as a green jacket with brown breeches, natural leather accoutrements, shot bag and powder flask. Their weapon was the German short-barrelled rifle, which could not take a bayonet; they carried short swords for personal protection. They communicated by using hunting horns.

In January 1775 Colonel Fawcet went to Cassel to negotiate the raising of 12,500 Hessian troops with the Landgrave. Johann Ewald and his jägers were selected to be part of this force. The 12,500 Hessian mercenaries were formed into twelve regiments of five companies each; there were also four battalions of grenadiers. All were regiments of the line. Initially there were two companies of jägers and some artillery.

Captain von Heisler brought over to America in August 1776 the first of the two jäger companies while the second, under Captain Ewald, arrived in October. These companies were found to be so useful that, in the following year, they were increased to 1,037 men organized in five companies, one of which was mounted. The whole force was under the command of Lieutenant Colonel von Wurmb but were detached to various units on an independent-basis.

Captain Johann Ewald first saw service during the last stages of the Seven Years' War. He served throughout the American Rebellion and was present with Lord Cornwallis when he capitulated at Yorktown in 1781. He went on to serve in the Danish service as a lieutenant general. A true exponent of light infantry tactics, he wrote several books on the subject. In 1785 he wrote *A Treatise on Guerrilla Warfare*, a book of which Frederick the Great spoke very highly. In 1790 he also produced *A Treatise upon the Duties of Light Troops* and *Conversations of a Hussar Corporal, a Jäger and a Light infantryman Upon the Duties and Services of Light Troops*. There were several others that Robert Craufurd probably read since he was fluent in German. The central theme in all of Ewald's tactics was the superiority of the attack over defence.

The Light Battalions
In North America three light battalions, known as composite flank battalions, were formed.

The regiment was an administrative unit and, when shorn of its staff, was drawn up as a battalion with various sub-divisions. There was a depot unit, usually composed of two companies responsible for recruiting and training. In the earlier part of the century the regiments were normally named after their colonels but by the latter part they were numbered. In times of conflict regiments often formed a second battalion, usually raised on a short-term basis. The famous 60th Royal American Regiment was unusual in being given a name and in having four battalions; later, in the early nineteenth century, it would have double that number.

The size of the battalion depended on recruitment, funding and casualties. The nominal size was 1,000 men, divided into ten companies, each of 100 men. The battalion was sub divided into grand divisions composed of a quarter of the men. Each grand division was divided into platoons, two or four composed of approximately thirty men or more.

When in line the battalion's ten companies would have the grenadier company on the right of the line and the light company on the left. The light company wore caps of varying designs, often modified cocked hats. The grenadiers wore mitres hats, leaving the centre, or battalion companies, wearing tricorne or cocked hats, so that these companies were referred to as the 'hat men'.

When a light battalion was formed it was made up from all available light companies combined into a composite light battalion to function on a short-term basis.

The South
In early 1777 the 3rd and 4th Battalions of the 60th moved to Florida where they were reinforced by drafts from the 1st and 2nd Battalions. In command of the Royal Americans was Augustin Prevost.

The southern colonies contained a higher proportion of loyalists than the northern colonies and Prevost was ordered to clear all the rebels out of Georgia and advance on South Carolina. A balance between rebels and loyalists was kept until the Spanish, who governed Florida, decided to enter the war on the American side. In discussions between the governments Spain had offered to remain neutral if Gibraltar was returned to her. When the British government refused Spain declared war.

At Baton Rouge, on the banks of the Mississippi, the 3rd Battalion of the 60th and units of local loyalists came under attack and fought a fierce action. The Spanish captured Mobile and Pensacola. Meanwhile, Augustin Prevost was mounting his main campaign on the port of Savannah in the colony of

Georgia. Both sides believed that Savannah was the key for the control of the south. While General Prevost marched his force north along the Atlantic coast and concentrated upon the defence of Savannah, the rebels had occupied Augusta, Georgia, and moved down the Savannah River. Marc Prevost encircled the rebels and overwhelmed them in a good tactical move in the battle of Briar Creek. Marc Prevost had sixteen men killed or wounded while the rebel General lost 3,000 men killed and over 200 taken prisoner.

By October 1779 the French had also entered the war supporting the rebel cause and a French fleet under Admiral d'Estaine attacked Savannah. Prevost's garrison of some 2,000 fit men faced a combined rebel and French assault force of some 11,000 men. But when they attempted to take the key Spring Hill redoubt their attack was not co-ordinated, due to heavy fog. The redoubt was held by the 4/60th in a fierce hand-to-hand fight. The rebels were finally beaten in a counter-attack by the Royal Americans led by Major Glazier. The total Franco-American losses were 1,500. Admiral d'Estaine was wounded severely and the French sailed away with their troops. This had been the most successful British battle in the south. Augustin Prevost captured Charleston in May 1780.

Many young officers probably arrived in America with very fixed ideas on soldiering but were to have their expectations drastically re-appraised. They had discovered that, in the majority of battles, the light battalions had become prominent due to the adaptation of tactics to suit American conditions. Both sides could lose heavily in a mass battle, but the rebels could make good their losses as they were untrained citizen volunteers whereas the British regiments needed men trained in all the disciplines and their line of communication was across the stormy Atlantic. Supplies, material and, importantly, reinforcements were always in demand. Men had to be conserved and mass attacks were considered wasteful of precious manpower. Britain could not afford pyrrhic victories when attacks by the flank battalions proved far more effective and less costly. So attempts to bring the rebels to battle in a mass action were avoided and new tactics were planned, making full use of the infantry dispersed to cover while there was never any threat of rebel cavalry. There was an increase in morale and an increased level of esprit de corps. To quote Matthew Spring:

> The backbone of the elite Advanced Corps comprised the flank battalions, which were unanimously considered 'the flower of the army'. Flank company officers – especially light company officers – were among the youngest, toughest, most dynamic and ambitious young gentlemen in the army, seeking preferment by embracing the most active, dangerous and demanding line of duty.

In June 1779, a fresh, young impressionable Lieutenant Moore arrived in America with the Duke of Hamilton's regiment which, unwittingly, became involved in one of the most bizarre episodes of the war. They were ordered by Sir Henry Clinton to build a fort on the Penobscot river as a base to blockade the port of Boston, the rebels' main supply port. There was some sporadic fierce fighting during which Moore earned himself the field rank of captain. It proved a disaster for the rebels in their attempts to destroy the fort. Although they had the men and the ships, nothing was done without their querulous officers having a meeting. They conducted everything by committee, with John Paul Revere refusing to take orders from anyone, and, as an artillery officer, he was hopeless. When the Royal Navy appeared the rebels burned all their ships and made a run for it. The episode was such an embarrassment that it is hardly mentioned in American histories. But for young Lieutenant Moore it was his baptism of fire and an introduction to a new weapon, the rifle. No doubt he kept this well in mind when he finally set up the training camp at Shorncliffe to raise and train the light regiments and the 95th Rifles

The Sixtieth

At the end of the American Revolution, and the British surrender to the Americans and the French at Yorktown, the British Guards' band played a popular tune entitled 'The World Turned Upside Down', which the French found very amusing.

The 1st and 2nd Battalions continued to serve in the West Indies and in Canada. Having been raised on Governor's Island, New York in 1755, it is the only regiment in the British Army with direct historic links to the United States of America. In 1794 the 1st Battalion, which was then stationed in Canada, became the first unit in the British Army to be equipped completely with rifles, which were probably of Prussian manufacture.

Chapter 5

The French Revolution 1793

After the American war it was apparent to all that tactics had changed to such an extent that light troops were becoming an essential element with France, Austria and Germany incorporating light or skirmisher regiments in their armies.

In 1792 the Prime Minister, William Pitt, assured the House of Commons that 'there never was a time in the history of the country when from the situation in Europe we might reasonably expect fifteen years of peace'.

Less than a month later there began a series of hostilities, which lasted almost continuously for twenty-three years, against the armies of Revolutionary France and Napoleon. The new Republican army consisted of eager and untrained volunteers, fired by a surge of new-found patriotic fervour. With improvised tactics that emphasized skirmishing and using the terrain to their advantage they took on each battle as it came, determined to fight to the bitter end to destroy the old order, or *ancien régime*, disregarding the old rules of warfare. With little or no baggage train to slow things down, they foraged and lived off the land.

The Auxiliary Regiments

The Army was designed to be a small professional force and sufficiently limited to support the authority of those in power but not large enough to cause any problems regarding their loyalties. In times of war the army could be augmented by auxiliaries, or hired mercenary regiments and supported by militia, yeomanry and fencibles; large standing armies were felt to be vulnerable to the influence of republicanism.

To save money, and control the size of the Army, regiments were raised and disbanded to suit the circumstances. At any period the larger part of the Army served abroad in colonial conquests or garrison duties, leaving only sufficient troops in Britain for internal security.

As Verner states in the *History of the Rifle Brigade*, 'No minister ventured to bring foreign soldiers to England'. Hence any corps which had recruited from such sources was condemned to perpetual foreign service, save for brief periods when HQ staff and a reduced cadre of officers and NCOs were brought to England or, preferably, the Channel Islands, for the ranks to be reinforced by recruits from the continent. No sooner was this effected than they were sent back to America or the West Indies. This was the experience of the 3/60th in 1793, of the 4/60th in 1796 and the 1/60th in 1797.

Craig, who succeeded Murray as Adjutant General, wrote to Dundas in 1793 emphasizing the need for foreign light troops. 'Our men,' he wrote, 'were too few and too valuable to be employed in skirmishing and outpost work, which involved a steady drain of casualties and to recruit foreigners was easy.'

The war in Flanders had exposed how the Army was out of date in organization and training. Old fighting techniques were obsolete and consequently the army received a severe mauling. To combat the *tirailleurs* who swarmed everywhere in their fire and move pattern of attack it was decided that, without the necessary skilled people to train light infantry and skirmish troops quickly, it would be easier to employ auxiliary mercenary units from the Electorates of Germany, but many Electors and proprietors saw an opportunity to make a profit. It was thought that these continental jägers had, for some unknown reason, a special innate ability that made them the best sharpshooters, superior over all others. They were thought to have special sharp eyesight that gave them a 'keen eye'. In the diary of Christian Ompteda, a colonel in the King's German Legion, there is a comment that officers accepted that the lower ranks, who were recruited from the peasant class, had long eyesight and were expert shots. The reason was more likely the very long tradition of hunting game in central and southern Europe. With large forests full of game, shooting to 'fill the pot' was a necessity of life. Trained from boyhood in stealth, tracking, woodcraft and shooting skills, they made natural skirmishers.

Before their introduction in the French army, light troops had been used in Europe by the Austrians who had hired many mercenary irregulars. Frederick of Prussia said he was confident of beating the Austrian regular troops, but found the Croatian light troops skilful, cunning and elusive opponents.

In December 1797 the famous 5th Battalion of the 60th Royal Americans was raised at Cowes, Isle of Wight, and saw continued service for twenty years. Command was given to Lieutenant Colonel Baron Francis de Rottenburg (later lieutenant general) and late of the Hompesch Fusiliers.

Many troops, British and particularly foreign, were quartered on the Isle of Wight during this period. The island was bristling with camps and cantonments, most of them tented, as barrack building for the regular quartering of troops in Britain had been almost non-existent before 1795. Albany barracks, built in 1796, were brand new when the intakes for the 5th Battalion arrived. The barracks were three miles (a league) from Cowes; the remains of the buildings are now part of Parkhurst Prison.

The Act to raise the Battalion speaks of 'the present juncture of affairs rendering it expedient to facilitate the speedy raising of the battalion' and it was completed speedily by turning over to it en bloc a number of existing foreign regiments and individuals who had taken service under His Britannic Majesty.

The 5th Battalion was raised in two phases. Phase one began in 1797 when the initial intake of seventeen officers and 300 other ranks assembled at Albany Barracks on the Isle of Wight. They were the remains of a Hompesch battalion, foreign riflemen raised for service in British pay during the 1793 Flanders campaign. Many of these corps were very much depleted in strength, some to not much more than a company. Some corps split their numbers between the other four battalions and the new fifth battalion.

Most of the foreign corps, if not in holding units on the Isle of Wight, were on active service in the West Indies and were absorbed in to the various battalions of the 60th. Twelve British officers from these corps transferred to the battalions of the 60th, Captain G. W. Ramsay (ex-30th Foot), who raised Ramsay's York Rangers and transferred to the 3rd/60th on 30 December 1797, was appointed commanding officer.

The second phase came when, at intervals, numbers of riflemen were absorbed into the 5th Battalion from various other corps which included Hardy's York Fusiliers, Waldstein's Chasseurs, Ferdinand Hompesch's Fusiliers, Lowenstein's Chasseurs and the Royal Foreigners. There were several Hompesch regiments with the main corps stationed in the West Indies and, by 1 May 1797, on Antigua and about to be absorbed into the 2/60th. There were other units of Hompesch's mounted riflemen, one of which was serving in Egypt. At the time of phase one Lowenstein's Chasseurs were on active service on Martinique in the West Indies.

Foreigners were recruited, or 'entertained', as auxiliaries and a varied lot they were. They included French Royalists, who fought with conviction and with the French qualities of zeal and élan, together with mercenaries gathered by the worst type of 'bringers' or 'crimps'. Some corps were considered as British corps. This ruling was given in November 1795 in favour of Hardy's Royal York Fusiliers, whose commissions were signed by the King, but the same ruling covered Ramsay's York Rangers. However, Irvine's York Hussars' commissions were signed by the Duke of York.

The decision to add a fifth battalion to the strength of the 60th Regiment would establish a skirmish battalion now armed with rifles, the first in the British Army. It made use of some of the better German jäger corps and, consequently, a well-trained, rifle-armed battalion was formed and was operational very quickly. The benefit to the Army was that these regiments or part regiments came as fully trained riflemen, variously uniformed, accoutred and armed with their own German rifles ready for use.

Count Charles de Hompesch (later lieutenant general), a former Prussian Hussar colonel who, with his younger brother Ferdinand, (who had served originally in the French 77th Regiment) offered to raise for the British Army two companies of *chasseurs a pied* and three squadrons of hussars in 1794.

All the Hompesch corps were classed as German, being mainly recruited from Germans of the various principalities and states of the Holy Roman Empire but also Austria, Hungary, Switzerland, Poland, Holland and Alsace.

After fighting in the Duke of York's campaign in the Low Countries in 1794–95, where they earned a good name but suffered heavy casualties, the chasseurs were disbanded. In September 1794, when the French drove off some Hesse-Darmstadt troops at Boxtel, the occasion on which Lieutenant Colonel Wellesley of the 33rd had his baptism of French fire, the Loyal Emigrants beat off three attacks while two chasseur companies attached to Hompesch's hussars defended their post magnificently, hanging on after the Hessians had given way in disorder. They suffered heavy casualties but their tenacity was beyond praise. All this was witnessed by Colonel Wellesley, giving him first-hand experience of the effect of rifle-armed chasseurs.

Hompesch's Fusiliers, raised and commanded by Ferdinand Hompesch, served in St Domingo in the West Indies in 1795. They took part in Abercrombie's bloodless reduction of Trinidad. By 1797 the unit was in Antigua and mustered seventeen officers and 528 other ranks. By 1 May it had been absorbed into the 60th, 500 other ranks going to the 2/60th. Those companies of the Hompesch Fusiliers that remained on the Isle of Wight were placed on the establishment and became the nucleus of the new fifth battalion of the 60th. All the Hompesch regiments' uniforms were of typical continental designs. The fusiliers' uniform was a short green jacket with red facings and blue breeches. Uniquely it was the first regiment in the British Army to wear a black felt shako.

Hompesch's mounted riflemen, or dragoons, served in Ireland alongside the 5th Battalion, under General Moore to suppress the rebellion of the United Irishmen. Both Baron Francis de Rottenburg and Robert Craufurd (later to command the famous Light Division in the Peninsular War) served with Ferdinand Hompesch's Fusiliers. In Craufurd's case it was for a short period only and planned as a career move as he was concerned at his slow promotion after returning to the Army from politics. A miniature exists of Craufurd in the uniform of the Hompesch Fusiliers with light infantry wings below the shoulder straps. The portrait is in the Royal Green Jackets' Museum at Winchester.

To quote the *Brief History of the King's Royal Rifle Corps*:

> The raising of this battalion (fifth), and the appointment of de Rottenburg to its command mark not only a distinct epoch in the history of the regiment but an important stage in the development of the British Army. Just as Bouquet, in 1756, had introduced radical

changes of dress and tactics into the newly raised 60th Royal American Regiment so did Rottenburg in 1797 introduce a system new to the British Army, which contributed not a little to the successful issue of the Peninsular Campaign.

De Rottenburg prepared for Field Marshal HRH the Duke of York, recently appointed Commander-in-Chief, the *Regulations for the Exercise of Riflemen and Light Infantry and Instructions for their Conduct in the Field* illustrated by excellent diagrams which, with a memorandum by the Adjutant General, was published in 1798. This book became the textbook or training manual for the training of the 5th Battalion and formed the basis upon which subsequent rifle and light infantry battalions were organized and trained. It was this work that largely influenced Lieutenant General Sir John Moore who, in regard to his training of the famous Light Division, wrote to the Adjutant General on 30 August, 1803, 'I mean to make De Rottenburg the ground work, noting in the margin whatever changes we make from him.' (See appendix 2)

His simple but effective tactical system quickly drew attention and when the drill was subsequently embodied in a book and published, the Duke of York had the Adjutant General translate it from German into English and approved it as the official light infantry manual. It remained in use for many years.

De Rottenburg's system of tactical drill was an uncomplicated one, clearly influenced by the drill manual written by Oberstleutnant von Ewald.

The key to de Rottenburg's training was 'pairing'. All riflemen of each platoon 'paired up' and stayed with their partner so that they became familiar and dependant on each other. Both went into action primed and loaded but only one would fire at any time; the second would cover the first whilst he loaded. This way they could not be caught in that vulnerable situation of both being in the process of loading and therefore defenceless. It was not mass fire that was required from riflemen but accurate aimed fire.

Extracts from de Rottenburg's Manual

1. When acting in line of battle with closed ranks and files, light troops were governed by the same regulations as applied to the army's foot (heavy) troops. Before being instructed in the light manoeuvres they had to be taught how to hold himself, to march, face, wheel and &c as regular infantry.
2. Marksmanship: the hallmark of a good rifle corps. The true rifleman will never fire without being sure of his man, (target - aim). A few well directed shots that tell will occasion greater confusion than thousands fired at random and without effect.

3. Targets used should be at least five feet in diameter; for if it were smaller, the unpractised recruit would be apt to miss so often as to despair of hitting it. To become expert a man should find encouragement and even amusement in this practice.

   Another disadvantage of it being too small would be that the rifleman could not become acquainted with his rifle, as in missing a target altogether he would not ascertain whether he had shot too much to the right or too much to the left; whereas a target of a proper size and painted in circles being easily hit the rifleman sees at once the fault he has made and learns to correct it. He should begin by firing at a distance of fifty yards and increase by degrees to three hundred. Practise shooting standing, kneeling, sitting, squatting, lying down on both back and front and against moving targets.

   [Shooting practice against moving targets was provided by mounting a target on a sledge or a truck on wheels which was drawn backwards and forwards by a person placed under shelter.]

4. The recruits now progressed to the execution of various manoeuvres performed by skirmishers. Formed in line, two men deep, they were taught to expand their frontage to the right or to the left, an anchor file at one end of the unit holding fast whilst the rest of the formation extended themselves in the appropriate direction. Similarly extension from the centre of a unit could be carried out; the middle file would hold their ground while the men to their left and right moved outwards.

   All of these manoeuvres were executed in quick time of 120 (30-inch) paces per minute, and to preserve that control which is requisite and restrain the dispersion (inherent to light troops) particularly *tirailleurs* which in the field after firing of a shot would take place.

   Each skirmish unit would have a larger proportion of officers and NCOs than a line battalion.

5. At close ranges supervisors could shout their instructions to their men. For communicating over longer distances, however, they carried whistles with which to signal their intentions and, to command a sizeable unit deployed over a still greater frontage, officers utilized regimental buglers. By playing distinctive tunes a whole variety of commands and even pieces of information could be relayed across the battle zone. These included directives for a unit to extend, halt, close ranks, charge, incline to the left or to the right, open fire, cease fire, retreat, withdraw, disperse and form line, column or square. The signals for passing intelligence included calls that indicated that

the enemy had been sighted and whether they were infantry, cavalry or both.

In prolonging the frontage of a unit the eventual spacings between files could be varied to suit prevailing conditions. They were usually deployed two paces apart, but the regulations laid down that in a particular case, when they are required to cover the front of a corps, or mask a manoeuvre the commanding officer will signify at what distance the files are to form from each other, before he gives the order for them to extend themselves. There were, however, three specific distances in the manuals: loose files, which had six-inch intervals; open order, where the files were two feet apart; extended order, where the spacings were six feet across.

6. Once they had mastered the art of extending their frontage light infantry recruits were taught the remaining part of the basic drill; the section that effectively combined shooting with movement. While half the unit remained in close order in reserve, the skirmishing companies, having deployed in their extended two-deep line, would advance, the reserve keeping some fifty paces to the rear. Once they came within range of the enemy, although the manoeuvre was executed at the usual rapid speed, progress was relatively slow. Both men in each file of the skirmishing line would start off with their rifles loaded. The leading man would take aim and at his direction fire. The man behind would run six paces in front of him and slightly to the right. Meanwhile his colleague now in the rear rank would load and when he had finished would call ready to the soldier in front who would then fire. The sequence could be continued as long as was required and ensured that at least one man of each pair of soldiers had his rifle loaded and ready to fire at any given moment. To execute a retreat the process was simply reversed and the distances run by each soldier in the movement phases of the sequence increased to twelve paces.

7. A similar device to the skirmishing line described above was the 'chain'. This was usually used when contact was first made with the enemy. The object of this branch of the duty of light troops is to scour a tract of the country by means of numerous detached bodies, clearing the woods and enclosures of the enemy's posts and, in a word, to establish a complete chain of your own troops by occupying as far as circumstances will permit every advantageous spot taking particular care however that your own posts are so stationed as to have easy communication and the power of mutually supporting each other.

When serving as a chain, three-quarters of the light infantry corps would deploy in a formation similar to their usual battle line, the only difference being that the men would be grouped together in fours rather than pairs and the intervals between each of the divisions would be increased to ten paces. The remaining quarter of the light infantry unit would form a solid reserve and march some fifty paces behind the line in order to give support to any part of the chain that was attacked.

Guidelines for the conduct of the vanguards were also laid down so as to reduce the possibility of a corps being surprised when on the march and to make the gathering of intelligence easier. A light infantry vanguard was to consist of several bodies of troops. The first of these – recommended to be half a platoon (about twenty-five) men strong – kept some 500 paces directly in front of the main force. (This distance was reduced to 300 paces at times of poor visibility.) Two hundred paces in front of this unit was to be another half platoon, with an NCO and six men probing another hundred yards forward from them and towards the outer flank. This elaborate arrangement enabled the light infantry to scour the countryside ahead on a frontage of at least 1,000 yards and greatly reduce the chances of the column they were escorting being surprised and ambushed.

Like the works of Emmerich and Ewald, de Rottenburg's manual concluded with detailed sections on the conduct of patrols, sentries and picquets, providing a fairly comprehensive system of operation for light infantry in and between battle zones.

In 1774 a French writer, M. Mesnil-Durand, advocated the use of small columns covered by a strong line of skirmishers instead of the three-deep lines. It was not until 1784 that this system was favoured and generally taught. Napoleon Bonaparte was a student at the military school in Paris and appreciated quickly the possibilities of this method. In 1796 chance gave him the opportunity. Napoleon used and improved these new tactics as he realized that they were well suited to the structure and composition of the new French Revolutionary Army. These tactics and methods became known as 'Napoleon's tactics'. The Army included hundreds of highly motivated Republican volunteers who had little or no formal military training but had plenty of dash and élan.

In the new French army regiments of light infantry were formed known as *voltigeurs*, or vaulters; *chasseurs* (hunters) *a-pied* and *a cheval* (foot and horse); *tirailleurs* or sharpshooters; and corps of *léger*, or light troops, such as the famous 9th Léger which took part in Desaux's victorious advance at Marengo.

As the light troops were deployed in a more extended order, so did the collective effect of their firepower diminish. It could not be compared with the blasting effect of the well-delivered volley. Napoleon compensated for this by seeking to increase the fire effect by the use of dense lines of skirmishers. He had the willing manpower and was not concerned by losses.

Napoleon could see the limitations and flaws in the Prussian tactics which he exploited with his own tactics. His key was speed. The Prussian style of heavy masses of battalions was ponderous in the battle positioning manoeuvres and it was whilst in this process that the main weakness became apparent, especially when moving from column into line formation. It was during these cumbersome manoeuvres that they became vulnerable to sudden worrying attacks to the exposed flanks, which could cause severe disruption and inhibit the pre-battle momentum. Napoleon used his light troops in large numbers, deployed at speed, to constantly worry the front and flanks of the enemy, to wear them down and cause disruption and disorder in their ranks.

These tactics plus rapid manoeuvre of his troops, superior intelligence gathering, revolutionary fervour and élan, combined with Napoleon's power of quick appreciation of events and ability to act upon a changing situation, gave him many victories.

The war of 1793 against the French armies of the First Republic, where the Duke of York's force in Flanders suffered an ignominious defeat, revealed all the weaknesses of the Prussian system against the new methods employed by the emergent French forces.

The light troops' functions were described in the *Reglements* of April 1792.

> While battle lines are being formed and batteries placed, the commanding officer orders the light infantry to advance ahead of the line, so as to discover the positions of the enemy's guns and to diminish their effect. The light troops are placed in small thickets, behind hedges, ditches or small rises according to the nature of the terrain. They are commanded to fire at the enemy's batteries and try to kill the gunners. These men do not form in troops so as not to draw artillery fire, but separate, benefiting from any feature that may afford them cover, and remain attentive so that they can quickly re-group at the first signal of their officers.

Chapter 6

The Duke of York

Any commander entering a campaign would hope or even expect that his support staff were efficient, that his troops would be well trained and proficient, his officers also well trained and competent, and that his men would be well fed and their needs catered for. The Duke of York reflected after the disastrous Flanders Campaign that the army was wanting in all areas.

In 1792 the Prime Minister, William Pitt, assured the House of Commons, 'That here never was a time in the history of the country when from the situation in Europe we might more reasonably expect fifteen years of peace.' Less than a month later began a series of hostilities, which lasted almost continuously for twenty-three years against the armies of the new French Republic and Napoleon.

The threat of invasion of England and Ireland was never stronger than it was at the end of the eighteenth century. The French Assembly of the First Republic, already at war with Prussia and Austria, declared war on Britain on 1 February 1793.

In the eighteenth century the post of Commander-in-Chief of the British Army existed only in time of war and so, from 1783, the end of the American war and for the next ten years, the post was vacant. In 1793, when Republican France declared war on Britain, the post was offered to Lord Amherst, his right by seniority. He took command of an Army that was in a state of confused negligence. During his short, inept and muddled administration basic disciplines collapsed and training procedures were neglected and unregulated. In cavalry and infantry regiments the colonels ran them as private and personal ventures. Officer appointments were in a lamentable condition, unsupervised and based solely on a financial and much abused system where nepotism was rife and where financial considerations bought preferment and rank.

It was in 1795 that Frederick, Duke of York, the second son of King George III, became Commander-in-Chief. He had spent five years in Europe being tutored in the art of war, Prussian style, by the Duke of Brunswick and by 'Old Fritz', Frederick the Great. He was well schooled in the Fredrician principles of war. But after the disastrous Flanders Campaign 'the grand old Duke of York', had a short sharp introduction into the French Revolutionary method of making war, a sharp salutary lesson in the failings and faults of the British Army.

He now became the centre of discussion, lobbying and representations that were occupying the time of those who were concerned at the state of the Army as it was about to enter into what could be a prolonged war with France.

Horse Guards

The supreme headquarters of the regular army was at Horse Guards in Whitehall, London. The senior permanent officers were:

The Quartermaster General   (Army)
The Adjutant General   (Army)
Secretary at War   (Civil)

Artillery came under the command of the Master General of Ordnance at Woolwich.

Dundas had been Quartermaster General in Ireland since 1779 and had grown increasingly contemptuous of officers returning from North America or the Caribbean who thought they had been introduced to the new way of making war. Dundas could not accept the move begun by General William Howe in 1776, to get as much of the army as possible to adopt his light infantry tactics. Dundas was a great believer in the Prussian system, felt nothing but bitterness towards officers returning from America, 'who had put the grenadiers out of fashion with their showy exercise and airy dress and independent modes they have adopted'. Dundas did much to hinder the progress and adoption of light infantry.

Horse Guards was where the Duke of York would find those who currently administer the running of the British Army. Also found there were the Secretary at War and his civilian staff. Both the Quartermaster General and the Adjutant General had extensive responsibilities regarding the areas of general discipline and administration, which often overlapped and were not defined. As an example, any unit of troops proposing to march some distance could not plan their own route; they had to submit in advance details to the Quartermaster General who would then allocate a given route that the march must strictly follow – hence a 'route march'. The regiment's quartermaster would control the march, billets for the officers and campsites for the men.

The civilian Secretary at War was concerned primarily with all financial aspects of the service. There were others who contributed to the running of the service but who were not responsible to those at Horse Guards. They were the engineers and artillery, who came under the command of the Master General of the Ordnance at Woolwich. He was also responsible for the control and dispensing of weapons and ammunition as well as covering the administration of the Royal Wagon Train. The actual movement of men and materiel was, however, covered by the Secretary at War, except when the men were being shipped abroad when the Transport Board took control of affairs.

A new post was created due to the threat of a French invasion. That was the post of Barrackmaster General, who was not based at Horse Guards but had an office farther along Whitehall. His position was created for the massive building programme to construct a series of barracks across the southern counties of England. These were built mainly to house the new militia regiments that were being raised and were expected to come from all parts of Britain. To avoid any element of speculation and pecuniary exploitation he created a totally new position, used for the first time, that of quantity surveyor, to estimate the costs of labour and materials.

The network of sub-divisions of command of the Army's control did not end at Horse Guards but continued with the individual regiments which were to a great extent self-governing and controlled by the regiments' colonels who had the funds for the purchase of uniforms, shoes and other necessaries; they could also control the purchase of arms. Rations and fodder for the animals came under the responsibility of a civilian post, that of Commissary General who was under the control of the Treasury. The responsibility for the Militia and the Volunteers involved the Home Secretary who took a major role in planning the defence of the Kingdom, with the threat of French invasion. It was also his responsibility for public order in the absence of a civil police force, which involved the Army to maintain order.

At this period the Secretary of State for Foreign Affairs was supposed to keep a watching brief on all campaigns in Europe while the Colonial Secretary supervised military operations in the colonies. But in 1794 the post of Secretary of State for War was created and he assumed responsibilities for total global strategy.

The King, George III, took a personal interest in military matters and during his reign effected an appreciable influence on military policy. Now that his son Frederick Duke of York was Commander-in-Chief, he took an even stronger interest. It was the King who advised the Duke of York to make his plans for change in a calculated fashion, not to implement drastic measures but to make the changes slowly so as not to upset Horse Guards and the regimental colonels' private fiefdoms.

Since the Civil War, when the army under Cromwell had virtual control of the country, the government had been deeply suspicious of the Army and its influence. It had suited the government to control the finances allocated towards the Army and restrict its size to a minimum. It also suited the government to ensure that the Army was never concentrated in large numbers but dispersed in numerous detachments. Without any form of civil police force it was left to the Army to keep the 'King's Peace', performing the duties of public order control, suppression of food riots and supporting the customs and excise with anti-smuggling duties. Consequently the regiments were dispersed across the country with always a substantial force permanently in Scotland and in Ireland. There were also many troops serving abroad, scattered in foreign postings, such as North America, the West Indies, Gibraltar and India. The government saw no need to have large divisions of troops as the protection and safety of the country was the task of the Royal Navy, the 'wooden walls of England'.

The involved structure that ran the Army was intentional; it was designed to spread control to several spheres of influence, all of whom came under the eventual control of the government. The fear was that the Army would be able to run itself. The British Army therefore was a relatively small force in 1793 when war was declared with France. It numbered 40,000 men.

The dispersal of the Army into small scattered independent bodies had the effect that it was virtually impossible to organize regular training of separate units even at brigade strength. Commanders could never develop tactics or test their effect with full-scale manoeuvres. Even at brigade strength the problem arose that when regiments did meet on the field they discovered that they had been functioning on their own for so long that they had all developed diverse and different forms of drill systems and evolutions.

The British Army, unlike the Prussian and Austrian armies, did not carry out large annual camps for the exercise of manoeuvres to give the troops experience in large-scale battle tactics and the officers in organizing and handling large formations of troops and all the logistical problems that go with such assemblies. Such exercises also gave commanders the opportunity to test new tactics and elaborate manoeuvres. British officers who needed such experience had to seek it abroad and go to the continent, as did the Duke of York.

If smaller scale manoeuvres were planned, even at brigade level, the problem was always the difference in the way the regiments conducted themselves and carried out their evolutions. Before contemplating any movements senior commanders would have to meet and agree a common form and a uniform system. To quote Captain T. Reide in his *Treatise on the Duty of an Infantry Officer and the Present System of British Military Discipline.*

> We never had any general system of discipline, ordered by authority to be implicitly complied with: on the contrary (a few review regulations excepted) every Commander-in-Chief or officer commanding a corps, adopted or invented such manoeuvres as were thought proper. Neither was the manual exercise the same in all regiments, nor marching in slow or quick time properly regulated. The consequences of

which were, that when 2 or 3 regiments were in the same garrison or camp, they could not act in brigade or line, till the general officers commanding established a temporary uniform system.

And to quote Sir Henry Bunbury:

Men of the present generation can hardly form an idea of what the military forces of England were when the Great War with France started in 1793. Our army was lax in discipline, entirely without system, and very weak in numbers. Each colonel of regiment managed it according to his own notions or neglect it altogether. There was no uniformity of drill or movement, professional pride was rare; professional knowledge still more so.

This was the first lesson that the Duke of York uncovered regarding the competence and state of the Army that entered into the Flanders campaign with such an amateur basis his forces were no match for the French. Youthful and full of energy, the young Duke was thrust into the depths of a bureaucratic imbroglio that would defeat most men.

As John Watkins, the Duke's personal secretary, recorded:

Error and abuse had for so many years prevailed ... general reform was rendered absolutely necessary ... The King, who ever since his accession, saw and lamented the corruptions which prevailed ... His Majesty however, was too prudent a man to recommend any sudden innovations of great magnitude ... It was his opinion, that the important work of reorganising such a complicated machine ... should be carried out progressively, to avoid raising the passions of the people against measures, the beneficial tendency of which they could neither perceive nor understand. To this sage principal the Duke of York cordially acceded.

Observing his father's suggestion the Duke of York planned his programme of reforms at a slow and steady pace. Sir John Fortescue was to cite him as the person who 'did more for the Army than any one man has done for the whole of history'.

The reforms carried out by the Duke of York eventually affected every sphere and aspect of the service, ranging from recruitment to rations. Importantly, the major reforms began to affect the core of the army, training and drilling the regular infantry and the training, selection and composition of the officer corps.

To obtain a commission in the Army was at the time dependent on the connections, personal wealth and social standing of the applicant which would ensure that undesirable elements who had property, land and wealth should have control of the regiments to preclude any undesirable persons who might have republican or democratic interests. Subsequent promotion again was based on a person's ability to purchase a higher rank. As one officer stated, 'An officer who had the money could purchase up to the rank of lieutenant colonel in three weeks or a month.'

The standard of the officer corps deteriorated and by 1794 the purchase system was corrupt and out of control. There was also the system whereby any officer who could collect enough volunteers to enter the Army could gain promotion just on the strength of enlisting men. This became important in 1793 when large numbers of new regiments were being raised quickly.

To counteract the undesirable practices that prevailed in the officer corps the Duke of York introduced a number of important reforms. His first task was to appoint a Military Secretary to serve as the sole channel of communications between himself as C-in-C and the rest of the service directly rather than through the Secretary at War, or some other official outside the Army. It had the effect of stifling interference by politicians and other civilians in matters of discipline and other issues.

The Duke implemented changes to the recruitment of officers but he dared not abolish the purchase system completely as it was too well established. The Duke succeeded in increasing the numbers of free commissions and decreed that no subaltern could be promoted to the rank of captain without first having at least two years serving as a lieutenant. For higher ranks a minimum of six years was required.

To improve the general education and professional knowledge the Duke founded a Military College at High Wycombe, which eventually grew into the Staff College of later years. The Duke also established a school for military cadets between the ages of thirteen and sixteen, a course which lasted four years. This school eventually developed into the Royal Military College, Sandhurst.

A second and most important area that needed attention was that of drill, manual exercises (arms drill) and evolutions, none of which was standardized – and this was in 1790, three years before the war with France.

In 1797, which was four years after the Duke of York experienced all the failings of the British Army in the Flanders campaign, he issued a series of directives on the training of light troops. In addition to several copies of the 1792 *Regulations* relating to light infantry companies being despatched to every foot regiment, a circular to senior officers directed that:

> His Royal Highness thinking it highly expedient at the present juncture, that Light Infantry Companies ... throughout the whole country should be diligently exercised, and prepared as much as

possible in those movements and manoeuvres, which are more peculiarly adapted to them, than to the Heavy Infantry, is therefore pleased to direct that you should give immediate orders for all Light Companies, attached to the several battalions in the district under your command, to be frequently taken out, in separate bodies, and practise in firing ball at a mark and in such other different exercises as they are principally formed and intended for when opposed to an enemy.

It was not only the Duke of York who expressed doubts about a regiment completely composed of riflemen. He expressed his views to the Hon. William Stewart of the Experimental Corps of Riflemen:

A Rifle Regiment, from its composition, must always be subject to serve as Detachments and can seldom if ever act together as a corps. It is on this principle that a corps of Chasseurs with a proportion of Rifle Men has generally esteemed preferable to a Regiment composed wholly of Rifle Men.

After the 1799 campaign in Holland the Duke of York had noted all the deficiencies in the Army, including that it was deficient in a skirmish force. So he became very interested in the plan put forward by Colonel William Stewart of the 67th for an Experimental Corps of Riflemen. The Duke agreed to this plan but on the provision that it was only to be a temporary arrangement and not a permanent corps. Being schooled in the Prussian system of rapid mass firepower, the Duke was reluctant to see a regiment totally armed with rifles, which had been proven to be no match for the musket in a rapid rate of fire. As a compromise it was suggested that one platoon of each light company could be armed with rifles.

General John Moore was then the commander of the forces in Southern England, an area that in previous times was well known for invasions and hence as the 'Saxon Shore'. His responsibility was the protection of southern England against any threat of an invasion by the French. In 1802 Moore sent an order to Colonel Stewart to move his new rifle battalion, now the 95th, from East Blatchington to the new camp which he thought could be adapted to their needs. The camp was at Shorncliffe, near Hythe in Kent, and was to become well known as the training centre for light troops.

Colonel Stewart developed the training and instruction programme. He wrote to the Duke for advice on the subject of a training manual and the C-in-C suggested to Stewart the *Study and Explanation of a small Treatise on the Science of Light Troops*, which had been compiled by General Jarry and published with

HRH's sanction. (During 1803 Jarry was giving personal tuition to a group of officers from the 95th at the Royal Military College.)

The Duke of York began his programme of developing the new light regiments under the guidance and command of General John Moore. Moore's own regiment, the 52nd Oxfordshire Regiment, was the first to convert, followed by the 43rd Monmouthshire Regiment. Then came the 51st Yorkshire, 71st Highland and 85th Buckinghamshire Regiments.

Chapter 7

Aimed Fire
The Experimental Corps of Riflemen

The drums of war were beating across the Channel, calling all citizens to not only defend the new republic but to spread the word, the idea, to the four quarters of the world. The threat of an invasion of England was never stronger than it was at the end of the eighteenth century. The French Assembly of the First Republic, who were already at war with Prussia and Austria, declared war on Britain on 1 February 1793, stating at the same time that William Pitt was an enemy of the human race.

The following year the revolutionaries threatened to invade Britain, the latest in a series of invasion scares during the eighteenth century. All this had William Pitt running scared; as Master of the Cinque Ports he enjoyed the residence of Walmer Castle which, he pondered, was only a short distance from the cliffs of France. So, at his own expense, he formed the Cinque Ports Artillery, a voluntary body raised to man the guns of Walmer Castle and the other four ports.

The government viewed Pitt's expensive and disastrous failures in supporting the French Royalist cause with trepidation and there was even more concern at Horse Guards. As the instrument of government, they viewed with alarm the Army's and the Duke of York's failures in the Low Countries. The Duke had tried his best and worked hard at it, made obvious by the battered state of his scabbard, but was beaten on all counts by the dismal failure of the Army's organization.

The country, especially the south of England, was in a near state of panic at the threat of invasion. The Duke of York was at Horse Guards with senior Army commanders and was being pressured into taking up the challenge from the French, England's traditional enemy. The Duke of York had already made many changes and improvements to the Army's lot, but it was his policy to make changes slowly so as not to disturb the delicate balance of the individual colonels' personal control of their regiments.

In 1799 Colonels Eyre Coote-Manningham and the Honourable William Stewart approached the Duke of York, pointing out the importance of having a regiment in the army 'furnished with a rifle arm and trained in the special duties of riflemen'. All were aware that during the Helder campaign a few companies of riflemen might have tipped the scale more than once, especially during the advance of Moore's brigade upon Egmont op Zee. Due to the absence of riflemen the advance failed and the best officer in the Army was very nearly lost. Due to the threats coming from the French it was decided to expedite plans to form the Experimental corps of Riflemen and the new light regiments. A new rifle and an improved light musket for the proposed new light regiments were being selected and the design of new uniforms was also being decided, all within the first twelve months or so of the new century.

In January 1800 the Adjutant General wrote to Colonel Manningham informing him that the Duke of York proposed to place him in command of a corps of detachments from fourteen line regiments 'For the purpose of its being instructed in the use of the rifle and in the system of exercise adopted by soldiers so armed'. Manningham was reminded that it was neither a permanent nor a distinct corps but a corps of experiment and instruction. The Duke, no doubt advised by Sir John Moore, had accepted the plan to form a training corps and the famous circular was issued by Horse Guards on 17 January 1800 to selected commanding officers of regiments, requesting volunteers, officers, sergeants and rank and file. They also called upon thirty-three of the Fencible regiments in Ireland to each give twelve active young men as volunteers to the corps, receiving ten guineas each. It should be borne in mind that a farm labourer at that time had a weekly wage of about eight shillings.

The term 'corps' used at this period was applied arbitrarily to any unit of indeterminate size or function. The Experimental Corps was not a gazetted regiment, although some sources misleadingly consider it to be a regiment, even to the point of illustrating a non-existent uniform. All the men were on detached training duties from their own regiments and still wore their parent regiments' uniforms with their distinctive facings and lace. When assembled they must have appeared a motley group. They were still under the command of their own commanding officers who continued to be responsible for their pay and uniforms.

First formed as the Experimental Corps of Riflemen in February 1800 and originally raised as a temporary training unit, its single purpose was the training of selected volunteers in the use of the rifle and light infantry drills and duties through range practice and field exercises. The original intention was that the trained riflemen would return to their individual regiments' flank companies and form platoons armed with rifles. The rifles used at this time would most likely have been imported rifles from Prussia, or they could have been the heavy rifled muskets made by Durrs Egg.

On 20 February 1800 orders were issued to the detachments of eleven of the regiments quartered in the counties of Kent, Sussex, Essex, Suffolk and

Norfolk to march to Horsham, a small market town in Sussex which was on the marching route from Portsmouth to Chatham. Horsham had one of the new barracks being built in all the principal towns across the south of England to accommodate mainly the militia regiments being raised due to the crisis. On the 21st the remaining four detachments belonging to regiments quartered in Scotland were ordered to embark at Leith, proceed to the Thames and land at Gravesend for Horsham, which was a six day march, covering twelve miles per day on average. The detachments began to arrive during the first week in March and before the end of the month all had assembled.

When the Horse Guards circular requesting volunteers to join the Experimental Corps was issued to selected regiments it was hoped that the volunteers would be those who would benefit most from the training. Unfortunately many colonels saw this as an opportunity to dispose of the undesirables and misfits. These were rejected and returned to their units, and exchanged for more suitable men. From the Marching Order Books, used to record the regiments' movements, are entries that indicate 'unsuitability' as six of the regiments were asked to replace fifty-two men who were found 'inefficient'. On 15 July a sergeant had to return a number of rejected men via Bristol to Ireland.

The first parade was on 1 April 1800. The men were formed into seven companies, an awkward number that must have presented a motley sight. Ten of the companies were infantry of the line and more or less clothed alike, apart from facing colours and lace. In 1800 King's Regulations stipulated red coats with regimental facing colours, white breeches with gaiters, black shoes (not boots) and bicorne cocked hats. But there were four Highland regiments, the 71st, 72nd, 79th and 92nd, all of whom wore the kilt.

At the end of April they marched off to the training camp at Swinley in Windsor Forest about five miles west of Chobham Common for field exercises and light infantry training under Lieutenant Colonel William Stewart. In 1800 much of this countryside was open heath land but by 1900 it was covered by fir trees.

As random as the common musket – Ezekiel Baker

Before the start of training a committee of field officers including Colonels Manningham and Stewart were directed by the Board of Ordnance to assemble at Woolwich on 1 February 1800 to select a suitable rifle for use by the new riflemen from the forty pieces presented. The principal gunsmiths from England including Durrs Egg, Henry Nock and Ezekiel Baker were invited to attend with their rifles, with additional rifles from America, France, Prussia, Holland and Spain produced and tried. After exhaustive tests the rifle designed and made by Ezekiel Baker of Whitechapel in East London was chosen. It was generally considered a fine rifle and proved accurate up to 300 yards and more importantly was robust and soldier proof and would stand up to the rigours of campaigning.

Whilst it was in the training camp at Swinley Horse Guards considered the corps to be a successful experiment and accepted the proposal to have a permanent rifle-armed regiment in the British Army. Orders were issued in June 1800 for recruits to be obtained from the fencible regiments then stationed in Ireland. From its first inception it was the intention of Horse Guards to form the new regiment as a *corps d'élite*. It was envisaged that only men with the right qualities should be selected by each commanding officer while, with officers, a double selection process was intended.

Was this somewhat hurried decision made as a desperate measure? It could have been that the prospect of imminent invasion and the drum-rolling from France was forcing the matter. Did the prospect of swarms of French *voltigeurs* and *tirailleurs* laying waste to the Kent countryside sharpen the concentration of those at Horse Guards? Manningham and Moore must have been forcing the question, with drawing-room discussions that went unrecorded.

But before this could be implemented Colonel Coote-Manningham, at Stewart's request, had persuaded Horse Guards that the corps could be used in the forthcoming expedition to Ferrol in northern Spain. The expedition was under the command of Sir James Pulteney and Admiral Sir Borlase Warren. A detachment of three companies of the corps under the command of the Honourable William Stewart embarked from Portsmouth on 5 August 1800.

On 25 August the corps, with the 52nd Regiment, landed near Ferrol on the north coast of Spain near Corunna, seized control of nearby heights and covered the main landing of the expeditionary force, later repulsing a Spanish attempt to regain the heights. This action is almost unique in the annals of British military history. The embryo regiment distinguished itself in action before it was even gazetted as a regiment and 25 August, the date on which the riflemen of the future 95th first came under fire, is observed as the regiment's birthday.

The decision to form rifle companies met with substantial opposition, mainly from those who had had unfortunate experiences twenty or so years previously in the war in the American colonies. Of the rifle-armed bushfighters they had encountered in 1776, many were deadly shots but not trained soldiers, lacking the new riflemen's skills and so could not be compared.

Nevertheless, it was not a precedent as Amherst had previously given the order to arm with rifles all the light companies in each of the four battalions of the 60th Royal American Regiment. Before that, Colonel Bouquet of the 1/60th during the French and Indian war had favoured the use of a number of Dutch-made rifles from Pennsylvania while, in 1797, the fifth battalion of the 60th was hurriedly formed as a battalion of jägers from several foreign units who came already armed with their Prussian-made rifles, known as the Hompesch rifle, an example of which can be seen in the Royal Green Jackets Museum.

One of the most noted and vociferous critics of the rifle companies was Lord Cornwallis, he who had surrendered at Yorktown in 1781, thus ending the revolutionary war. In 1800, as Commander-in-Chief in Ireland, he was asked to report on the proposal to draft men from the line regiments in Ireland to form a rifle corps. In his reply he gave his considered opinion that the corps of riflemen would be 'a very amusing plaything', and that he was opposed to the reduction of the line regiments for such a measure. But he was overruled when the drafting of fifteen or twenty men from each regiment was authorized. Cornwallis added that he considered that in the new corps only one man in every ten should be armed with a rifle and quoted Colonel Wumb in support of his considered advice. Wumb was in command of a corps of German jägers (Hessians) during the American war and had recommended, in 1775, that flintlock muskets be substituted for the rifle with which the jägers were armed. Needless to say, General Cornwallis was overruled and the project went ahead, supported by HRH the Duke of York and Sir John Moore and steered by Colonel Coote-Manningham.

The Duke of York was obviously very keen on the idea as may be judged by his reaction to a visit he made to a field exercise carried out by the Corps of Dutch Riflemen in October 1800. They impressed him greatly, so much so that he directed Colonel Manningham and Lieutenant Colonel Stewart to acquaint themselves with the system that their commanding officer, Colonel Hyde, was acting upon. So it seems that 'Bentinks' jägers served as something as a model for the rifle corps.

Meanwhile, those members of the Experimental Corps who did not go to Ferrol but remained at Swinley broke camp and marched to a camp at East Blatchington, now part of Seaford in East Sussex. The corps were at East Blatchington Barracks from August 1800 to April 1801. Sir Charles Napier, then a junior officer, noted that the early life in the corps was the reverse of exhilarating. The barracks were a collection of hurriedly erected huts as part of the anti-invasion plans, at a small fishing hamlet on the bleak downs near Seaford.

After the abortive expedition to Ferrol where, nevertheless, the Rifle corps distinguished itself, the three companies were directed to Malta where they were dispersed to other regiments either posted in the western Mediterranean or Egypt. Then followed a period of 'marking time' when the mists of time cloud events or, more accurately, a lack of written records creates uncertainty regarding the corps. It appears that, after the dispersal of the Ferrol companies, the corps seems to have been recreated in the course of the autumn with the remaining members at East Blatchington being joined by 290 recruits from the disembodied Irish Fencibles. On 25 August the new Rifle Corps was officially gazetted and numbered the 95th (Rifles) Regiment, but was known and continued to be referred to as the Rifle Corps for a number of years. By the end of 1800 the Rifle Corps numbered 435 NCOs and men.

During this period the personnel still wore their old regimentals as they continued to be clothed by their respective colonels. Those of the Highland regiments still wore the kilt. Training was interrupted when a strong detachment was sent as marines to support Nelson's successful campaign against the Danish fleet at Copenhagen. Many years later in 1951 the Rifle Brigade and the Royal Berkshire Regiment (formerly the 49th) were permitted to use the naval crown, subscribed '2nd April 1801', on their cap badges in recognition of this duty.

In June 1801 the Corps, now 539 strong, marched to Weymouth Barracks whilst King George III was in residence during one of his convalescent periods; Colonel Coote-Manningham was an aide-de-camp to the King, They were there all summer until September and then marched back to East Blatchington, a good route march, to continue training.

In 1801 the Standing Orders of the regiment were drawn up. Known as *The Green Book Standing Regulations of the 95th* they included new procedures that must have startled the old school of 'die hards', the martinets and exponents of powder, pomp and pipe-clay. There were provisions for careful and systematic training in musketry (rifle shooting) to classify men according to their skill at firing at marks; white tufts on the shako for recruits and green tufts for marksmen; medals for good conduct and for bravery; the establishment of the company system which gave company commanders direct and separate control of their commands and for the formation of a regimental school with periodic lectures and examinations on military subjects as well as encouragement of athletic exercise and what would be termed today as a form of assault course.

Training was based on the use of several manuals, the most important of which was *Regulations for the Exercise of Riflemen and Light Infantry and their Conduct in the Field*. This was first written in German by Baron de Rottenburg, Colonel of the 5/60th, after a manual by Colonel von Ewald.

From 1802 to 1804 they were based farther along the coast at Shorncliffe Camp, near Folkestone, for intensive light infantry training under the command of Sir John Moore. They also acted as a rapid reaction force to any invasion threat. Sir John Moore was noted for his humane approach to soldiers' military conduct, his fairness over punishments, his abhorrence of flogging indicative of his understanding of the troops and his aim to foster an *esprit de corps*. Illustrating this was his order regarding departures to foreign parts. It was then the general custom when a regiment received orders for foreign

A 95th Rifleman, *c.*1810.

Colonel Coote Manningham.

Colonel Bouquet.

Sir John Colborne.

Sir John Moore.

Baron Francis
de Rottenburg.

Robert Craufurd.

Baker Rifle.

Riflemen of the 5/60th in two firing positions – kneeling and standing. They are wearing the 1812 uniform with red facings and green trousers instead of blue pantaloons.

Sergeant of the 1/60th Royal American Regiment in 1758. His short coat has the blue facings of a royal regiment but is without lace while his accoutrements are plain leather.

Uniform of a line infantryman just arrived from England in 1758. He wears a long coat with lace, a tricorne hat and all his accoutrements are pipe-clayed.

A light infantry soldier in America. His coat has been cut down to form a jacket without any lace and his tricorne hat has been cut to form a cap.

Typical uniform of a German jäger: green jacket with red facings. All accoutrements are in natural leather. He carries a short sword.

A grenadier with tall mitre hat, typical of the uniform of Braddock's advance guard of the 44th and 48th Regiments' Grenadier Companies.

Main entrance of the Portuguese fortress town of Almeida.

Hessian line troops hired to support British forces in America.

service to shut the gates and confine the men to barracks to avoid desertions. When the 51st sailed from Cork to Gibraltar (then a hated posting) in 1792, Moore ordered the gates to be thrown open so that the soldiers might make merry and enjoy themselves and get drunk on 'pongo' before their departure, adding at the same time that if there were any poltroons in disguise amongst them they might be off. It was only good soldiers he wished to take with him. On this occasion not one deserted.

The command also included the 1/52nd, the 1/43rd and the 1/71st who were to be the first of the new light infantry regiments that were part of Moore's plan to combat the voltigeurs. Whilst they were training they were also to be part of what would be termed today as a rapid reaction force to combat any French landings near the beaches. On the alarm being sounded they were to parade at their alarm posts in light marching order without baggage. Included in their duties when not on field training exercises were outpost duties, guards, picquets and patrols for all of which they were specially trained.

When Colonel Coote-Manningham was away from Shorncliffe, Lieutenant Colonel the Honourable William Stewart would assume command. He was the author of the *Green Book Standing Regulations*, which became a model for all light regiments. Stewart was respected as a very capable officer but it was noted that on occasions of assuming total command his zeal apparently became unbearable. Sir Charles Napier, then a junior officer in the Rifle Corps, commented, relating to the duties of the duty officer inspecting each Martello Tower on the beach:

> He ordered that all the Martello Towers on the beach should be visited a certain number of times, day and night by the subaltern on duty.
> Napier was the first to report.
> 'How is this, sir? Not a quarter of the duty performed.'
> 'It is impossible.'
> 'That word is not in the military dictionary.'
> 'But in arithmetic, Colonel it is, to walk forty-five minutes along a beach with legs deep in shingle.'

Rifle Green

Patterns for uniform clothing were decided in May 1801 and a clothing warrant was issued dated 20 May 1801. 1800 was a time of change to King's Regulations regarding uniforms for the infantry regiments of the line with the long coats and cocked hats being replaced by short jackets and shakos for NCOs and rank and file.

The uniform for the 95th was new to the British Army as it was designed to make them inconspicuous on the battlefield, a reversal of the usual practice. It tended to follow the European pattern for chasseurs and jägers by using a dark bottle-green material, known later as rifle green, dull buttons, no lace and black leather accoutrements. Because of this dark, almost black aspect, they became known by other regiments as 'the Sweeps'. The French who later saw them darting from cover called them 'Grasshoppers'.

Part of the hurried developments taking place at this juncture was the suggestion that red as a uniform colour for infantry was unsuitable. That suggestion probably met with a fusillade from Horse Guards. Modified plans suggested that the new light infantry regiments planned should be also dressed in green, but Sir John Moore had his own views on that subject. (The appellation of Green Jackets was traditionally applied in the past to both the King's Royal Rifle Corps and the Rifle Brigade.)

In 1797 the 5th Battalion of the 60th was formed with an intake of 365 from Hompesch's Chasseurs a' Pied Regiment in British pay. They retained their original jäger uniforms of green jackets, blue pantaloons and an Austrian-style belltop shako, the first regiment in the British Army to wear a shako. In 1799 they were supplemented by a draft of 550 from another hired regiment, Lowenstein's Chasseurs, who wore grey uniforms with green facings. The battalion was attested to serve in the British Army as the 60th Regiment but only permitted to serve on foreign postings as they were recruited from foreigners, mainly German speaking. The uniforms of both regiments looked distinctly foreign and were kept until worn out.

During the war with France from 1793 to 1815 many cases occurred of mistaken identity, or what is termed today as 'friendly fire'. It was the Duke of Wellington who during the Peninsular Campaign recommended that the uniform design of British regiments should look distinctly British, even when seen in silhouette against the sky line, to lessen such mistaken identities.

The Hamilton-Smith Tests 1800

An experiment was carried out in 1800 through controlled tests on the range of the effect of aimed fire on coloured targets, representing the different colours of uniforms, being red, green and grey. The tests proved that grey was the target most difficult to discern and registering least number of hits. It was therefore presumed that grey was the most suitable colour for a uniform and recommendations were made for its adoption by the new rifle regiments and other light regiments.

The tests were supervised by Charles Hamilton-Smith of the 60th Regiment, a well-known military illustrator of regiments and their uniforms, who used a company of riflemen from the newly-formed sixth battalion of the 60th. These riflemen were from a detachment of Lowenstein's Chasseurs who had recently been drafted into this new battalion for the Helder Campaign. They wore grey uniforms faced with green and retained their Prussian-made rifles.

Towards the end of 1800 a new regiment was embodied from the Experimental Corps of Riflemen and gazetted as the 95th (Rifles). A decision had to be made on what colour should be chosen for the new uniforms. Bottle green had already been adopted in 1795 for the uniforms of two companies of riflemen of the North Riding Militia of York. In the event grey was not selected and it was decided to adopt bottle green or the darker version known as rifle green as a good camouflage colour for uniforms. The regiment's first colonel, Coote-Manningham was probably instrumental in deciding on green.

In certain conditions rifle green looks almost black and black uniforms, as worn by the Brunswick Oels Jägers, are also difficult to distinguish, especially when seen against the dark greens and deep shadows of the verdant woods and countryside typical of northern Europe. (I know that my old dog, a black Labrador, was difficult to see when he ran through the undergrowth.)

In 1809, at the beginning of the Peninsular Campaign, Horse Guards decreed that all the rifle regiments should be dressed alike as soon as possible, all in green but with individual facings and buttons. This regulation applied to the 95th, the 60th, who kept their blue pantaloons for full-dress parades for a number of years, the light battalions of the King's German Legion, who kept their grey trousers, and the Corsican Rangers whose uniform was almost identical to that of the 60th.

Sir John Moore, the father of British light infantry, could have been the key figure in deciding against the adoption of a camouflage colour for the new light regiments, the 43rd Monmouthshire Light Infantry, the 52nd Oxfordshire LI and the 71st Highland LI. He did not want the new light regiments to become singled out as a *corps d'élite* to become a specialized skirmish force only, as were the rifle regiments. He wanted them to feature very much as an integral part of the line infantry and be adaptable like the French voltigeurs. They should be able to adapt swiftly from the skirmishing role and picquet duties to forming up with the line troops as part of an attack column or a defensive line or square. Moore wanted the new light regiments to be trained so that they were equally familiar with the drills and duties of light and line troops and keeping their red coats or, more properly, jackets would help to establish and emphasize that fact.

From the first conception of the Experimental Corps of Riflemen to its gazetting as the 95th Rifles took less than a year. Such a rapid realization was due to the work of Colonel Coote-Manningham and Sir John Moore, both great believers in forming such a *corps d'élite*. Their faith in the new regiment was vindicated when the 2/95th was raised in 1805, at the height of the invasion crisis. The 3/95th was raised in 1809. The 1/95th was 'blooded' in 1806 when it was led by Brigadier General Robert Craufurd in the ill-conceived campaign in Buenos Aires.

A further vindication was what could be called a French testimonial. Casualties amongst French officers were very high. A report from Marshal Soult, Commander-in-Chief in Spain to the Minister of War survives. Dated St Jean de Luz, 1 September, 1813, it reads:

> The loss in prominent and senior officers, sustained for some time past by the Army, is so disproportionate to that of the rank and file I have been at pains to discover the reason, ... armed with a short rifle, the men are selected for their marksmanship, they perform the duties of *sacouts*, and in action are expressly ordered to pick officers, especially Field or general officers ... This mode of making war and injuring the enemy is very detrimental to us ... I saw yesterday battalions whose officers had been disabled in the ratio of one officer to eight men.

In this report Soult was referring in particular to the riflemen of the 5/60th Royal Americans but it applied equally to all riflemen of the 95th and the King's German Legion light battalions.

Colonel Dumas, on Soult's staff, claimed in support of this that 'Les Riflemen' killed all officers between 25 July and 31 August 1813, a total of 500 officers and eight generals. And it all began with Tom Plunkett of the 1/95th.

Chapter 8

The 95th Rifles and the Baker Rifle

The young Lieutenant Colonel Wesley of the 33rd Foot, later the Duke of Wellington's Regiment, had had his 'baptism' of French fire at Boxtel in 1794 during the war against the armies of the First Republic, where the Duke of York's disastrous campaign in Flanders suffered an ignominious defeat. The campaign exposed all the weaknesses of the Prussian system against the new tactics employed by the emergent French forces. It was here that Wesley, later Wellington, experienced for the first time the heavy casualties and total disruption caused by the new French tactic of using hordes of *tirailleurs* and *voltigeurs*, albeit armed with short muskets and carbines but very few rifles.

These light troops' functions were described in the *Reglements* of April 1792:

> While battle lines are being formed and batteries placed, the commanding officers order the light infantry to advance ahead of the line, so as to discover the positions of the enemy's guns and to diminish their effect. The light troops are in small thickets, behind hedges, ditches or small rises according to the nature of the terrain. They are commanded to fire at the enemy's batteries and try to kill the gunners. These men do not form in troops, so as not draw artillery fire, but separate, benefiting from any feature that may afford them cover, and remain attentive so that they can quickly re-group at the first signal from their officers.

Almost the first order that Wesley made when taking up command in Portugal was to divide up the 5/60th so that every division would have at least one company of the battalion as sharpshooters. He also ordered all the light companies, the flankers, from the 3rd Division to be combined into a composite light battalion under the command of Major Woodgate of the 5/60th. His other act was to build up the structure of the Light Brigade by increasing it to divisional strength and renaming it the Light Division. This gave his army the necessary light infantry capability to combat the *voltigeurs*.

'As random as the common musket'

Of the 37,383 British, King's German Legion and Hanoverian infantry directly under British command and control at Waterloo, by far the greater number were armed with the smoothbore flintlock musket known as the 'Brown Bess'. The exceptions were those of the 1st, 2nd and 3rd battalions of the 95th Rifles and the 1st and 2nd light battalions *(Scharfschützen Korps)* King's German Legion which were armed with the British Baker rifle. In the Hanoverian Brigade of Colonel Ompteda's 2 Brigade of the King's German Legion, was also a Jager Korps of 331 men, presumably armed with Prussian rifles.

On 18 June 1815 both the 95th Rifles and the Baker Rifle itself, which was originally designed and made for the regiment, were only fifteen years old. In the following year the Duke of Wellington ordered that the regiment be taken out of the line and, without a number of precedence, be re-named the Rifle Brigade (which was still its name when this author enlisted).

The rifle as a personal weapon was well known during the eighteenth century and was used mainly by hunters in the forests of central Europe, and by those hunters who enlisted and became hunter *schuzen* in the armies of Middle Europe, the *Grenz* and *Jäger* of the German Principalities, Prussia, Austria and Croatia.

The rifle was also a well-known weapon in use in the American colonies where it had been introduced and manufactured by Dutch and German colonists. It was distinguished by its small bore and very long barrel, and known as the Pennsylvania long rifle. It fired a very small ball, big enough to kill without making a big hole in the pelt and was used by hunters and frontiersmen who had emigrated to the colonies and lived as trappers in the forest wilderness that spread across North America and Canada, or New France.

The word 'rifle' is derived from, or is a corruption of, the Low German verb (now obsolete) *'riefein'*, meaning 'to cut a groove'. It was the German and Dutch gunsmiths of Pennsylvania who were the main producers and suppliers of rifles in the colonies and from that source many rifles were eventually traded with the French and the Indian nations who used them against the colonists, settlers and the troops, both British and provincial during the Seven Years' War.

The ballistic principle of the rifle was well known and had been proven. To achieve accuracy, the bullet was made to spin or rotate on leaving the barrel. This was caused by engraving or gouging out precise grooves or 'turns' in a helical form to ensure accurate flight and range. The hunter or rifleman was thus able to aim his piece inside the bore of the barrel. By ensuring that the bullet was a tight fit when rammed in, these 'turns' imparted rotation to the bullet when fired, which was necessary to ensure accurate flight and range. The hunter or rifleman was now able to aim his piece with some certainty of scoring a hit.

Because of the extra care needed when loading the rifle, it took longer to load and make ready than did a musket. This worried the military but not the hunters, since they usually hit their target with the first shot.

With the musket's smooth bore there was always plenty of 'windage' or loss of propellant gases, and the best a musketeer could do was to give his bullet direction rather than aim. In fact the British musket could not be relied on to hit a mark at a hundred yards. When fired, the ball was liable to fly anywhere at random within a variable arc. But fired all together in a fusillade, the missiles (weighing fourteen balls to the pound) had sufficient force and direction to inflict heavy and murderous casualties on men in massed ranks fifty or a hundred yards away. Although the object aimed at was seldom the object hit, like Picton at Waterloo many became casualties by being struck by wild bullets or grapeshot.

So, with its faults and limitations understood and accepted, the musket, made in great numbers, earned its place as the standard infantry weapon and held it for many years. The rifle was considered a specialist weapon for the hunter and sharpshooter. That it was far more accurate than the musket was well known, but the musket could be produced cheaply and in quantity, and was more robust, being able to tolerate the rough handling it got, especially in the cut and thrust of battle when it was often used as a bludgeon.

The Arms Available Determine the Tactics

The musket's deficiencies led to the 'wall of fire' tactics developed to perfection by the armies of Frederick II, The Great, of Prussia. From 1740, for nearly sixty years, the Prussian system was adopted by most European armies wanting to emulate Frederick's successes. The British Army of the eighteenth century based its tactics on a modified version of the Fredrician system. The high command had seen the Prussian troops executing their manual drills and manoeuvres on the drill fields of Potsdam, impressive in their massed ranks, resplendent in their uniforms, marching dutifully (or robotically) into position with the balance, or goose, step.

But behind the spectacle of parades, bands and pomp was a military structure that was harsh, brutal and dehumanizing, even for the eighteenth century. Drill and yet more drill in preference to field exercises was the method of training the line infantry regiments. Training was based on the fear of authority. Its aim was to instil unquestioning obedience as the object was to move to orders only, never to take independent action, and to hold officers and NCOs in more fear than any enemy. The discipline stripped the men of any self-respect and deprived them of any dignity. Yet it is difficult to imagine what other training methods could have been used that would condition men lacking in any form of motivation to march determinedly into battle, in regimental formations, sweating in heavy restricting uniforms and finally to stand to their front and be shot at very close range, and all without question.

The key to the Prussian system was its harsh, iron discipline and drill, with everyone acting in unison. It enabled troops in great numbers to perform their complicated evolutions, bring to bear as many muskets as possible on the enemy, and deliver a wall of fire in the form of rolling volleys or by divisions, all at great speed. Their will and steadfastness would hopefully crush the will of the enemy. The ultimate objective was that with so many large balls hurtling towards an enemy some were bound to find a target. The complicated evolutions were executed in the heat and din of battle where commands were smothered by the crescendo of cannon fire before they got beyond the second man and everyone disappeared in clouds of acrid smoke.

So long as the traditional formations and manoeuvres of the eighteenth century were adhered to by both combatants there was no particular need for arms of greater precision. The ritual of the system became such that it was considered against the tenets and gentlemanly rules of warfare to deliberately 'pick off' individuals. Everyone took their chance.

Early Recognitions

Colonel Christian von Ompteda was one who recognized the deficiencies of the Prussian system and the need for light troops. Some interesting observations were noted in his diary whilst stationed at Gibraltar.

3 February 1807, Gibraltar

Sir Hew Dalrymple had a company drawn today from each of the four English regiments and formed a battalion there – from which was drilled partly by himself and partly by other English staff officers under his instructions. The intention was to impress on them the first principles of dressing and wheeling. They seemed to be imperfect in many essential particulars. Good as Sir Hew's idea was, the success did not seem to be answering. It is certain that for some time the English regiments, whether under special orders, or by spontaneous requirement of their commanders have been perpetually drilled. The patience of the men is something astonishing, and it is pitiful to see the purposeless exercises which are required of them, which reminded me of Guibert's remark with respect to cavalry: 's'aimer dans la poussierre du menage' When I see the quick, active and smart Englishmen being perpetually tortured with the clumsiest system of Prussian regulation step, I reflect on the serious possible results such training might have when opposed to the nimble and dexterous enemy.

21 February 1807

I marched the first company of the battalion today up to the Windmill Hill to give them some instruction in the elementary principles of skirmishing, which at the same time are pretty exhaustive for a form of tactics so surrounded by obstacles. It afforded me real pleasure to see with what zest the men took up this exercise, and how quickly they grasped the leading ideas. I might look on this as the victory of free rational movement over the system of soulless mechanism.

Some commanders had a very singular and non-regulation attitude to musket-fire, as did Colonel Mainwaring of the 51st Regiment, later the King's own Yorkshire Light Infantry. On 1 August 1809, during the expedition to Walcheren, he addressed the battalion before an action and added that they should observe his old favourite maxim of firing low: 'You will hit them in the legs and there will be three gone, for two will pick him up and take him away.' It was not enough to save the day!

The Prussian tactics had proved very successful and, therefore, as very suitable for all battles, and not only on the great northern plain of Europe. They were designed to be universal and it was expected that there would be no need to adapt to other particular conditions or terrain. But by restricting the musket to such limited and singular use, and by not encouraging marksmanship and loading skills, a serious flaw was built into infantry skills, destined to bring unexpected and serious reverses.

Scharnhorst summed it up when he remarked after Prussia's disastrous war with France in 1806: 'Before the war we taught the men to load quickly, but not well, to fire quickly, but without aiming. This was very ill-considered.'

Serious reverses there were, and some salutary lessons were learnt, sometimes at great cost. Many of the reverses occurred in the colonies and Canada in 1755 during the Seven Years' War and in the American Revolution in 1776. One notable exception happened in 1759 when Wolfe's troops finally defeated Montcalm's across the Heights of Abraham with 'the most perfect volley ever fired'.

The European tactics of Frederick the Great did not always travel well. The massed volley fire by platoons corresponding to half companies or sections, by bodies of disciplined troops, was at a loss when caught in ambuscade and attacked by 'irregulars' who might be called rangers, marksmen, skirmishers, sharpshooters or rebels (colonists). They fought, usually, in small groups and often independently, in a fire and move mode, using the terrain to their advantage, and always dressed in clothes, without bright colours, that blended in with nature.

This new experience of war against irregulars who fought like hunters, who never sought a pitched battle but chose their ground, who struck in small groups and stealthily dispersed, came as a shock to Army command. It was a new land with a new type of men, who had formed out of the terrain a new method of fighting, with a new weapon, the rifle.

The Army attempted to adapt by creating new light regiments, but these were a stop-gap. When conditions became peaceful these regiments were either disbanded or reverted to garrison duties where their hard-won skills and experience as light troops were lost.

The 'Old School' still believed that massed bodies of disciplined troops were the only answer against motley bands of irregulars who fought in a clandestine manner.

Reactions

Finally, the war in Flanders exposed how out-of-date the Army was in its organization and training. Its old fighting techniques and tactics were obsolete and it received a severe mauling from the French. The *tirailleurs* and *voltigeurs* swarmed everywhere in their 'fire and move' pattern of attack, totally confounding the opposition. Their sudden worrying attacks to the exposed flanks caused severe disruption and disorder, and completely inhibited the pre-battle momentum of movement.

As a hurried stop-gap it was decided to fall back on the expedient of 'entertaining' foreign mercenary troops contracted in ready-made regiments raised by *Colonels Proprietaire*. Almost all of these hired regiments were expected to function as light troops and skirmishers. Some saw the recruiting of these units as a compromise or as a stop-gap, whilst others thought of them as expendable, since it was well known that skirmishing was dangerous.

Craig, who succeeded Murray as Adjutant General, wrote to Dundas in 1793 emphasizing the need for foreign troops: 'Our men were too few and too valuable to be employed in skirmishing and out-post work, which involved a steady drain of casualties, and to recruit foreigners was easy' or, as others expressed it, 'the importing of cheap cannon-fodder from Germany'.

All the regiments had a short and most violent existence. Many were eventually posted to the disease-ridden West Indies. Some of the best regiments, such as the Hompesch's Fusiliers and Prince Lowenstein's Chasseurs, were amalgamated and taken into British pay to form the fifth battalion of the 60th Royal American Regiment.

The 5/60th was expected to serve eventually as part of the Army's American commitment along with the other four battalions, but the Peninsular campaign would change that. There was a major distinction: whereas the other four battalions carried light companies the 5/60th was raised as a light battalion of skirmishers and all were armed with rifles. As Dundas instructed the Duke of York, 'It is further His Majesty's intention that no difference should be established between this battalion and the other four, except to what may arise from the manner of arming them with rifles instead of common musquetes.'

The 5/60th became the first regular battalion in the British Army to be armed with rifled weapons, and this marks an important development in the creation of the Service's skirmisher arm. It should be noted that all foreign troops recruited to the 5/60th brought with them their own rifles, known as the Hompesch rifles, which were of Prussian manufacture. At that time no British rifles were being made.

According to Howard Blackmore in *British Military Firearms* many of the foreign levies were experienced in the use of the short thick-barrelled rifle of the continental jäger. Some brought those arms to Britain and the demands of others for similar weapons led the Ordnance to once more seek supplies of rifles.

In October 1798 Sir John Sinclair and General Sir Ralph Abercrombie presented a plan to Secretary of War Henry Dundas. Included was a proposed major set of reforms regarding light troops. General John Money also wrote to Dundas on the subject of light troops. Money was a veteran soldier who ended his military career in the army of the nascent French Republic and had been impressed by the French light regiments, especially by the successes of the Republic's forces in Flanders, which he saw as largely due to the excellence and number of chasseurs.

A plan to form a *corps d'élite* of riflemen was initially put to the Commander-in-Chief in December 1799, after Colonel William Stewart of the 67th Foot, later the South Hampshire Regiment, had also written in detail to the Secretary at War outlining a plan for creating and training a body of skilled marksmen armed with rifled weapons.

As an observer attached to the Austrian forces in Italy in 1799, Stewart had witnessed at first hand the growing importance of light troops, notably riflemen. Stewart's proposals were received warmly and subsequently adopted. Colonel Coote-Manningham, veteran light infantry officer who served with distinction in the West Indies, served as Colonel-in-Chief of the Experimental Corps of Riflemen with Stewart as Lieutenant Colonel.

Obtaining British Rifles

The Duke of York was aware of the strong support for the creation and use of rifle companies from the many requests from promoters of the concept. He was convinced of the rifle's usefulness and was generally in favour of special corps to train in the skills needed. But he was also aware that the Board of Ordnance had a problem finding sufficient supplies of suitable rifles of good quality. There was a limited number of gunsmiths in Britain who had the expertise required to manufacture rifles, and in the necessary quantities; it was very much a 'cottage' industry.

In 1804 the Adjutant General had to advise one correspondent that 'Even in the event of his Highness approving of the formation of rifle companies there is little possibility that such an arrangement could at this time be effected, as in a recent instance of a similar nature it had been found impossible to obtain the supply of rifled arms'.

As usual the Ordnance turned to Germany to augment its supply and, in August 1798, through the agency of Paul and Haviland le Mesurier, ordered 5,000 Prussian 'rifled muskets' with bayonets at 35 shillings each (£1.75). At that price good quality weapons could not be expected and many were broken and inferior and so the price was reduced to 33 shillings (£1.65). The Hompesch rifle cost 32 shillings, but usually neared £2 each while, by comparison, the Long Land Pattern musket was much cheaper at approximately 15 shillings (.75p). Again by comparison, 15 shillings was the weekly wage of a skilled shipwright of that period.

The Board of Ordnance was very much aware of the urgent demand for a suitable rifle, especially after the report presented by Colonels Manningham and Stewart regarding the formation of the Experimental Corps of Riflemen and so it was decided to prepare a series of evaluation tests at Woolwich.

On 1 February 1800 a committee of field officers assembled at Woolwich to select a rifle to be used by the rifle corps. All factors had to be considered as well as handling characteristics and accuracy. These included its maintenance and its tolerance to the inevitable rough handling it would get on active service. Small-bore rifles, such as the American long hunting rifle, were generally considered unsuitable as military weapons because the bore quickly became clogged during a high rate of fire and needed constant cleaning.

The principal gunsmiths of England had been invited to attend with their rifles while rifles from America, France, Germany, Spain and Holland were produced and tested. The committee reported in favour of a rifle submitted by Ezekiel Baker of East London and it was eventually adopted for use by the new rifle regiment, the 95th Rifles, the 5/60th and, during the Peninsular campaign, it was also issued to the light of the King's German Legion, the Brunswick Jägers and some companies of the Portuguese *Caçadores*. It remained the standard British rifle for the Army until 1839 when it was superseded by the improved Brunswick rifle, the last weapon to fire ball shot (or rounds).

Even after the acceptance of Baker's rifle in 1800 there was always a shortage of British-made rifles. The problem was that the rifles were virtually hand made in the gunsmith's small workshops, and precise tooling of the rifling proved exacting work.

These were the numbers manufactured in the seven years from 1803 onwards:

1803	44
1804	325
1805	1,663
1806	3,379
1808	3,997
1809	986

Ezekiel Baker recorded the following notes during the test firing of his rifle;

At a range of 100 yards, thirty-four shots were fired at a target in the shape of a human figure six feet high, and thirty-two rounds punctured the target. The target was moved to two hundred yards and twenty-two hits out of twenty-four were noted.

Accuracy was all with the Baker rifle. The main cause of concern that military commanders had about the use of rifles was that, compared with the smoothbore musket, it took far longer to load, thus giving a slower rate of fire.

Rifles were not suitable for use in the Prussian tactics of rapid fusillades of massed fire by platoons or rolling volleys. Generally a musket could be loaded, primed and fired at a rate of five rounds per minute, whereas the rifle could fire only two rounds a minute or, in the hands of an expert rifleman, three rounds per minute. It was during loading that riflemen were particularly vulnerable. Whilst loading, a section of riflemen could be overwhelmed by an opposing section of chasseurs armed with light muskets.

To compensate for this drawback, Colonel de Rottenburg, commanding officer of the 5/60th, devised special skirmishers' training drills and fieldcraft. His training manual, *Regulations for the Exercise of Riflemen and Light Infantry and Instructions for their Conduct in the Field*, became the basis of the training at Sir John Moore's camp at Shorncliffe. Special emphasis was given to weapons training, proficiency and marksmanship was encouraged and rewarded. (See Appendix 2.) In field training the core of the system was grouping the riflemen into 'comrade' pairs, whereby each rifleman was covered by a second man who was loaded and primed and able to provide cover whilst the first man reloaded. Each section operated in pairs with each rifleman keeping to the same partner. This plan of mutual covering fire functioned in an advance and in a withdrawal. If the situation became untenable, such as with the appearance of cavalry, a quick stealthy withdrawal to thick cover was always advised. If the ground was open, and there were enough riflemen, a rallying group could be formed.

The concern that commanders had that riflemen could be overwhelmed by a fast-loading, musket-wielding enemy was perhaps placing too much stress on caution. In March 1810, prior to Massena's invasion of Portugal, the Light

Division fought a successful action near the frontier at Barba del Puerco. The outcome proved that the confidence Sir John Moore and his followers had in the rifle was justified. Wellington was relieved that all went well and sent a despatch stating how appreciative he was of the way the 95th conducted themselves. Craufurd was reluctant to compliment or pass on praise from others, but in this instance he issued a complimentary order:

> Brigadier General Craufurd has it in command from the commander-in-chief to assure Lieutenant-Colonel Beckwith and the officers of the 95th Regiment who were engaged at Barba del Puerco that their conduct in this affair has augmented the confidence he has in the troops when opposed to the enemy in any situation. Brigadier General Craufurd feels particular satisfaction in noticing the first affair in which part of the Light Brigade were engaged during the present campaign. That British troops should defeat a superior number of the enemy is nothing new, but the action reflects honour on Lieutenant Colonel Beckwith and the regiment, inasmuch as it was of a sort which riflemen of other armies would shun. In other armies the rifle is considered ill-calculated for close action with an enemy armed with a musket or bayonet, but the 95th Regiment has proved that the rifle in the hands of a British soldier is a fully sufficient weapon to enable him to defeat the French in the closest fight in whatever manner they may be armed.

The Baker Rifle

The Baker rifle was thirty inches long in the barrel, compared to the Brown Bess Long Land Pattern at forty-two inches and had a calibre of 0.615 inches against the Bess's calibre of 0.75 inches. The musket had a flintlock and a 17-inch sectioned socket bayonet whereas the Baker rifle had a flintlock and a sword bayonet called a spadroon, always referred to as the sword. This was twenty-seven-and-a-half inches long overall, the blade being twenty-three inches with one cutting edge, and a stirrup-guarded brass hilt and spring-loaded clip for attachment to the rifle's muzzle. The first pattern had a weak knuckleguard, and a modified version was introduced which was a copy of a German design. The rifleman's mode of fighting meant keeping a distance, using the range of the rifle, and avoiding becoming embroiled in close actions. The sword was seldom required or used, as bayonet charges were the province of line troops, but it was useful for personal protection, for making bivouacs and cutting firewood, and could be used effectively for defence in forming square or rallying groups. The Baker rifle was not usually fired with the sword fixed since the piece became too muzzle-heavy, making it impossible to hold anything like an accurate aim.

The thirty-inch barrel was rifled with seven grooves which made only one quarter of a turn, giving the ball a slow twist in that distance.

The balls were twenty to the pound, and the weight of the arm was nine and a half pounds. It was sighted to 100 yards and, by means of a folding sight, to 200 yards.

Loading and firing the baker rifle was almost the same procedure as for the musket but for complete accuracy the procedure differed slightly. The firing orders were: Handle Cartridge, Prime, Load, Draw Ramrod, Make Ready, Present, Give Fire. The major difference was that line infantry fired their muskets on the order, whereas the Rifles fired independently or when a suitable target presented itself.

All riflemen carried in their pouch a quantity of prepared cartridges. These were for emergency use when rapid fire was required and accuracy was of secondary importance. The cartridge was made of a bees-waxed paper tube that contained a measured quantity of gunpowder and a lead ball bound together. The lead ball was made to fit the 0.615 inch bore of the Baker rifle. The drill was for the rifleman to bite off the end of the cartridge and pour a little powder into the barrel from the muzzle. The lead ball was then inserted, followed by the cartridge paper which was rammed down by the ramrod which was removed from the stock under the barrel. Tamping down the wad and charge created compression and the secret of good loading was to make a very tight fit of ball and charge so that there would be as little 'windage', or escape of explosive gasses as possible.

For accurate aimed fire, special greased patches were kept in a patch box, a compartment in the rifle butt. They were usually made from soft chamois kid skin, or woven linen, and greased on the underside only to make contact with the grooves in the barrel and thus reduce friction. In addition, a fine grained specially dried powder was carried in the rifleman's powder (cow) horn for the exclusive use of priming the rifle. It was important to keep the priming powder dry. As well as failing to ignite, damp powder would increase in weight, up-setting the rifleman's calculations of quantity in ratio to range.

Both regiments, the 95th and 5/60th, initially had problems with loading caused by the tight fit of the lead balls and patches. Small wooden mallets were used to hammer the ball in.

Major Davy replaced Colonel de Rottenburg as commanding officer of the 5/60th prior to their sailing to Portugal. The battalion were based in New Barracks, Cork, in Ireland and, on 11 June 1808, had its Prussian and Hompesch rifles replaced by a new issue of the Baker rifle, eight years after its trials and acceptance. They had four weeks to get familiar with the new arm.

It was at this time that they had problems with loading and so Major Davy applied for 450 mallets, the same as issued to the 95th, one per rifleman, and also replacement powder flasks.

The balls were manufactured (many at the old Shot Tower, South Bank, London) from the softest available lead, which was preferred to lead salvaged from old roofings or guttering pipes which would be full of impurities that could spoil the smooth surface of the ball and affect its trajectory. Many riflemen carried the necessary mould and lead to be able to make their own rounds on active service. A pouch would contain fifty rounds of ball ammunition.

It was important to keep the rifle clean and free from corrosion, and each rifleman was issued with a cleaning kit. Attached to the belt, on brass chains, were a picker and brush for cleaning the touch hole and priming pan. There was also a rag and tallow, a spiral brush of hog's hair that could be attached to the ramrod for cleaning the rifling, a cleanser of crimped brass wire and a small oil bottle.

All rifles were marked individually with an identifying serial number, and each rifleman was responsible personally for its safety and cleaning. Unfortunately, many commanders of line regiments did not encourage the practical use of arms. The troops had plenty of manual exercises, or arms drill, with rigid loading procedures drilled by numbers, but very little weapons training. They 'went through the motions' but practice on the range was not considered necessary, leaving many to fire their first shots on the battlefield.

Marksmanship with the Baker rifle in the Rifle regiments was, and still is, considered of prime importance. It was at the old Bisley contests that they showed their skills. Surtees mentions in his memoirs that when recruits went on the range their first shots went from a range of fifty yards mounted on a 'horse' which sounds like a form of wooden trestle. The pre-1939 Army used a tripod structure, the purpose being to keep the rifle steady so that the recruit could concentrate on correct aiming and sight setting; as for the old SMLE, getting the blade of the foresight in the centre and level with the 'u' or in this case the 'v' of the rear sight, as the manual might say.

For the 95th Rifles a training manual was prepared by Colonel William Stewart entitled *Regulations for the Rifle Corps formed at Blatchington Barracks under the command of Colonel Maningham 25th August 1800 and known as the Green Book 95th (Rifles) Regiment*.

The usual position for firing in the line regiments was to stand and present the muskets to the front. Riflemen were taught to fire from all positions, standing, sitting, prone, kneeling and supine, all based on exploiting and making the best use of cover. Live firing against targets at varying ranges was practised, as was firing at moving targets mounted on trolleys, and what is known today as 'snap' targets.

Sergeants were armed with rifles and not spontoons, and were usually the best marksmen in their platoons. Many junior officers preferred to carry and use rifles, not only for self-preservation but because it gave added firepower to their units and they would present a less obvious target, compared to the sword-wielding French officer.

Marksmanship was recognized by the award of a plume. All riflemen wore a black leather cockade, above the bugle horn badge, to which the feather plume was fixed. Recruits and poor shots were called first-class shots and wore just the leather cockade. Second-class shots wore a small white plume. Third-class shots wore a small green plume. Any drop in proficiency and the rifleman reverted to a lower class. Riflemen were also awarded brass and silver medals of merit which hung from white and green ribbons and were worn on the left breast. These were not given lightly and had to be earned by high standards of proficiency, conduct and meritorious service.

Major Davy in his Regimental order of the 5/60th condensed the rifleman's *raison d'être* into a brief summing up that was issued prior to sailing to Portugal, a campaign which would involve the battalion in all the major battles and actions for the next six years, up to the capture of Toulouse in 1813. Many did not survive the long and arduous campaign to see England and Germany again.

Regimental Order   Cork Harbour on board
                                the transport *Malabar*
                                27th June 1808

'The True Rifleman' will never fire without being sure of his man, he should if possible make use of force balls, and only load cartridges in case of necessity, as when a brisk fire is to be kept up. And he will recollect that a few well-directed shots that tell will occasion greater confusion than thousands fired at random and without effect, which will only make the enemy despise our fire, and inspire him with confidence in proportion as he finds us deficient in skill and enterprise.

Major Davy, CO

When in Portugal Major Davy made a request for more NCOs. He added that he had plenty of buglers but action conditions had exposed the need for additional NCOs. This need occurred in both rifle regiments. When in action the Rifles often operated in numerous small detachments, sometimes spread over large areas, with each group having an officer in command supported by a sergeant and a corporal and always a bugler.

Article II of the 95th Regulations describes in detail the organization of the rifle companies of which there were eight (the 5/60th had a similar organization) each divided into two platoons, each of two half platoons or squads. Regulations specifically stated that each squad would be commanded by a sergeant, assisted by a corporal. The Regulations go on to state:

> in every half-platoon one soldier of merit will be selected and upon him the charge of the squad devolves in the absence of both non-commissioned officers of it; as from among these four chosen men (as they are to be called) all corporals are appointed, the best men alone are to be selected for this distinction.

Chapter 9

Sir John Moore,
the Father of Light Infantry

The Duke of York introduced many changes and improvements to the Army of which the most outstanding was the establishment of the light infantry regiments and the controversial creation of a new regiment to be armed with the rifle.

Sir John Moore has always been recognized as 'the father of light infantry', which is misleading to a certain extent and based on the somewhat exaggerated recognition he received from former brother officers of the famous Light Division.

Although Moore did play an important part in the actual creation of the new light regiments and made a significant contribution to their future roles, he was not alone in this new development. There were others who also played their parts in formulating ideas, organizing training schedules, writing manuals on the role and training of light troops, on their special duties, and on the tactical use of light troops.

The role of light troops was becoming more important in warfare and was highly developed on the continent, especially in the armies of the German states and Austria. The young William Stewart, keen to gain experience, went as an observer to the Austrian army during their campaigns and particularly noted the use of light troops as skirmishers and the role of the rifle-armed jägers.

Moore was no stranger to the use of light troops as they were used extensively in the West Indies; his long service there gave him useful experience in the suppression of the insurgents on St Lucia. His policy was to keep up a constant attack and relentless pursuit, never allowing the rebels time to regroup. He applied the same tactics when in Ireland in 1798, during the United Irishmen's rebellion. Under his command were the new 5th Battalion of the 60th Royal American Regiment and some German auxiliaries, including a Hompesch unit. It was in Ireland that he designed several light infantry movements for the use of an Irish militia unit; this was sixteen pages of simple drills and evolutions. He was already forming ideas for his version of light infantry who were intended to be an integral part of the infantry line and not a separate special élite corps. Moore considered them to be more multi-purpose soldiers, more adaptable to demands and more flexible in their drills and formations.

Leading up to the establishment of light troops there were several exponents of light tactics who had prepared instruction manuals, all of whom had some influence on the decision by the Duke of York to give the order to form the Experimental Corps of Riflemen and give command to two of these exponents, Colonel Coote-Manningham with Colonel William Stewart as his second in command. Both had formed the plan to raise the corps with the aim of introducing the rifle into the infantry on a trial basis at first.

An important manual for the training of light troops was written by Baron Francis de Rottenburg, Colonel of the 5/60th, *Regulations for the Exercise of Riflemen and Light Infantry and Their Conduct in the Field,* based on the manual written by von Ewald. The Duke of York had de Rottenburg's manual translated into English so that it could be circulated and used. Another important manual on the subject of light troops was *Instructions Concerning the Duties of Light infantry in the Field,* written by General Jarry who had served previously in the army of Frederick the Great. Both manuals became the basis of the training programme of the 95th and the other light regiments whilst at Shorncliffe.

> *The Channel is but a ditch. Anyone can cross it who has the courage. Let us be masters of the straits for six hours and we shall be masters of the world.*
>
> Napoleon Bonaparte

On 21 May 1802 General Moore was appointed as commander of all the troops in the Southern District of England, which was known in the Second World War as Southern Command, and in a previous era as 'The Saxon Shore'. His main task was to prepare the southern counties for the anticipated invasion by the French.

Moore's headquarters was at Fort Amherst, Chatham, and Shorncliffe Camp was in his area of command. He wrote to Stewart on 2 October 1802, issuing him with a route for 'the march of the Rifle Corps under your command to Shorncliffe', adding that he would find that place suitable for 'target practice and field movements'. Moore had inspected the camp previously and discovered that an enormous redoubt was under construction as part of the preparations for the expected invasion. Moore immediately put a halt to this construction. He expressed the view that it assumed they would wait in the redoubt expecting the French to attack them. Moore knew that if the French had successfully got ashore they would not spend time attacking fortifications but make all speed and march on London which was the prize. Moore's policy was the same as that expressed by Field Marshal Rommel in 1944: 'get them while their feet are still wet, don't let them establish a foothold'. Failing that, Moore decided to fall back, leaving nothing of use but a barren landscape or scorched earth, and to attack the French on their flanks. Hundreds and thousands of volunteers were raised to gather up all food and fodder and destroy the rest. Sir John Moore was sceptical. He expected them to be of little use and no more than a worthless rabble, and rather than impede the French march on London their main pre-occupation would most likely be to loot and pillage before the French arrived.

These volunteers were nothing like the force of trained partisans, proposed and envisaged by General Money. They caused much debate and misgivings, and many proposals were put forward regarding their quick and specialized training. The most practical and prophetic were those suggested by Colonel George Hanger. In 1805, the year of the withdrawal of Napoleon's invasion army from Boulogne, and the battles of Austerlitz and Trafalgar, Hanger published a pamphlet with the curious title *A Plan for the Formation of a Corps Which Never has Been Raised as yet in any Army in Europe, in Which Corps, Singly Shall be Composed all the Strength, Activity, Energy and Skill of Four Corps, Namely, a Regular Battalion, a Corps of Light Infantry, a Corps of Sharpshooters and a Corps of Rifle Marksmen.*

This Corps was to be composed of 1,200 men and:

> it shall in itself comprise all the solidity, activity and skill of three distinct corps, namely the strength, solidity and force of fire of a regular battalion in close order, the activity energy and rapidity in charge of British Light Infantry, acting either at open order or double open order as particular cases and situations may require, together with the destructive skill of a rifleman, *acting a la debandade*, nay, more, they shall act at such loose order as to imitate the subtle art of the Indian, who endeavours always to steal away the life of an enemy without exposing himself to danger. One company of this force was to be enlisted solely from artificer and workmen, carpenters, sawyers, spadesmen, hedgers and ditchers etc. Three hundred men were to be armed pioneers.

Further, on the volunteers, he continued, 'All regiments were to be dressed alike and similar to the line. The 400,000 volunteers then raised were to do two months training.'

Moreover he proposed that they should carry out three field-days a week with regular troops. Then he added:

> I think the goose step may be dispensed with, and that absurdity, the lock step, totally laid aside, so destructive and detrimental to the national vigour and energy of British troops. Their evolutions should

chiefly be confined to marching in line, marching in column, from column forming the line and from the line to form one of the various columns, these being the only evolutions I am acquainted with that are ever put in practice on the day of actual battle.

Let every officer join hand in hand to recommend and patronise the formation of a corps that can perform every duty that is required of a British soldier, from the grenadier to the irregular marksman. Speaking relatively to the defence of this country in case of invasion, I with confidence assert that such corps are wanting, the nature and features of our country evidently point out their utility and efficacy, look only for instance, to the counties of Essex, Kent and Sussex.

Colonel Hanger's plan, if a little verbose, was very much in line with the ideas that Sir John Moore had when he began his training of the new light regiments at Shorncliffe Camp.

Moore's plan for the 95th and the other light troops at Shorncliffe was to act as a rapid response unit to attack the French on the beach as they attempted to land. Moore decided that his own regiment, the 52nd Oxfordshire Regiment, would be the first to convert to light infantry and with a new colonel in command. The new colonel would be Kenneth Mackenzie who had seen service as a light infantry officer in the West Indies and in the Mediterranean area. He had previously joined Thomas Graham's newly raised 90th Perthshire Volunteers Light Infantry in 1794 and had fought directly under the command of Moore at the second battle at Aboukir in the Egyptian campaign. Mackenzie eventually became the main influence on the training at Shorncliffe and organizer of the tactical drill as well as developing the regimental structure and discipline of the new light troops.

Vigour and Rapidity

The British Army has always been capable of adapting to new methods of warfare – in the end, some would say. Light infantry regiments were created out of a need, a desperate need, to adapt to changes that were reshaping tactics. Flexibility was the new order. To steal a march on your enemy required mobility and quick command decisions backed by rapid reaction and response. It was the new pattern.

During the dominant Prussian period of Frederick the Great, light troops did not feature in battlefield tactics. The rules of eighteenth century choreographed battles, according to Fredrician principles, reduced the role of light troops. They became subordinate to the Prussian grenadiers and troops of the line with their ponderous evolutions, as they massed in four deep lines of battalions, giving fire with rolling volleys in head-on confrontations.

Developments leading up to the French Revolutionary Wars saw the French experiment, introducing many changes to their battlefield methods and tactics, with the new criteria being flexibility combined with speed. No longer was there a rigid adherence to a single pattern of tactics. Instead, there were decisive tactical moves with the ability to utilize columns and mixed-order formations rapidly for attack, and fall back to linear tactics for defence. There was an increase in the number of *voltigeurs* and other light troops who could deploy as skirmishers like lots of worrying, stinging insects, creating chaos with constant harassing attacks on all flanks before returning quickly to take their place in the line or column. Not knowing quite what to expect from the new French army stunned the British high command, who were completely thrown off balance by the nonconformity of the new French tactics.

There were some who were aware of the Army's shortcomings during the latter part of the eighteenth century. Its inability to respond to these new tactics was amply demonstrated during the Duke of York's campaign in Holland. One of these critics, and the author of much on the subject, was Colonel George Hanger, an experienced and eccentric soldier and onetime hunter and sportsman who was at the same time a person with some sound ideas and suggestions regarding light troops and other military matters. He published, in 1794, *Reflections on the Menaced Invasion* (a much abbreviated title) in which he made many sound suggestions regarding the Army's defensive preparations against the threatened invasion by the French Revolutionary forces.

He summed up this new attitude to tactics:

> Vigour and rapidity are the only means of rendering *a coup de main* successfully; in such a military enterprise you must advance rapidly towards the object you wish to attain, and that object not be at too great a distance; stop for nothing one moment; vigorously attack any force that opposes you, and push on.

A summing up that in modern terms would have been understood by many, including the German General Staff, who would have recognized it as an outline of 'Plan Yellow', the first phase of the attack on France through Belgium in 1940.

The creation of light infantry regiments was the aspiration of a small number of forward thinking military theorists, including General Sir John Moore, at one time a major in the 60th and Colonel of the 52nd Regiment. He is given the distinction of being the prime mover in the creation of the new light regiments, leading to the eventual formation of the Light Brigade.

Moore was known as a modern soldier and an enlightened one who was aware of the many developments and speculations of the military theorists. It is known that many of his views on discipline and training were contrary to the accepted practices and standards held at that period. He knew that there were better methods of improving morale and discipline, and that 'flog and hang' was not the way. He was very much aware that the Army was in need of change. It had to change: it was, at the end of the eighteenth century, in need of review and drastic reorganization.

The creation of light troops, i.e. regiments specially trained and properly equipped, whose prime function was to protect the main force while being an integral part of that force, was an aim he had nurtured through a decade of neglect following the American Revolution. His motivation was based on close observation, practical experiences and the lacklustre performance of troops in such theatres of war as the West Indies, Ireland, Egypt and Corsica, and inspired by the writings and exploits of many light infantry leaders and 'bush fighters' such as Wolfe, young Amherst, Major Rogers and his rangers, Lord Howe, Henri Bouquet and the 1/60th, Tarleton, Simcoe, Fergusson and his sharp-shooters, von Ewald and his Hessians, Colonel Baron Francis de Rottenburg of the 5/60th, Generals Dumouriez, Jarry and Money. General Jarry became the first commander of the Military College at High Wycombe.

Sir John Moore was the catalyst. Many had ideas and had written manuals which they promoted but Moore had influence. He was on good terms with the King and also with Amherst's successor, the Commander-in-Chief, Frederick, Duke of York, whose total support he could claim. In turn, the Duke respected Sir John Moore's views and looked to him as a sounding-board and sought his advice, knowing he was aware of new developments. With such influence and support, Moore was in the position to make things happen and was able to select personally the most suitable officers who were conversant with light tactics and could support him in the creation of the new light regiments. Lieutenant Colonel Kenneth Mackenzie was selected by Moore, who had served with him previously and knew him as a keen experimenter in light infantry drills and tactics. In 1803 Moore chose him to be the commanding officer of the recreated 52nd Light Infantry.

In 1796, at the age of thirty-five, Moore was promoted to the rank of brigadier general and appointed Governor of St Lucia, an island in a constant state of unrest and rebellion. Moore was on the island for two years, which almost broke his health. Whilst at Fort Charlotte he wrote to Sir Ralph Abercrombie and stressed that what the British Army needed was not a new drill, but a new discipline to rejuvenate it.

> There was already too much drill, and the Army had become a mechanical instrument in place of a living co-operative organism. Its discipline was based on 'flog and hang' and its drill on the theatrical movements of the Potsdam Grenadiers.

This, of course, was a reference to the regime of 'powder, pomp and pipe-clay' and the all-pervading influence of the Prussian drills, all executed to the balance step.

In 1799 Moore was appointed Colonel of the 52nd Regiment but he had to relinquish his command in 1801 and join Sir Ralph Abercrombie's expedition to Egypt. It was there that he gained a reputation for his excellent use of light troops and it was in the course of this that he had occasion to observe the Corsican Rangers. Moore noted 'the perfection of their movements and their utility', which impressed him so much, that from this date on, he appears to have had in mind the creation of a similar force in England. The Corsican Rangers were a multi-national light infantry regiment with some British officers that functioned from 1799 to 1802 and earned a distinguished record. They were re-raised as a rifle regiment commanded by Hudson-Lowe (the same), which existed from 1803 to 1816, serving extensively at Maida and in the Mediterranean area, and known as one of the best foreign corps. Their uniform was almost identical to the later uniform of the British Army's own jäger battalion the 5/60th.

The threat of the forthcoming war with Republican France, the imminent danger of invasion and the inevitable clash of meeting on the battlefield had driven on those that had grasped the opportunity to express their views and anxieties for the need for changes in the Army. Fortunately, the Duke of York was of the same mind and was receptive to all the views and advice being offered.

The immediate threat of invasion had sharpened people's attention and emphasized the need to act swiftly, to 'bite the bullet' and go ahead. So, by 1801, the 95th was formed and, by 1803, the new light regiments were under training. Battle would be a testing time for the Army and for Sir John Moore. Would his reasons for creating the light regiments be justified, and would these regiments prove themselves in battle? Had they the mettle for all that was expected of them?

Chapter 10

The Peninsular War 1808–12
The Light Division in Action on the Côa,
July 1810

Napoleon Bonaparte had proclaimed the Continental System, which was intended to stop all countries trading with Britain by closing their ports to British ships. It was his way of attacking Britain through its trade. Most complied with this order, except Portugal which was a trading partner of long standing.

Napoleon decided to act and in conjunction with Spain, he invaded Portugal and captured the port of Lisbon. The French emperor then turned against Spain. The result of this was that the Spaniards sought help from their former enemy, Great Britain.

Arthur Wellesley was in Cork, Ireland, with 9,000 men waiting for orders to sail on an expedition to South America, another attempt to expand British trade interests to the detriment of Spain, a longstanding enemy of Britain. Spain had now become an ally, a change of plan that would give Britain the opportunity to send a force in the support of Spain and a way of attacking the French on mainland Europe.

Sir Arthur Wellesley received revised orders and set sail for Spain, eventually making a beach landing at Mondego on the coast of Portugal. His plan was to march south and secure the port of Lisbon as it was essential to have a port as a communications link to Britain for supplies, material and troops.

After landing in Portugal, Wellesley organized his command and revived the practice of combining all the light companies of the 3rd Division into a composite light battalion under the command of Major Woodgate of the 5/60th. He also formed the Light Brigade, a formation of three regiments, the 43rd, 53rd and 95th (Rifles) Regiments, all of which had trained at Shorncliffe Camp. They were under the command of Brigadier General Robert Craufurd.

The Convention of Cintra
After two battles Wellesley captured Lisbon. He now had the measure of the French and made plans to drive them out of the peninsula with the assistance of the Spanish army and the people. However, Wellesley was not of senior rank in terms of service and was replaced by Sir Hew Dalrymple and Sir Henry Burrard who decided, after dining on board ship, that enough had been done

and, to avoid any further bloodshed, to agree to an armistice with the French. This would allow the French to return home with their arms, colours and all honours, including the loot they had plundered, in British ships.

There was outrage in Britain at this and Burrard, Dalrymple and Wellesley were recalled for trial, although Wellesley was not a party to the humiliation. In the meantime Lieutenant General Moore was sent to take command of the army of 35,000. He was about to march to Madrid when captured despatches disclosed the worst, that the French had taken Madrid and that a large force was about to cut across his rear and his lines of communication with the coast. Moore's only recourse was to withdraw since his force was outnumbered by a superior French force, and he could not rely on the Spanish. He made a forced march back on his line of communications to the ports of Vigo and Corunna. It was the beginning of winter and, in horrendous conditions, the army marched along the narrow tracks that weaved their way through the snow-covered Galician mountains with the French in pursuit.

A strong rearguard was formed by the light regiments and Paget's cavalry and both put a fearsome defence. The army eventually reached Corunna, but had to wait for the ships to come from Vigo. The French caught up and attacked on the outskirts of Corunna and there was a fierce fight with the British troops giving vent to their anger at the suffering the French had caused. The French were driven back, the ships arrived and evacuation began. In the last throes of the battle General Moore, leading at the front, suffered a mortal wound. His light troops had proved their mettle.

Dalrymple, Burrard and Wellesley were tried for the incident of The Convention of Cintra at the Royal Hospital Chelsea. However, Wellesley had had no part in agreeing the armistice and was sent back to command in Portugal.

It was 1810 and his forces were in cantonments on the Portuguese side of the frontier. At this time Wellington decided to increase the size of the Light Brigade of three regiments into a Division of seven regiments with a troop of horse artillery in preparation for his assault against the French. There was constant conflict with numerous actions centred round the fortress town of Almeida on the Portuguese side and Ciudad Rodrigo on the Spanish side.

An account of the new Light Division at this period illustrates their mode of action.

The Light Division on the Agueda, February–July 1810

The original Light Brigade was conceived as an élite force, and much was expected from them. They were to act, as Sir Charles Oman said:

> as a protective screen for the whole army, a vanguard, its tactical
> skirmishing line thrown out in front of the main force was designed

to harry the French and keep their *tirailleurs* and *voltigeurs* at bay until the actual moment of battle, and at the same time hide the dispositions of the British main body.

In a withdrawal they were to be the rearguard to protect stragglers and act as a shield to ward off enemy advance patrols.

The Light Brigade, with the addition of two of the recently trained Portuguese Caçadores battalions, the 1st Hussars of the King's German Legion – probably the finest in Wellington's army – two light dragoon regiments, and Hew Ross's troop of Royal Horse Artillery with six guns, was enlarged to form the Light Division. It came to be regarded as an élite force and was respected as the finest in Wellington's army.

The Watch on the Agueda, February–March 1810

The Light Division would be a type of flying column, placed on special detached duties in very sensitive areas, spread out over a wide front. A special type of commander would be required, one with a strong sense of purpose, single-minded, a good organizer with the ability to extemporise, or in modern terms, to 'think on his feet'!

It was the latter that gave Wellington doubts about Craufurd, since he knew that Craufurd was prone to interpret orders when Wellington expected full compliance. It was probably for this reason, and to obviate any doubts in orders, that Wellington wrote to Craufurd several times during the period January to March 1810. At the end of January Wellington despatched a general order to Craufurd in which he expressed his overall view of what faced Craufurd and what he expected from him and the Light Division.

> I don't think the enemy is likely to molest us at present, but I am desiring in maintaining the Côa, unless he should collect a very large force, and obviously intends to set seriously to work on the invasion of Portugal. If that would be the case, I don't propose to maintain the Côa, or that you should risk anything for that purpose, and I beg you to retire gradually on Celerico, where you will be joined by General Cole's Division. From Celerico I propose that you should retire gradually along the valley of the Mondego upon General Sherbrooke's Division and other troops will be there. If you should quit the Côa bring the (King's German Legion) Hussars with you.

Did Wellington think that this order was ambiguous? Unable to predict the future turn of events, Wellington had to suggest limits to which he expected Craufurd to go without restricting his judgement. Knowing Craufurd could be headstrong, he did not want the order to offer him any reason to deviate and take risks. It was obvious to Wellington that by using the words 'unless he should collect a very large force, and obviously intends to set seriously to work on the invasion of Portugal', he intended Craufurd to hold the ground only until it was prudent to withdraw and not to maintain or defend it in a sense of 'at all costs'. The problem for Wellington was how good would Craufurd's judgement be in assessing the right time to withdraw. A French attack across the Agueda would be in far superior numbers and he did not want Craufurd to let his reason be governed by any headstrong dash into a vainglorious escapade.

Wellington needed the Light Division's presence on the right or east bank of the river Côa for as long as possible and perhaps his initial order might induce Craufurd to quit the Côa prematurely. In a follow-up letter Wellington affirmed his intentions and qualified his view on a withdrawal, saying he wanted Craufurd to retire only if faced with a force 'so formidable to manifest a serious intention of invading Portugal'.

On 8 March 1810 Wellington sent Craufurd a third letter in which he gave him additional information on the role he expected the Light Division to play in the overall plan, and gave him full responsibility for making all the decisions regarding the dispositions to be made along the east bank of the Côa.

> The line of cantonments which we took up, principally with a view to the accommodation of the troops during the winter, and their subsistence on a point on which it was likely that it might be desirable to assemble the army, will not answer our purpose of assembling on the Côa, if eventually that should be deemed an object ... I have long intended to alter our dispositions, as soon as the season would permit the troops occupying the smaller villages on the Côa and as (soon as) I should be able to bring up the Portuguese Light troops of your division to the front. Since we took the position which we now occupy, our outposts have come in contact with those of the French; and although there is some distance between the two, still the arrangement of our outposts must be made on a better principal, and the whole of them must be in the hands of one person, who must be yourself. I propose, therefore, as soon as the weather will allow of an alteration of the disposition of the advanced corps, that your division, with the Hussars ... under your orders, should occupy the whole line of outposts, with this, the Portuguese corps shall be brought up to the front as soon as the state of the weather will allow them to march. I am desirous of being able to assemble the army upon the Côa, if it should be necessary. ... and 'till we shall see more clearly than I can at present what reinforcements ... (the French) have received and what military object they have in view ... I am adverse

to withdrawing from a position so favourable as the Côa affords, to enable us to collect our army and prevent the execution of any design on Ciudad Rodrigo. I wish you then to consider of the parts to be occupied in front of and upon the Côa, to enable me to effect that object ... you must be a better judge of the details of this question than I can be, and I wish you to consider it, in order to be able to carry the plan into execution when I shall send it to you.

Wellington by now must have felt that he had explained fully his intentions and what he expected of Craufurd. Underlying this, and at the forefront of Wellington's thoughts, was the conservation of the Peninsular army, small in comparison to the might of the French 'Army of Portugal'.

The area that Wellington expected Craufurd to maintain straddled the frontier, forming a corridor five leagues (fifteen miles) wide between the rivers Côa and Agueda from Ciudad Rodrigo to about ten leagues (thirty miles) north, where the Côa and Agueda rivers joined to continue north and eventually flow into the river Douro. In this total length the Agueda was crossed by only four bridges: at Ciudad Rodrigo, Navas Frias, Villar and Barba del Puerco. There were additional crossing places where it was possible to ford, but only when the river was not in flood, which was difficult to predict, since it will rise or fall by many feet within a few hours. Both the Côa and the Agueda were surrounded by hills which cut through deep-sided ravines with hillsides heavily strewn with rocks. The tracks followed a narrow twisting path up from the bridges; the land between the rivers was a mixture of rough scrubland, small woods, poor farms and vineyards. There were a few poor villages, some deserted, some still occupied. Leach describes them as 'The poor villages peopled by the most wretched, dirty, idle, ignorant, priest-ridden peasantry anywhere to be found'.

These observations were made by a young officer from a Protestant culture, describing very simple backward peasant people, farmers, goatherds, shepherds, desperately scraping a meagre living off the poor land. But even so, all was not quite what it seemed, for these 'poor wretched people' would waylay and murder any French deserters or stragglers who unwittingly came their way.

So it was expected of Craufurd that he should cover this extensive area with fewer than 5,000 men, while on the east side of the Agueda the French were increasing in numbers by the day. Picquets had to be placed at strategic points and cavalry had to mount vedettes to cover outlying areas, watch fords, gather information and keep in communication with the forts at Almeida and Fort Conception, and the garrison at Ciudad Rodrigo.

Craufurd had to observe and report back all French movements and dispositions, keeping a discreet distance, not provoking the French, and at the same time fending off any inquisitive French reconnaissance incursions. The Light

Division had to be preserved intact and not risked in any aggressive or foolhardy action of the sort that is inspired only by dash and the quest for glory.

It was on 6 January 1810 that Craufurd first crossed the Côa with the 1/95th. They marched to Villar Torpin, Regada and Cinco Villar, and formally moved positions during January, February and March to other villages. Deep snow covered the landscape. Craufurd's policy was to keep the picquets on the move to different outposts so that they could become familiar with all paths, tracks and roads that ran between the Côa and the Agueda. Signalling beacons were set up as a warning system.

The first foray came on 16 February when a French force from newly occupied San Felices de los Gallegos came to Barba del Puerco, probably looking for signs of the Light Division. They left the following morning. A second typical encounter happened on 27 February 1810 when Captain Creagh's company of the 1/95th was ordered to march from Escarigo and reconnoitre the village of Barba del Puerco, six leagues (eighteen miles) north of Ciudad Rodrigo. On reaching the village of Bouza a reconnoitring patrol was sent forward the five miles to Barba del Puerco. This was an important post: here was one of the few bridges that crossed the Agueda and consequently it was frequently in contention. In the village Creagh's company found a detachment of about 200 French cavalry and infantry. There was a skirmish and Creagh's patrol was forced to fall back to Bouza, and his company withdrew as ordered, to Escarigo where he was joined by Captain Leach's company and a third company which had been sent from Villar Torpin in support. The three companies advanced towards Barba del Puerco with Leach's company sent forward in advance to reconnoitre the village again. They discovered the French had left after pillaging the houses, so they established a picquet post there and sent a small party down the steep track that led to the long, narrow, stone bridge. The local priest offered the information that there was a strong French force at San Felices de los Gallegos, a village about four miles farther on. It was occupied by most of General Jean-Gabriel Marchand's 1 Infantry Brigade, belonging to the division of General Loison, 'the butcher'.

The information proved correct and so the three companies of the 1/95th entered Barba del Puerco but Craufurd withdrew them the following day for unexplained reasons. These constant changes of local picquets, especially at Barba del Puerco, were found very unsettling by local commanders, including Colonel William Cox, governor of Almeida who, in a despatch to Major General George Cole at Guarda, wrote, 'I know not what are the General's motives for this continual change, the poor inhabitants are the sufferers'. The French were totally baffled. Later, on 4 March, an attempt was made to occupy the village but heavy rains made this too difficult.

On 8 March Craufurd had decided to post a stronger detachment at the village of Barba del Puerco and the bridge but, on the 9th, Maucune's brigade pre-empted this plan. A French force headed by 150 cavalry took the bridge before midday, occupied the village and went on to Villarde Cierv. Maucune's 6th Léger and 69th Ligne almost caught and cut off a detachment of the 1st Hussars, King's German Legion, who managed to get back to Fort Conception, hotly pursued almost to the fort. After carrying out their reconnaissance the French turned foragers, and retired carrying off all they could find back to Felices de los Gallegos.

On 11 March, the 1/95th were ordered to advance on Agueda, supported by the 1st Hussars, KGL. They occupied the villages and crossing-points from Ciudad Rodrigo to the Douro. Lieutenant Colonel Beckwith re-occupied Barba del Puerco, posting O'Hare's company on the bridge with Lieutenants Mercer, Coane and Simmons in support on the hillside above. Craufurd considered that four companies were sufficient to hold the village and the bridge whilst the river was in full flood. Villa de Ciervo was occupied by Leach's company and another company occupied Escallias. The 1st Hussars maintained constant patrols along the river, watching the fords and noting any changes in water levels. Captain Ross's troop of horse artillery concentrated at Fort Conception.

Craufurd implemented his policy of constantly moving the companies to keep all bright and alert, and also so that they would become familiar with the topography, including the many paths and tracks that led from the Agueda to the Côa, which could prove most useful in a sudden withdrawal.

With the 1/95th on the Agueda, the 1/43rd and the 1/52nd were placed in the villages farther back and nearer the Côa, in positions where they could move forward to give support if needed. Craufurd had positioned all units very carefully in pre-determined locations so that they were able to offer mutual support and would also be able to move back quickly if threatened by a large French force, or if the water level dropped to allow the fords to become usable. All units were in sight of each other and able to communicate with a signalling system based on beacon fires. The Portuguese army had a signalling section and eventually set up and operated a semaphore that ran from Almeida, Elvas and Abrantes to Lisbon.

The Action at Barba del Puerco – 19 March 1810

The Light Division had been well trained by Craufurd, who recognized that with light troops speed was of the essence. Napier states that for the Light Division:

> only seven minutes sufficed for the Division to get under arms in the night, and a quarter of an hour, night or day, to bring it in order of

battle to the alarm posts, with the baggage loaded and assembled at a convenient distance in the rear. And this not upon a concerted signal, as a trial, but at all times and certain.

This may have been so: there is no doubt they were well drilled and quick but reminiscences remind us that this was not always the case. There were instances when, at night, with the alarm raised and apart from those off-guard, who slept in their clothes, many turned out in various stages of undress and *déshabillé*, which was the case on the night of 19 March 1810.

Earlier that day General Loison sent General Claude Ferey's brigade 'to disperse the enemy's advance posts on the Agueda and push on as far as possible towards Almeida'. Ferey's brigade, which included two battalions of the 82nd Ligne, with the Hanoverian Legion, left San Felices de los Gallegos and reached the eastern side of the chasm leading to the bridge before midnight. There had been continuous rain all day, the troops were drenched and the roads must have been a quagmire, which might explain why it took all day to travel the four and a half miles from San Felices. The moon was obscured by rain clouds and the river Agueda was swollen and in full flood, with the water crashing against the rocks, the sounds magnified by the walls of the chasm. The constant roaring of the waters drowned out the sounds of Ferey's advancing column who concealed themselves behind rocks near the bridge.

Captain O'Hare's company was guarding the bridge, with Lieutenants Mercer, Coane and Simmons. At eight o'clock that evening Lieutenant Simmons took the guard and posted the sentries. Twelve riflemen with Sergeant Betts were placed in rocks about 150 feet high above the bridge. Riflemen Maher and McCan, as double sentry, were positioned behind a rock fifteen yards from the bridge. They had orders to fire shots to raise the alarm and withdraw immediately to the twelve-man position if the French stormed the bridge. There they were to 'hold until reinforced'. All that night it must have been a problem to keep their powder and weapons dry.

Lieutenant Simmons then crawled across the bridge to look for any French amongst the rocks on the east side. What with the driving rain and the blackness he was unable to see anything, so he returned and clambered up the gorge to an officers' tent. The main body of the company was sheltering in a small church, drying themselves round a fire. At eleven o'clock the officers 'doing the rounds' reported all quiet. As they retired they must have felt confident that they were secure against a surprise attack.

Captain John Kincaid of the 95th records in his memoirs:

> Ferey at the head of 600 chosen grenadiers burst forth so silently and suddenly, that, of our double sentry on the bridge, one was taken and the other bayoneted without being able to fire off their pieces.

But another account states that, under cover of the rushing waters, General Ferey, at the head of 600 chosen grenadiers, rushed the bridge in apparent silence, knocked down and bayoneted one sentry but that the second managed to fire off a shot to raise the alarm before he was taken prisoner. The shot alerted Sergeant Betts's picquet, who managed to return fire before being over-run, in the course of which Sergeant Betts was shot in the mouth.

Another account states that it was the shot from the twelve-man picquet that raised the alarm. With all the dash and élan they could muster, the 82nd Ligne, with their drums beating, charged up the track from the bridge over-running the twelve-man picquet. The track up to the village was very steep with rocks scattered about, but in spite of the steepness the French had the momentum and were making rapid progress up towards the village. The earlier shot had also alerted O'Hare's company who tumbled out of the church, and 'had barely time to jump up and snatch their rifles when the enemy were among them'.

There was no time to come to order. Lieutenant Mercer and about fifty riflemen threw themselves at the French in a fierce hand-to-hand bloody fight, each fighting for dear life. Mercer was shot as he was putting on his spectacles. Accounts can vary in the confusion of battle and by tricks of memory, as in the case of Rifleman William Green, who recalled, 'I saw our officer stretched on his back, his sword in one hand, and his spy glass in the other. I said "Mister Mercer, are you wounded?" But his spirit had fled.' One wonders how Mr Mercer managed to put on his spectacles with both hands full and what was he doing with a spy glass on such a dark night?

Lieutenant Simmons took command. The riflemen were scattered amongst the rocks, and were difficult to see in the blackness in their green jackets, whereas the French made easier targets due to their white crossbelts and brass breastplates. The fierce fighting continued for about fifteen minutes, with Simmons and the men being pushed back up the hill towards the village.

O'Hare arrived to take command as more French poured over the bridge. O'Hare called out for the men to make a stand, 'We shall never retire. Here we stand. They shall not pass over my body.' But the French were being urged on by their officers, who were whipping the men with the flat of their swords. O'Hare's men were on the verge of being overwhelmed and the French ready to over-run Barba del Puerco when, on the crest of the hill, appeared Colonel Beckwith, distinguished by his tall stature and dressed in night-gown, slippers and a red nightcap. He brought with him the remaining three companies, not many of whom were attired in full uniform. Simmons remarked that the sight of these companies 'was the pleasantest sight I ever beheld.' The men turned out of their houses, many wearing shirts and cartridge belts slung over their shoulders. They formed up and fired a 'thundering discharge'. Fixing swords, they charged the French who by now were shattered and in total confusion as they retreated towards the bridge. Colonel Beckwith urged the men on and was about to roll a huge boulder down the hill when a bullet shot a hole in his nightcap.

The French were bloodied and in confusion, some throwing away their muskets as they rushed back over the bridge in a minor rout; others managed to take some of their wounded with them. Once across the bridge there were 1,000 troops of the 66th Ligne and the Hanoverian Legion waiting to give support and who kept up a random musketfire across the chasm to little effect.

General Ferey's bold attempt to 'disperse the enemy's advance posts and push on as far as Almeida', was thwarted by what must have surprised him as very stubborn resistance by such a small force. He withdrew his force back towards Salamanca. Ferey learned from this encounter that the constant movements of the Light Division were only routine moves of the same troops, which he still found baffling. Sir William Cox, the governor of Almeida, who was temporarily saved by this action, travelled up from the fortress to see for himself the scene of the action. He noted, 'The bodies of two officers and seven men have been found dead, a sergeant and five men taken prisoner; and three have been taken who were not wounded of the French.'

Another eyewitness said there was one captain, Capdevielle, a subaltern, and seventeen soldiers 'stretched upon the rough ground'. The recorded British casualties included one officer, Lieutenant Mercer, and three other ranks killed, and ten wounded. The French had two officers and forty-five other ranks killed and wounded.

Wellington must have been relieved that all went well since he sent a despatch to Craufurd in which he stated how appreciative he was of the manner in which the 1/95th Rifles had conducted themselves in the action. Craufurd, who by nature very seldom handed out praise, did in turn issue a general complimentary order:

> Brigadier General Craufurd has it in command from the Commander-in-Chief to assure Lieutenant Colonel Beckwith and officers of the 95th Regiment who were engaged at Barba del Puerco that their conduct in this affair has augmented the confidence he has in the troops when opposed to the enemy in any situation. Brigadier General Craufurd feels particular satisfaction in noticing the first affair in which any part of the Light Brigade were engaged during the present campaign. That British troops should defeat a superior number of the enemy is nothing new; but the action reflects honour on Lieutenant Colonel Beckwith and the regiment, inasmuch as it was of a sort which the riflemen of other armies would shun. In other armies the rifle is considered ill calculated for close action with an enemy armed

with a musket and bayonet; but the 95th Regiment has proved that the rifle in the hands of a British soldier is a fully sufficient weapon to enable him to defeat the French in the closest fight in whatever manner they may be armed.

It was praise that all had earned well. Of the four understrength companies, only three, totalling 200 men, fought off and held their post against 600 first-class French troops. The fourth company was covering the right flank and the village was immediately reinforced by one company of the 43rd and two companies of the 52nd in case of further attacks. But a day after they arrived Craufurd decided to pull out the infantry and leave Barba del Puerco in the hands of the 1st Hussars. This sudden decision must have indicated that the water level in the Agueda had dropped considerably, which would have made the fords usable and thus exposed the flanks of the defenders.

On 25 March 1810 intelligence reached Craufurd that the remainder of General Loison's Division had moved from Salamanca and joined up with those at San Felices. Loison was known to the Portuguese as the notorious general who, before the Convention of Cintra, had permitted, even encouraged, atrocities to be perpetrated by the troops under his command, 'as would have disgraced a band of untutored savages'.

In April 1810 the 1/95th were reduced in strength from ten to eight companies, as a recruiting party was sent to England to find replacements. The 95th had arrived in Portugal less than nine months previously with 1,100 men and were now down to 800, mainly due to sickness from 'Alemtejo fever' (malaria), during the autumn of 1809. Losses to the French were 'trifling'.

The build-up of French forces continued through early April. For the Light Division and Craufurd it was a relatively quiet period apart from the occasional probe by an increasing and more belligerent French cavalry. By May their numbers had increased to an estimated strength of 5,000 but even so they never managed to break through Craufurd's outnumbered cavalry. The cavalry patrolled the long line of country through which the Agueda flows, from the fords on the extreme right at Fuente Guialdo, to their left where the Agueda flows into the Douro, near Escalhao. Most of Craufurd's forces were stationed behind the Azava, which had brought them farther south. Towards the end of April the Light Division was brought up to strength with the addition of the 1st and 3rd Caçadores.

Masséna's forces, styled the Army of Portugal, were pre-occupied in their preparations for the siege of Ciudad Rodrigo. Craufurd was one who continually pressed for an attack against these forces. Some at headquarters wanted to mount a 'lightning rush' on Salamanca to destroy Marshal Ney's siege train and blow up his magazines. Herrasti, the Spanish commander at Ciudad Rodrigo, was pleading for the town to be saved. Even Wellington pondered the idea of a relief attack but observed that, even if this were possible, and even if it succeeded, what would be the cost? Anyway he needed time, and the delays that were occupying the French and the siege itself would give him valuable time.

On 25 April French columns advanced to the walls of Ciudad Rodrigo to prepare for the investment of the town. Two days later Wellington learned of the advance and began to concentrate his army along the Portuguese frontier. His headquarters were advanced from Viseu to Celerico where the 1st Division was posted under the command of Lieutenant General Brent-Spencer.

Marshal Andre Masséna, fifty-two year old Prince of Essling, 'the Old Fox', commanded the Army of Portugal. It was to be composed of three distinct corps: II Corps, commanded by Marshal Ney, the Duke of Elchingen; and VIII Corps commanded by General Junot, Duke of Abrantes. The cavalry was commanded by General Montbrun. Masséna proclaimed in rhetorical style that they came not to invade Portugal but to rescue it from the English, whom he said he would drive into the sea and plant Imperial eagles in Lisbon: he had a force of 110,000 men and it was useless to resist.

To Wellington this was just so much bombast, but he was impressed by 110,000 Frenchmen. It underlined his need for time to complete the training and allocation of the new Portuguese army, time to complete the preparations for the forthcoming onslaught, and time to construct 'Fortress Lisbon', the Lines of Torres Vedras.

The build-up of the French forces and the investment of Ciudad Rodrigo kept the Light Division fully occupied with patrols, scouts and picquets. As Captain Leach recalled, they were on constant stand-by, had to sleep fully accoutred, and were always under arms one hour before daybreak. By 10 June the Agueda became fordable in all parts. The French were busy building redoubts in preparations for the siege.

As the French were absorbed in their preparations it allowed Don Julian Sanchez and the *guerrillero* who broke out of Ciudad Rodrigo on the 23 June, with a body of mounted guerrillas and arrived at Gallegos, to hover around the French army, losing no time or opportunity, 'of annoying and incommoding it'. Putting it not so euphemistically, this meant he was raiding, plundering and murdering all unfortunates who came his way.

Craufurd still maintained his dangerous position. By doing so he gave encouragement to the garrison at Ciudad Rodrigo. He also protected the still inhabited villages between the Azava and the Côa from marauding French foraging parties.

On 18 June, the French VIII Corps occupied San Felices and other points, and all the villages from Sierra de Francia to the Douro.

A week later the French batteries opened up against the fortress, the defenders returning a tremendous cannon fire. French cavalry closed upon the Azava. Craufurd withdrew all his outposts to the left (east) bank. This brought the opposing patrols extremely close to each other near the bridge of Marialva.

Marialva Bridge, 4 July 1810

Wellington decided to increase the Light Division's cavalry capability by adding the rest of the 14th and 16th Light Dragoons to make up the regiments to full strength. They and Lieutenant Colonel Talbot joined Craufurd on 1 July 1810.

Three days earlier, a Spaniard managed to get through French posts with a message from Herrasti, the gallant commander of besieged Ciudad Rodrigo, requesting urgent help.

All were pleading with Wellington to relieve Ciudad Rodrigo – the besieged forces, the Spaniards, the Portuguese, and even his own staff. He even had to suffer the taunts of Masséna, who was accusing him of being fainthearted and cowardly. Masséna moved his troops as if to appear open and vulnerable to attack, but Wellington recognized this *ruse de guerre* and was not going to fall into Masséna's trap. He was unmoved and adamant, much to the chagrin of many of his officers.

Wellington and General Brent-Spencer visited the outposts to observe for themselves. Gallegos was one of these outposts. Every evening Craufurd withdrew the infantry to a wood on heights behind the village towards the river Duas Casas and bivouacked, and then at daybreak returned to occupy the village. French patrols could see these moves and mistakenly thought they were reinforcements moving up.

As Ciudad Rodrigo still held out, French infantry pushed on to Azava. Leach recalled that their cavalry, 'were eternally in motion in large bodies towards our chain of posts, and we were often under arms waiting for them'. Craufurd positioned his cavalry at Gallegos and concealed his infantry in the woods of Almeida, two miles in the rear. From there he could fall back, either to the bridge of Castello Born by Villa Formosa, or to the bridge of Almeida by San Pedro. Not wanting to withdraw further and lose more ground, Craufurd carried out a scheme of deception, hoping to gain time. On the evening of 2 July he manoeuvred his troops on rising ground in single ranks, sending cavalry to the rear to raise dust, and marched the files of infantry slowly in succession within sight of the French who would, he hoped, be deluded into thinking that they were many brigades coming to the relief of Ciudad Rodrigo.

He gained a respite of two days, but on 4 July a strong body of French cavalry assembled at Marialva. Masséna ordered general Junot to cross the Azava at Marialva Bridge on that day for a close reconnaissance with about 15,000 men. Shots were exchanged between the cavalry patrols at the bridge.

The 1st Hussars kept up a continued skirmish. Captain Kraukenburg, 'an officer of the highest merit', distinguished himself. He formed his squadron on suitable ground near the small, narrow bridge and allowed a number of French Dragoons to cross. Then he charged them putting them into confusion, killing and wounding many of them and also taking prisoners.

Craufurd had drawn up the Light Division on the heights. Captain Ross's horse artillery opened up on Junot's troops who were advancing with caution. Facing superior numbers, Craufurd decided to make tactical withdrawal across the Duas Casas, covered by skirmishers from the 95th who held off the French cavalry. Two hundred riflemen and a troop of cavalry were left on the heights as a picquet. The remainder were placed near Val de la Mula, behind the Turon rivulet which marked the frontier between the two countries.

What surprised Leach and others at the time was that Junot, who was well known to be a general of a rash and ardent temper, displayed so much caution against the Light Division of only 4,000 men and far from support. What Captain Leach did not appreciate was that Junot, warned of constant 'reinforcements' that moved into the Light Division's positions, thought Craufurd's force was much larger than it really was, and decided, uncharacteristically, on caution and called off the advance.

Why Masséna, who had such a strong force, permitted the Light Division to remain so long between the Azava and the Duas Casas when French cavalry could easily have cut them off from the crossings on the Côa, did surprise Leach and his fellow officers. The Light Division remained for some days near Val de la Mula with cavalry vedettes on the Duas Casas.

On 10 July 1810, after sixteen days of furious bombardment, Ciudad Rodrigo surrendered to save the town and its inhabitants from the maelstrom of rape, looting, killing and destruction released from the pent-up tensions of the stormers. It was realized that, with no response to their Spanish commander's pleas for succour, Wellington would not be mounting a relief force. In spite of constant criticism, he knew the paramount need was to preserve his small army. He could only wait and watch until the town surrendered.

The Action at Villar de Puerco, 11 July 1810

After the surrender of Ciudad Rodrigo, the French increased their reconnaissance patrols between the town and the frontier. These patrols had to report on any changes to the Light Division's outposts and they also foraged for food and supplies in the deserted villages. After several such incursions Craufurd took these acts as an affront and was annoyed at the French boldness, so he planned an ambuscade. On 11 July, as on the three previous nights, General Godert issued orders for a strong patrol column, commanded by Colonel Armand, to move towards the Duas Casas river and reconnoitre the area near the village of Barquilla. They left before dawn, at 2.30am. In the van was a squadron of about thirty cavalry while following on behind were 300 (some reports estimate 200) infantry of the 3rd Battalion of the 22nd Ligne, commanded by Captain Gouache. Much farther back was Colonel Armand with three French battalions of *voltigeurs.*

The first part of Craufurd's plan was to march at night and to effect a complete surprise. They left Val de la Mula after dark with all accoutrements checked to stop rattling, with orders to stop smoking their pipes, and no talking; the wheels of the guns were muffled. Craufurd decided to use a large portion of the Light Division, which included two squadrons of the 1st Hussars, KGL under Captain Krauchenburg, two squadrons of the 16th Light Dragoons and three squadrons of the 14th Light Dragoons. The infantry was composed of the 95th Rifles, two companies of the 52nd Regiment, three companies of the 43rd Regiment and the 3rd Caçador Battalion. They crossed the Duas Casas river before 2am and continued through the night with Craufurd leading the column, finally in total silence, to within a mile of Villar de Puerco. Once there he posted five squadrons of cavalry in a wooded ravine to await further orders. A squadron of the 1st Hussars under Captain Gruben was concealed in farm buildings between Barquilla and Villa de Ciervo to cut off any French retreat. Several troops of the 14th Light Dragoons were positioned in the area of the planned attack. Several companies of the 95th marched to a wheat field, behind a ridge overlooking Villar de Puerco. There they were ordered to conceal themselves and lie down in the wheat. The remaining companies of the 95th, supported by a detachment of the 14th Light Dragoons, were positioned on high ground near Barquilla. Three companies of the 43rd were posted some distance behind the woods which were already occupied by the rest of the cavalry contingent. The 3rd Caçadores were positioned to cover a ford on the Duas Casas river, which was over two miles from Villar de Puerco. Captain Ross's two guns remained at Castillejo de Duas Casas, nearly a league away.

It seemed that Craufurd had deployed his forces to cover all possible eventualities, and it looked as if the French were in for a blooding and a nasty surprise if they came to the villages of Villar de Puerco and Barquilla again.

But how familiar was Craufurd with the local terrain? At dawn he had gone forward alone to the village of Villar de Puerco to reconnoitre. At about 4 o'clock in the morning, just as first light broke, he sighted French cavalry on the Barquilla road. The French infantry who were following had not yet reached the village. Why did Craufurd rely on only one pair of eyes, why did he not post vedtetes to cover the roads? Light Infantry tactics were always to send out scouts to cover the flanks and avoid surprise attacks.

Racing back, Craufurd decided to attack immediately with his cavalry, but without infantry or artillery support. Reaching Captain Krauchenburg, he ordered him to charge the French cavalry with his 1st Hussars, supported by Captain Ashworth and the 16th Light Dragoons.

Large groups of cavalry need plenty of space to manoeuvre with open flat country the ideal terrain. There was open country on the right that would have enabled the six squadrons to get between the infantry in Villar de Puerco and their point of retreat, but to Craufurd this route was too circuitous, so his orders were to take the most direct route to Villar de Puerco. That way the cavalry encountered many difficult obstacles.

They had first to gallop about a mile, then were forced to slow and string out to avoid stone walls, and then had to slip through a narrow defile flanked by a stone wall. Once beyond this gorge, Krauchenburg had to try to reform his troopers for an attack.

Craufurd's aide de camp, Lieutenant Colonel James Shaw-Kennedy, and Brigade Major William Campbell rode ahead to scout and observe the exact position of the French cavalry. As they galloped forward they could see the enemy dragoons in the distance, but reined in to stop and observe Gouache's infantry column just leaving the village of Villar de Puerco. At first the infantry were not very obvious as they were almost hidden by the high standing wheat.

The aides galloped back to Krauchenburg with the information, who decided to attack the 300 infantry first since they were out in the open and vulnerable. But negotiating the defile and stone walls and enclosures took time, during which the squadrons became separated.

Captain Gouache, aided by Sergeant Patois, reacted quickly after the initial shock of seeing the cavalry. The grenadiers were formed into a square by half sections, in among the wheat stalks, hidden by the rise, 'without confusion'.

They saw the dust cloud and heard the thunder of the horses and waited for the shock. Krauchenburg's squadron arrived first followed by Ashworth's. They were both surprised to find Gouache's troops formed in square. With sword in hand and the morning sun in his eyes, Krauchenburg ordered the charge. Ashworth was ordered by a staff officer to form in line with the 1st Hussars rather than behind them. Consequently, when they made their rough charge, Ashworth's Dragoons were extended too far and missed the square. Gouache waited until the cavalry were within thirty paces, and then gave the order to fire by file, which felled eleven men and horses. The two squadrons veered to either side of the square and headed off towards Barquilla in pursuit of the French dragoons.

Following on closely behind this first attack came a second squadron of the 16th Light Dragoons, commanded by Captain Belli. They, too, had the same difficulties negotiating the defile and other obstacles. As a result, their attack was delivered in rough order, without cohesion or strong determination. The clumsy attack was fortunate for the French for they had been caught in the process of re-loading their muskets. The Light Dragoons should have had some effect but they veered too much to the right of the square. They all got off lightly: the momentum sent them off in the direction of Barquilla and the French dragoons.

Craufurd by this time was beginning to get agitated and lose his composure. He called up Lieutenant Colonel Talbot, who arrived dressed in nankeen pantaloons, and ordered him to attack with Thomas Brotherton's squadron of the 14th Light Dragoons.

Talbot led the squadron off, experiencing the same problems with the defile and the obstacles. He charged the square, although they all had difficulty in seeing the French through the dust and smoke. Captain Gouache had difficulty also in seeing the charging dragoons through the clouds of dust, but he could hear them. His troops were now primed and loaded, bayonets fixed, and crouching down, using bodies of the horses and the dead and dying hussars as cover. The 14th Light Dragoons led by Talbot burst out of the haze, the low morning sun in their eyes. Gouache's men stood up as one and fired a volley. An eyewitness, Captain Charles Cox of the 16th Light Dragoons who took part in the attack, noted:

> It is impossible to do justice to the intrepidity of this body of men.
> They stood the second charge as well as the first, knocked down some
> by running fire, and bayoneted others.

Eighteen dragoons were either shot or pulled from their horses. Those who reached the square were bayoneted, both men and horses. Colonel Talbot was shot eight times and bayoneted as he broke into the second rank: he fell dead at the feet of the grenadiers. Talbot's quartermaster, McCormick, also fell mortally wounded. William Campbell, Craufurd's Aide de Camp, had his horse shot from under him. Unwounded but dazed, he made his way slowly from the disaster, saved by Gouache who prevented his men from firing. Captain Brotherton also had his horse shot and went down within a yard of the square with the horse on top of him. It was remarked that 'Such was the steadiness of the men composing it (the square), that not an individual left the ranks to kill or capture him', although Brotherton 'lay completely at their mercy'. The survivors of Talbot's charge withdrew in echelon by troop. Meanwhile, Craufurd, making what could only be construed as a miscalculation, decided that the remainder of the cavalry should attack the square again.

Lieutenant Colonel Arentschildt, commanding a squadron of the 14th Light Dragoons, was ordered to attack Gouache's square. Orders were sent to call up three companies of the 43rd from behind the woods. The companies of the 95th who had been lying in the wheatfield were ordered 'With scarce a pause between, to "fall in", "double" and "extend".' They doubled through the field and up the rise where they saw before them the village of Villar de Puerco, and, as it was happening, the disastrous charge of Talbot's squadron on the French square. They were too far away to be of any help and could only watch the sad spectacle.

As Arentschildt was preparing his squadron to advance against the French square he saw a number of cavalry detachments which, at a distance, he assumed were the French dragoons advancing to assist Captain Gouache. One group came down the road from the direction of Barquilla, a second group from Valdespino, and a third from Gallegos. He veered his squadron off in their direction to intercept them, only to discover they were Gruben's 1st Hussars, Butler's 14th Light Dragoons, and a unit from the 16th Light Dragoons, who had earlier taken off in pursuit of the thirty French dragoons, all of whom had been taken prisoner. Finding out their mistake took time, during which Captain Gouache moved his troops cautiously towards Sexmiro, safety and Colonel Armand, who was hurrying forward with his *voltigeurs* at the double to support him.

Craufurd now realized that there was no hope of making further attacks: what should have been a quick surprise ambush and defeat of the French had turned out to be a humiliating and successful French riposte. He gave the order to stand down and collect the dead and wounded, who numbered over thirty troopers killed or severely wounded, and a loss of thirty horses killed. Of the French, thirty-one dragoons had been taken prisoner. Captain Gouache's steadfast stand was made without the loss of one man. Both the French and British commands were full of praise for this gallant captain's bravery, which earned him promotion, and the Legion of Honour for Sergeant Patois.

There was no promotion for Craufurd, who had set up his ambush with the important initial ingredient, surprise, which was carelessly thrown away. On the occasion of this action he seemed to ignore some of the basic rules of light infantry and cavalry tactics, and showed that, under pressure, he could easily become ruffled, and that his judgement was flawed.

There are questions that need answers. Why did he carry out the first reconnaissance on his own and not send out cavalry patrols? Why did he insist on further cavalry charges against the French square, when this broke one of the basic rules of attacking without infantry or artillery support? Packed infantry in a square are a sitting target for horse artillery using grape shot. Why was there confusion with recognition of units, liaison and with orders?

Both Masséna and Wellington were full of praise for the courage and discipline displayed by Captain Gouache, Sergeant Patois and the 300 grenadiers of the 3rd Battalion of the 22nd Ligne. It was chapeau!, or 'hats off to the victors'. All those who took part at Villar de Puerco blamed Craufurd for the disastrous outcome. Many back at Wellington's headquarters considered the action at Villar de Puerco as a humiliation and wanted a scapegoat. What must have rankled many in the army was that the debacle was the product of Robert Craufurd and the Light Division – who were meant to be a superior force – although it was the cavalry that came in for the recriminations.

None of those involved wanted to be associated with failure and Craufurd suffered much criticism from his own officers and men. Captain Leach wrote, 'It seems incredible that 200 (?) French infantry on a plain surrounded by nearly 1,000 British dragoons and fully 800 British infantry not more than a mile distant, should escape without loss of a man', and 'a few discharges of grapeshot would have annihilated the square in ten minutes or caused it to surrender'. Lieutenant George Simmons, also of the 95th, noted in his journal: 'Our wise General had the 14th, 16th, and German Hussars all to assist, also horse artillery and seven companies of infantry, but let this party of Frenchmen slip through our fingers so shamefully.'

They all seemed to agree with what should have been done and that Craufurd had made many mistakes. Captain Charles Cocks was also very critical and wrote that many officers had told him that they thought 'Black bob' had lost his presence of mind. Cocks reiterated the general feeling that Craufurd should have quickly brought up the infantry and artillery to deal with the French, and that the 14th Light Dragoons had behaved with great élan and gallantry. He also remarked that Craufurd seemed to forget his own orders and arrangements, as the units of British cavalry were repeatedly pointed out by him as enemy dragoons.

General Stapleton Cotton, commander of Allied cavalry stated, 'Groundless malicious reports circulated of the misconduct of the 16th Light Dragoons in the affair of the 11th at Villar de Puerco.' Several high-ranking officers suggested that an inquiry should be held. Wellington intervened for the sake of calm and unity and to stop controversy getting blown out of proportion, and also because he needed Craufurd. Wellington observed that when Arentschildt prepared to charge the square, several Allied cavalry units made their appearance:

> The 16th had nothing to do with this mistake – the French infantry appear to have behaved remarkably well, and probably were so posted that no effort of cavalry could have forced them. It would really not be fair to the 16th to have any inquiry into their conduct in the affair.

Later that week he wrote to Craufurd:

> I have been much annoyed by the foolish conversations and reports and private letters about the 16th Light Dragoons. They appear in this affair to have conducted themselves with spirit and alacrity of

soldiers. They failed in intelligence, and coolness, and order, which can be acquired only by experience.

Wellington went on to express his bewilderment to Craufurd:

I can only say that I have never seen an attack by our troops in which similar, if not greater, accidents and mistakes have not occurred, and in which there were not corresponding accidents and failures.

Sergeant Costello wrote that the fight 'had brought our general into bad odour at headquarters', and continued 'some days after, Craufurd wore a troubled look on his face, as though he took our failure to heart'.

Wellington, in a private letter to his brother, William Wellesley-Pole, questioned Craufurd's actions at Villar de Puerco, but added that he would not make any public pronouncements which implied criticism of Craufurd. In hindsight, some felt Wellington should have reprimanded Craufurd and brought him to book. It might, they thought, have cooled Craufurd and made him feel more accountable – and perhaps he might then have displayed more caution and better judgement two weeks later on the Côa.

Craufurd, who was desperate to exhibit his ability to command with flair, was totally dismayed by the outcome at Villar de Puerco and wrote to his wife a week later lamenting the results, 'I had a little affair the other day which terminated unsatisfactorily'. He went on, 'the failure was attended with some mortifying circumstances, and occasioned by a series of unlucky accidents.'

After the action at Villar de Puerco, Craufurd and the Light Division detachments marched back to Val de la Mulla.

Chapter 11

The Peninsular War, 1808–12
The Light Division in Two Actions during 1811

The First is a Sharp Action at Sabugal, April 1811

'One of our most glorious actions'

From its gazetting in August 1800 Colonel Coote Manningham's 95th Regiment attracted a new type of soldier and officer, those who chose to become Riflemen. They were adventurous, sharp-witted, intelligent and literate, a cut above the norm. Foregoing the cachet of the old established regiments they chose the challenge of a new regiment with a new ethos, new training, a new and singular uniform and a new weapon, the deadly Baker rifle. To become *chasseurs* was to become an élite force. Amongst those who stood literally head and shoulders above others was Thomas Sydney Beckwith, noted as a man of mark. Kincaid wrote, 'Never was a leader more devotedly followed'. Lieutenant Colonel Beckwith was appointed commanding officer of the 1/95th in 1806.

There was now a lull in operations. Winter was approaching and Wellington was safe behind the lines of Torres Vedras, with Lisbon's Fort Julien by the sea as his final embarkation point if evacuation proved necessary, but Lisbon was fully operational with transports bringing in reinforcements and a constant flow of supplies from England.

It was at this time that Robert Craufurd, desperate to see his wife and children, decided to apply for permission for leave of absence to Scotland. This was despite reminders from Wellington that he would be vacating his command and that others, senior to him, would be expected to be offered the command of the Light Division. In one letter to Craufurd, Wellington wrote that 'It has not been an easy task to keep you in your command,' warning Craufurd that it might not be possible to keep his command of the Light Division upon his return. In a letter dated 29 January 1811, Wellington stated that, although he gave permission for Craufurd's leave of absence, he did not approve of it.

Wellington knew that Craufurd was the best person to lead the Light Division and was also a person he could trust. But what irked him was that other senior officers were also seeking permission for leave of absence.

Sir William Erskine

With Craufurd home on leave the Light Division was commanded by Major General William Erskine, an opposite to Craufurd and a person Wellington could not trust. In 1805 Erskine had been promoted to major general by David Dundas, as C-in-C of the British Army during the period when the Duke of York was in disgrace. Dundas thought highly of Erskine and sent him to the peninsula as a brigade commander. Wellington questioned the posting as Erskine's reputation was well known; he was thought of as highly unstable, was a drunkard and, consequently, was often incapable of conducting any business after dinner, other than a game of cards.

Colonel Torrens, military secretary to Dundas, replied 'that, while Erskine probably was a little mad, he was very clever during his lucid moments, although he looked a little wild when he embarked.'

Wellington had very little influence in the appointment of senior officers, which was based entirely on seniority, and he had to accept Erskine.

Erskine had additional problems with his eyesight, which was so bad that he was nearly blind. An example of Erskine's capricious behaviour can be cited when, on a later occasion, the Spanish guerrillas of Don Sanchez told him that a French supply column was making its way towards Ciudad Rodrigo. Speed was essential but Erskine delayed and failed to intercept the column that entered the town with the badly-needed supplies.

Masséna's attempt to subjugate Portugal had ended in ignominious failure. During the hard winter months he delayed trying to find a way through the lines of Torres Vedras, all the time expecting reinforcements that never materialized. Unable to find a way through and outwitted by Wellington, the bedraggled remnants of the Army of Portugal left in the night leaving 'mawkins', decoy sentinels stuffed with straw. The troops were sick, cold and starving. Dejectedly they began their retreat from the forbidding and impassable lines of Torres Vedras, leaving a trail of destruction, desolation and misery by taking their frustration out on any unfortunate Portuguese they met and sacking their villages. Only occasionally did Masséna show some of his old flair with some well-executed extractions from Wellington's grasp.

Known by his young mistress or *fille de chambre* as 'he with the flashing eyes', Masséna's eyes must have been downcast as he took stock of his options. He was leaving Portugal with a reduced force of 44,000 men. Even after Masséna's heavy losses from starvation and disease Wellington, with 38,000 men, was still outnumbered but his troops were being fed and were in better condition and, as pursuers, their morale was high. But ultimately it was not always a question of who had the larger number of men but who on the day could put more men in the firing line to present the maximum fire-power, as witnessed at Busaco.

Wellington's Pursuit

On 8 March 1811, with Masséna in retreat, Wellington set off in pursuit and set up his headquarters at Frenada where he could menace Almedia and Ciudad Rodrigo. Wellington now had to face the unwelcome problem that some of his best divisional commanders – Hill, Leith, Cotton and Craufurd – were all absent on leave in Britain. Giving Erskine, one of his least able commanders, command of the Light Division would inevitably lead to difficulties, and be an invitation to disaster. Indeed at a most critical time, at Sabugal, the Light Division was left without a leader.

Wellington's vanguard, the Light Division, caught up with a group of French stragglers on 19 March. The group included General Loison's *aide de camp*, a Portuguese who soon took on the look of a doomed man. His wife was with him, dressed in the style of a hussar, the military mode favoured by the fashionable young ladies of Paris and Madrid. As a Spanish beauty her time as a widow was going to be very short.

By the 22nd Wellington's roving gallopers had discovered that Masséna, who had gathered at Celorico, had given orders that his retreating army should march south-eastwards to Guarda and were not moving towards Almeida as expected. Patrols confirmed that French were moving *en masse* towards Castello Branco, a region with poor roads that were no more than rough narrow tracks and devoid of anything to offer the foraging parties. This was the very area that Victor starved in 1809.

At Wellington's headquarters there was speculation that there could be a French column with fresh provisions and supplies moving into this area.

Masséna could be in desperate trouble if forced to continue without replenishing his run-down stores. Since the retreat had begun his ragged army had lost or disposed of many of his wheeled vehicles, carts, guns, caissons and, drastically, over 600 horses.

From information eventually gathered from his roving gallopers, or spies, Wellington learned that there was no sign of any other French army or column; indeed the nearest force was south of Badajoz some 130 miles away, or due east at Salamanca, 100 miles away.

Dissension erupted amongst Masséna's senior officers. Outwitted by Wellington and faced with the humiliation of a forced retreat, arguments, disobedience and refusals began to test his authority. It became known that there had been explosive exchanges at the French HQ between Masséna and Ney over the route they should follow. Ney favoured going due east, the easiest and most direct route to Almeida, to secure fresh provisions and then move into Spain. Masséna wanted to take the south-eastern route which had a lot do with saving face and a reluctance to leave Portugal, especially by the route he used during his triumphant entry. Masséna chose the south-eastern route which meant crossing the mountains by impossible tracks to the Tagus. Ney disagreed to the point of insubordination and so Masséna had him placed under arrest and escorted back to Paris, where he received a mild reprimand from Napoleon.

On 24 March the 2/52nd joined the Light Division, having arrived at Lisbon on the 6th.

Exit Masséna

Wellington reached Guarda on 29 March to discover that Masséna must have had second thoughts as he was no longer following a south-eastern route but had changed direction and was retreating westwards. And so Ney was vindicated. The French were now in positions behind the upper Côa, which being nearer its source was narrower and easily forded. Reynier's corps of three divisions had reached Sabugal.

Next day the 95th, with some squadrons of light dragoons, had little trouble following the trail of death and destruction left by the French rearguard. The French were often accused of non-existent and unfounded terror but even so there were many examples of senseless butchery and torture of the Portuguese peasants and the wrecking of their churches and squalid houses. It demonstrated the spiteful vengeance of defeated troops who lacked compassion, honour and discipline. They were often encouraged by their superiors and the burning of whole villages was always carried out on higher orders. Kincaid recorded the horrors he encountered:

> 31st March, we found the body of a well-dressed female whom they murdered by a horrible refinement in cruelty. She had been upon her back in the middle of the street, with a fragment of rock placed upon her breast, which required four men to move.

Were these not true sons of the revolution? The terror was still living.

The French rearguard, a much stronger force, was driven out of the villages of Frexedas and Alverca. At night the 95th lit many fires over an extended area so that the French would think they were a much larger force. The only casualty so far was the adjutant, Mr Stewart, who was shot through the head by a French *voltigeur* from a window. He was buried in front of Colonel Beckwith's quarters. On 1 April the 95th advanced guard arrived near the bridge by the town of Sabugal. The French had placed advanced posts on the west side of the river. The 95th's picquets were placed at only half a musket shot, about seventy-five yards, from the French sentries.

War and now Fog

Wellington now realized that the French were standing firm on the Côa and so he planned to evict them from their last foothold in Portugal. He could crush

Reynier's II Corps now in its isolated position formed up just on the other side of the Côa and occupying a long ridge that ran parallel to the river. Northwards a bend in the river turned it away from the ridge, which at this point was crossed by a bridge that led to the old town of Sabugal with its crumbling Moorish castle.

His plan was for the Light Division to ford the Côa about two miles above the town with the intention of circling round to strike the rear of the French left flank, whilst two other divisions would launch a frontal attack. Trant's column of 4,000 and Wilson's mixed force were to move between and threaten Almeida and Ciudad Rodrigo, turning south as if to menace Reynier's rear.

The Light Division, supported by two cavalry brigades, were to ford the Côa at two points about a mile apart above Sabugal to launch a dawn preliminary attack on both of Merle's flanks. Colonel Beckwith's 1 Brigade was to attack the right of the flank and rear while Colonel Drummond's 2 Brigade would attack Merle's centre. Erskine, with the cavalry, could have crossed his command further up for it was expected that they should appear well to the rear of Reynier's left wing. They should then cut across the hills towards the village of Torre on the Alayates road and across Reynier's line of retreat. The cavalry were not expected to be attacked, as the French would be heavily occupied to their front. Picton's 3rd Division was to cross the Côa between Sabugal and the Light Division's crossing point and head the main attack against Merle's centre. The 5th Division, under the temporary command of Dunlop, with artillery was to take the bridge at Sabugal. The 1st and the newly arrived 7th Divisions were to take up positions in reserve and were not to make a frontal attack until the French were on the point of retiring. Alexander Campbell's 6th Division and one battalion from the 7th Division were above Sabugal, facing Loison's centre, and were to make a demonstration, or show of strength, of their presence with the objective of keeping Loison guessing.

Wellington's plan had the limited objective of catching Reynier's II Corps at Sabugal in a separated position, crushing it or giving it a severe mauling before VI and VIII Corps could offer support. But the best laid plans are at the mercy of the weather. As dawn broke on 3 April, and as all should have been making moves to their positions, they were faced by a thick blanket of fog that obliterated the landscape and clung to all but the highest points. From a vantage point, Wellington could make out something of the landscape but those below were unable to recognize any features.

The Thickening Fog of War and Erskine Vanishes
So dense was the early morning fog that units were having difficulty finding their correct starting positions. Divisional commanders, reluctant to venture blindly into the mist, delayed their start. The Light Division was left to its

own devices with Erskine ordering an advance but making no attempt to put Beckwith and Drummond's brigades in position to cross the Côa. Beckwith's Brigade consisted of four companies, about 300 men of the 1/95th under the command of Major Gilmour, and the 1/43rd under Major Patrickson, who were waiting on a track above the river unsure of their position when Erskine's *aide de camp* galloped up and, in a brusque manner, asked Beckwith 'why he did not cross'. So, without receiving the expected orders and without replying, Beckwith took his brigade forwards into the mist unaware that he was not at the intended ford. He had crossed at a point nearer Sabugal, too far to the left, where the waters were deeper and his men were up to their armpits in the freezing water as they crossed, keeping their Baker rifles and powder dry. Beckwith was now too far to the centre and not to the flank of Merle's position. At first there were sporadic shots from the enemy picquets and French balls were hissing and hitting the water.

Meanwhile Erskine decided to gallop off with the cavalry brigade into the fog. He was not seen again and played no part in the battle.

The skies darkened and a heavy rain fell, reducing visibility and all recognition of friend or foe as well as reducing the use of their muskets and rifles. The preliminary attack by the Light Division was made not only in the wrong place but too early, due to Erskine's incompetence. The fog had caused delays to the Divisions who were not in their opening attack positions leaving the Light Division precariously isolated and with Beckwith and Drummond both unaware of the critical situations they were in.

Colonel Beckwith and the four companies of the 95th fought their way up the rising ground in extended skirmishing order making good use of plentiful cover. The rising ground was scattered with some fine groves of big chestnut trees and there were cultivated areas and orchards, all interlaced with dry-stone walls, not ideal cavalry country. They were suddenly met by a violent storm of musketry and were about to face the usual noisy French attack with bugles and drummer boys frantically beating their drums. There were shouts of '*Vive l'Empereur*' and brave French officers 'dancing like madmen with their hats on their swords', encouraging their men forward. They had struck the left regiment of Merle's left brigade in the centre instead of the flank. Beckwith also encouraged his men but with assured calm orders, pointing out to them to shoot the officers; 'shoot that fellow', he urged some rifleman. The columns were easy targets. Officers and NCOs were the first to be shot, leaving the men leaderless.

The 43rd followed the 95th while Drummond's Brigade had headed off in the planned direction further to the right. Then it started to rain again as the mist began to clear and Colonel Beckwith could instantly recognize his predicament. But again he spurred on another charge to reach the summit of the hill. The French brought forward two short-barrelled howitzers and began firing canisters of grape and round-shot creating dense clouds of gun smoke, typical of howitzers. The number of French to his front began to increase as others menaced his flanks. These troops had been positioned down the hill further along the Côa, near to the point of the expected British attack and also to be near drinking water; battle is thirsty work. Their renewed attack was therefore made uphill and with such ferocity that the 95th faced being overwhelmed on both front and rear.

Captain Hopkins of the 43rd made a rapid assessment of the danger to Beckwith and took his company to seize some high ground close to the French guns, commanding the ascent to the hill. As the French troops were again storming up from below, his company fired a volley that threw them into confusion, but they soon rallied to be met by the rest of the 43rd firing platoon volleys in succession throwing the French into disorder again. Once more they rallied and launched another desperate attack as Captain Hopkins ordered load, fix bayonets, present, fire and charge!

Just then, attracted by the volume of fire, Drummond's Brigade decided to offer support. Ignoring Erskine's order 'not to engage' Drummond changed his line of advance and came up on the right of Beckwith and advanced with companies of the 2/95th, the 1st Caçadores and 1/52nd deployed in line with the 2/52nd held in reserve. The main body of the 43rd was now engaged heavily and Beckwith, who had sustained a head wound and had blood streaming down his face, rode amongst the front line of skirmishers directing fire. He was giving orders and encouragement in his avuncular manner as if in total command of the situation: 'Now my men, this will do … let us show our teeth again.' In praise of Beckwith's leadership Kincaid described the man in action:

> Throughout the fight, whenever danger was greatest, the calm sounding voice of that officer, Harry Smith's adored colonel, could be heard. 'Now my lads, we'll just go back a little if you please, no, no' as some of the men began to run, 'I don't mean that we are in no hurry, we'll just walk quietly back and you can give them a shot as you go along.'

The fight reached a frenzy and the French were falling in large numbers. A second charge carried the hill, overwhelming the French gunners. One howitzer was taken by the 43rd and the skirmishers were even moving down the hill to the French positions below when, suddenly, bugle calls sounded indicating that enemy cavalry were approaching. They came galloping in from all quarters forcing Beckwith's troops to fall back rapidly and take cover with the main body, which had reformed behind a low stone wall. With great courage the French dragoons rode right up to the wall and, brandishing their large dragoon pistols, were about to fire when the 95th and the 43rd rose up and fired a blinding fusillade, decimating the dragoons.

During this incident a strong force of French light infantry, having stormed up the hill, were intent on recapturing the howitzer; but, as they fought through harrowing fire from the 43rd, very few survived to make the attempt. Then the Royal Horse Artillery opened up with two guns from Captain Bull's troop and the 52nd charged in strength against the flanks of the main body, driving them back from the summit only to be faced by a fresh charge of cavalry, causing the 52nd to scatter, which did cause some disorder until the cavalry were repulsed.

Reynier now decided to send a stronger force of all arms, infantry, cavalry and artillery, nearly 6,000 men to outflank the Light Division, storm the heights and recapture the howitzer. But, as orders were about to be given, Reynier was shocked to learn that Dunlop's 5th Division had crossed the bridge and entered Sabugal and that British cavalry had appeared on the hills behind his left.

General Colville with the 3rd Division poured forth from the woods on Reynier's right, opening up a brisk fire on that flank. Reynier now feared the worst and, to forestall any possibility of being surrounded, gave the order for a general retreat to Rendo and the safety of VI Corps. Some had orders to leave at the double with others to make off as best they could. A strong French rearguard was organized by Heudlet's 2 Brigade from the 17th Léger and the 70th Ligne, with orders to oppose the advancing British vanguard in strength. The job of chasing the heels of the French fell to Picton's 3rd Division. As they began to press the French the rain, which had been on and off all morning, strengthened and turned into a torrential downpour, blanketing out any features of the countryside, so much so that, realising the futility, Wellington ordered the whole force to halt. He rode up to the Light Division and, as a compliment, ordered them into the town of Sabugal where they occupied the place just before the 5th Division entered, much to the latter's annoyance.

Erskine gave the Light Division little or no support and his cavalry could have played their part during the retreat of the French but they never made contact with the French or came near the British during the whole morning. But a squadron of the reliable 1st German Hussars came across and appropriated the private baggage of Reynier and General Pierre Soult. One officer of the 95th accused Erskine of being 'a shortsighted ass'; there were many such comments from all ranks. The men felt particularly unsafe under his command.

After the combat at Sabugal, Masséna continued his retreat, preparing to make a further stand to stay in Portugal and face Wellington at Fuentes de Onoro. Due entirely to the vagaries of the weather, Wellington's well-formulated plan never achieved the hoped for results. Reynier's II Corps was able to get away but only after receiving a sharp lesson in the excellent fighting qualities of the British and Portuguese light troops. Wellington's despatch recorded the action, with the highest praise ever received for the Light Division and, unusually, singled out Lieutenant Colonel Beckwith for special mention:

> Nothing could be more daring and more characteristic of British courage than the way Beckwith with a handful of men withstood and thrice repulsed and then pursued the whole Corps d'Armée placed in a strong position. I consider the action fought by the Light Division, by Colonel Beckwith's brigade principally, to be one of the most glorious the British troops were ever engaged in.
>
> Wellington

The 'most glorious' combat was due entirely to the supreme efforts of the Light Division and Colonel Beckwith's leadership. The 3,500 men of Beckwith and Drummond's brigades had unknowingly taken on the whole of Reynier's II Corps and inflicted heavy losses with much smaller casualties to themselves.

It was at this time that Major General Craufurd returned from leave in Scotland. Whilst he was in Lisbon glowing reports were filtering through of the Light Division's splendid action at Sabugal. Craufurd, who needed promotion was consequently always keen to do well and go for glory, was crestfallen when he read the reports of praise for Beckwith and the Light Division. He had never received such praise, even though Wellington thought very highly of him. Perhaps Wellington was indicating that Craufurd should have been there?

The Cost
The 43rd suffered most losses and earned most of the glory. All the praise was for Colonel Beckwith who, because of his coolness and his air of confidence, inspired others. As always he seemed to flourish when the situation became desperate, when quick judgements and resolution were called for.

The French lost 689 men killed and wounded of whom sixty-one, about ten per cent, were officers, shot due almost entirely to the presence of riflemen with their accurate Baker rifles. They also lost 186 unwounded prisoners.

Wellington's losses were 179, ten of whom were from the Caçadores. Of this total 143 were from the Light Division, of whom eighty were members of the 43rd Regiment. Picton's 3rd Division had twenty-five casualties, the Royal Horse Artillery lost one, and the 1st Hussars had two wounded. The figures indicate who took the brunt of the action. The 43rd's prize was one howitzer and the 52nd's two hams.

Conclusion
The day after the action at Sabugal Wellington wrote to Beresford, 'Really these attacks in column against our lines are contemptible'. In other words

the thousands of French conscripts, highly charged with revolutionary spirit, hurriedly trained, mostly on the march, and loosely disciplined with little knowledge of evolutions, were no match for trained and disciplined infantry who were able to offer concentrated firepower. To this should be added the fact that they were well-led infantry. But Wellington knowing their value, had also given his infantry that special sharp edge with the new regiments of light infantry and the specialist services of the rifle regiments, the 60th Royal Americans, 95th Rifles and the light regiments of the King's German Legion. Light infantry were not accorded the same importance by the French high command.

Half of Colonel Beckwith's brigade, some 1,500 men, were deployed as skilled skirmishers up against Merle's four *voltigeur* companies, about 350 to 400 men. They were driven in quickly by the 95th and the Caçadores and Merle's four supporting columns suffered heavy casualties. To quote Lieutenant Blakiston of the 43rd:

> Certainly I never saw such skirmishers as the 95th. They could do the work much better and with infinitely less loss than any of our best light troops. They possessed an individual boldness, a mutual understanding and a quickness of the eye in taking advantage of the ground which, taken together, I never saw equalled. They were much superior to the French *voltigeurs*.

In discussing the action years later Colonel Beckwith always maintained that if it was possible for one company commander to decide the fate of the action, it was Captain Hopkins of the 43rd who had decided it at Sabugal.

The Last Word

'There perhaps never was nor never will be again such a war brigade as that which composed the 43rd, 52nd and the Rifles,' wrote John Kincaid. Kincaid's remark remains apt today, even after many disbandments and amalgamations.

Postscript – The Sabugal Howitzer, a Disputed Trophy

When any member of a regiment captured a piece of an enemy's field ordnance or appropriated it if it had been discarded, it was considered to be the regiment's prize. To confirm it they chalked the regiment's number on the barrel.

The capture of the French howitzer by the 43rd Regiment during the action at Sabugal, and a counter claim made by the 52nd Regiment after the French counterstrike, led to an inter-regimental debate in the 1840s when the 43rd's claim was disputed by the 52nd. It is noted in the 43rd's regimental records that discussions took place between officers of the 43rd and Colonel Gurwood of the 52nd Regiment. There were also comments by Major General William Napier in letters to the *Naval and Military Gazette*.

There was strong evidence, supported by eyewitness accounts, which substantiated the claims made by the 43rd Regiment. In a letter, Lieutenant Hopkins wrote:

> The captured howitzer was left under the command of the 43rd and the Rifles, as every attempt of the French to carry it off was ineffectual, causing severe loss both in cavalry and infantry.

The 52nd's account mentions that a company of the 52nd, commanded by Lieutenant J. Frederick Love, later recaptured an abandoned howitzer, the 43rd having lost possession of it during the French counterstrike. The 52nd handed the captured howitzer to the Royal Artillery as was the practice. When the Duke of Wellington was asked to decide the matter he declined to give an opinion.

The Light Division and all the Light Troops in the Second Action at Fuentes de Oñoro, May 1811

Craufurd was a complex person who was desperate to prove himself and valued the trust that Wellington had in him as commander of the newly created Light Division. Earlier he had left the Army to enter politics but eventually decided to return to the Army. In the interim he had lost position in the scale of promotional advancement and had to re-start his career.

So, with Wellington watching him closely, it was an opportunity to demonstrate his ability and show that he was more than capable of carrying out Wellington's orders regarding the Light Division's special position on the frontier in 1810.

Craufurd was a first-class infantry officer but so far had demonstrated that he was less than capable of commanding cavalry and he could have sought Krauchenburg's experienced opinion of his plan before committing the cavalry to attack the French infantry.

But Craufurd's troubles were not over as he took up position with the entire Light Division on the east bank of the Côa river. The French were sending out very strong cavalry patrols who were obviously probing to test Craufurd's strength. It all pointed to the inevitability of a mass move forward of Marshal Masséna's forces. Had Craufurd remembered the doubts that Wellington had expressed at being caught out when too far forward?

Craufurd left his withdrawal to the last minute but it was almost too late as it looked dangerously as if his entire division would be swept up. So alarm!

There was a sudden headlong dash for the narrow bridge across the Côa. The Portuguese were the first to cross, almost in a panic as they fled, but the

Light Division was saved. Craufurd had again lost his composure and become agitated and hesitant, so the regimental commanders, Colonel Beckwith of the 95th and Colonel Barclay of the 52nd took control. Eventually they managed to get across, together with the horse artillery, with the 95th establishing firing positions on the west bank to keep the French at bay.

Much to the annoyance of Wellington, Craufurd had asked to take leave and go to England. Masséna and his Army of Portugal rolled relentlessly on until it came to an abrupt halt at the defensive lines around Lisbon completely unknown to the French, the Lines of Torres Vedras. Unable to pass the formidable lines Masséna was forced to withdraw.

In Craufurd's absence the Light Division was under the temporary and blundering command of the unstable Major General Sir William Erskine.

By 1808, Sir Arthur Wellesley, now in command of the British forces in Portugal, had come to terms with beating the French tactic of assault by an intimidating column. He kept his lines in dead ground during the opening softening-up artillery bombardment, moving them forward as two deep lines (which became *de rigueur*) to meet the column, with a heavy front of riflemen to kill off the French officers and gunners and also threw forward skirmishers to thwart the disrupting attempts of the *voltigeurs*.

The new light regiments acted like a sharp edge to blunt and wound the French advance and were so much valued by the Duke of Wellington that he decided to create the Light Division.

On 5 May the Light Division was at Fuentes de Oñoro after their successful attack at Sabugal had disrupted Masséna's carefully planned withdrawal. This was acknowledged by Wellington with a special Mention in Despatches of Colonel Sydney Beckwith of the 95th who steered the attack, no thanks to Erskine who galloped off into the mists chasing Spanish windmills and not the French. Masséna's retreat from Sabugal now left the fortress town of Almeida isolated and having to look to its own resources.

The temporary command of Major General William Erskine was over. After three months' leave Craufurd had rejoined the Light Division only the day before it was about to be given a special and difficult task. For this it had been chosen by Wellington because he knew he could trust Craufurd and the quality of the troops that he led. It was to be Craufurd's last action in the field before the assault on Ciudad Rodrigo.

Dispositions on 3 May 1811

Masséna's Army of Portugal, the same that Masséna promised would drive Wellington's army into the sea when he entered Portugal, had lost control of all that he had conquered, its fate being sealed at Torres Vedras. All that remained of Masséna's conquests was the town of Almeida that lay just on the east side of the frontier and was in sore need of fresh supplies.

South of Almeida, and key to Wellington's position, was the straggling village of Fuentes de Oñoro that stood in the path of Masséna's force attempting to relieve Almeida. Wellington was determined that the village should be held. Fuentes, with its maze of narrow twisting lanes and many ominously dead ends, was and still is only just wide enough for a donkey and cart and was to witness intense and bloody street fighting on 3 May. All art and skill was lost in the mayhem of vicious killing with sword, bayonet and butt of rifle and musket. The backstreet brawls of Cork, Dublin, Glasgow and London had been good training.

The village was held by 2,600 light troops from twenty-eight battalion light companies from the 1st and 3rd Divisions, except for Stopford's Guards Brigade. Of the twenty-eight, thirteen were British, four were Portuguese and six German, with skirmishers from the King's German Legion under Major Aly of the 3rd Line Regiment, and five companies of German marksmen from the 5/60th and three companies of riflemen from the 3/95th. All the light troops were under the command of Lieutenant Colonel Williams, the commanding officer of the 5/60th.

In the early afternoon Masséna ordered Ferey's Division of VI Corps (Loison's) to attack the village whilst II Corps (Reynier's) made a feint against Wellington's left near Fort Conception. The fighting was frantic with the action see-sawing back and forth as the French attacked with 4,000 men, fording the Dos Casas that at this time was unusually knee deep. Eventually the allies were driven back beyond the church. Additional support was thrown in with the 71st (Highland) Light Infantry, the 1/79th (Cameron Highlanders) and the 2/24th (Warwickshire) Regiments. The 71st, led by Lieutenant Colonel Cadogan, made a shock bayonet charge that drove the French back over the Dos Casas. By evening the village west of the Dos Casas was in allied hands. Wellington's casualties were 259, and Masséna's were 652.

The Light Division soldiers were familiar with the frontier from early 1810, when they covered the Côa area with patrols and vedettes. They often passed through Fuentes, getting to know many of the residents from their sojourn the previous year. The abandoned Fort Conception, just over the frontier on the Spanish side, was used as a base during their numerous scouting patrols. On that morning of 3 May they were on outpost duty when the French made moves towards the 6th and 5th Divisions in the north. Wellington sent the Light Division to cover these moves but, as it became obvious that it was a feint by the French the division was recalled.

On the 4th the morning began with a thick mist that lay across the low-lying Fuentes. When the mist lifted sporadic firing sprang up across the Dos Casas but did not last long as the time came to parley; a truce was agreed so that the two sides could exchange wounded and clear the dead, and small groups took the opportunity to talk and barter food, wine and tobacco. Simmons recalls a French officer who spoke to him by the Dos Casas:

> This place is appropriately named the 'Fountain of Honour'. God knows how many of our friends on both sides have drunk deep of its waters and with tomorrow's dawn most likely many more will do so.

Masséna was now aware that Fuentes de Oñoro was too strongly defended to be taken and, equally importantly, held. He considered alternative plans. Showing caution this time Masséna ordered a reconnaissance.

Wellington redeployed some of his forces but kept the 5th and 6th Divisions and Barbecena's Portuguese cavalry blocking all access to Almeida, which was not to be relieved. Masséna had declared in his customary manner that he was going to relieve Almeida and drive Wellington across the Côa. Wellington was determined that neither would happen, especially a retreat across the Côa that would have echoes of Craufurd's mad scramble the previous year.

Wellington also saw French movements to their left and realized that, on the 5th, Masséna would attempt to swing round his flank and attack the ridge at the south end. Wellington had expected this move earlier and decided to stop the French advance as far away from his main body as possible. The only force on the plain was Don Julian Sanchez's mixed force of Spanish irregulars at Nave de Haver. Wellington ordered the 7th Division (Major General Houston) to move to Poco Velho, three miles south of Fuentes, where he could cover the crossing of the Dos Casas and deny it to the French. Allied cavalry would support this move that had now extended his front to twelve miles.

At first light on the 5th, under cover of a thick mist, the main body of French cavalry swung round Poco Velho making for Nave de Haver and surprised Don Sanchez's force of horse, foot and some light artillery pieces. The Spanish picquets were nervous and created confusion when they mistook Sanchez's lieutenant as a Frenchman as he rode in front of the French taunting them and gesticulating; he was mistakenly shot by one of his own guards. In a state of fury Sanchez ordered a retreat. They took off at speed and headed for Freneda and took no further part in the action. At the same time the Cavalry of the Guard attacked the 7th Division's outposts in the scattered woods at Poco Velho, driving in two of Houston's battalions, the 85th (Buckinghamshire) Light Infantry and the 2nd Caçadores but not before receiving some withering fire. A squadron of the 16th Light Dragoons, and another of the 1st Hussars KGL who presented a front were eventually driven in with some loss. Two French infantry divisions, of Marchand and Mermet, stormed Poco Velho driving back the 7th Division in some disorder and forcing them to withdraw with cover given by the 1st Hussars. Major General Houston realized that the division was in a very precarious position and it became almost isolated at one point before Wellington sent a galloper with orders for it to fall back northwards with the Light Division covering its retreat.

First in the Field and Last Out

Earlier on the 5th Wellington had seen the moves of Solignac's division, as well as a large force of cavalry marching south. He now realized that he had extended his flank too thinly and too far and ordered Cotton's 1,400 cavalry, Bull's troop of horse artillery and Craufurd's Light Division to the right to support Houston.

Craufurd marched to a wood south-west of Poco Velho, keeping the riflemen to the fore to ward off the *voltigeurs*, who did keep their distance when they realized they faced rifles. The situation was becoming critical just as the Light Division, with Craufurd back in command, approached Poco Velho. Wellington had ordered them south to support the 7th Division soon after dawn, with orders not to extend the Allied front any farther to the south but to cover 7th Division's withdrawal to the north.

The 7th Division had been recently formed and was untried. As a light division it was commanded by Major General Houston and included two brigades, Sontag's brigade with the 2/51st Light Infantry, the 85th (Buckinghamshire) Light Infantry, the Chasseurs Britanniques and the Brunswick Oels Jägers, (the Black Brunswickers) while Doyle's (Portuguese) brigade included the 7th Portuguese Line (two battalions), 19th Portuguese Line (two battalions) and the 2nd Caçadores. These two brigades had a total of 6,990 men of all ranks.

Then came some fragmented action and wild fighting during which the Chasseurs Britanniques were charged by French cavalry but in good British style, fired off some platoon volleys and drove them off. As Simmons wrote, 'When Greek meets Greek there comes a tug of war', adding 'we were highly amused at the *rencontre*'.

As the Light Division kept the French infantry occupied Houston had the 7th Division in order of close columns and making a gradual retreat with the eccentric Colonel Mainwaring of the 51st telling his men 'to keep in step and they cannot hurt us'. They moved across the higher ground protected by allied cavalry and Bull's horse artillery troop. Although outnumbered, the light dragoons and 1st Hussars kept up repeated harrying charges.

Form Square

This situation was exactly what Sir John Moore had anticipated when he planned the training for the light regiments in 1801. He insisted that his new light regiments were to receive the same basic battalion training as all line regiments before their selective light infantry training. This would ensure that they were totally adaptable as all-purpose light troops and not some rag-tag-and-bobtail fringe group of rangers.

Robert Craufurd now formed the Light Division on the plain, in battalion columns of quarter distance ready to form squares on the command. When Craufurd gave the command to 'form the square' all the regiments' buglers would sound the call 'form the square', and, as it echoed across the plain, it would be followed by the order that they should face the front and march. The mobile squares were in echelon and all faced the direction of the march, continuing until given the command halt. When they all faced out to their individual fronts they presented a wall of bayonets to the 3,000 French cavalry, who were constantly hovering, shouting, waving their swords and gesticulating but failing to close in. At the same time the French cavalry were being attacked by allied cavalry who, although few in number, showed great courage. Meanwhile, Bull's troop of guns quickly unlimbered between the squares and fired off grapeshot to keep the French cavalry at bay before limbering up rapidly and galloping off. The riflemen of the 95th were extended on the flanks using cover of outcrops and low dry-stone walls keeping the *voltigeurs* at a distance; they could form rallying squares if necessary.

It was at this time that Captain Norman Ramsay's troop of guns who had unlimbered and were firing off shot rapidly to keep the French at a distance delayed too long and were cut off and surrounded by the French. The Light Division now had to rescue Ramsay's horse artillery. Ramsay gave the order to limber up and mount and, in a furious gallop, rode in what became known as 'the artillery charge' through the French horsemen. With sabres drawn and flashing pistols, they charged the French, the horses' nostrils flared, eyes bulging. The race was on, the gunners' heads bent over their horses' necks, limbers and 6-pounders rattling and bouncing, wheels bouncing they bounded to safety, scattering the astonished French.

Captain Brotherton's squadron of the 14th Light Dragoons rode up at the pursuing French cavalry and, with the assistance of the Royals, the 1st Dragoons, drove them off, in the process capturing Colonel Lamotte and some other prisoners. Colonel Charles Stewart, the Adjutant General, led this charge bravely, which enabled Ramsay's troop to reach the allied lines. Meanwhile, the 16th Light Dragoons and 1st Hussars, faced with overwhelming numbers of French cavalry, dismounted rapidly and, with their mounts, sought safety in the Light Division's squares.

After a stop-start march in perfect mobile squares covering a distance of about three miles, all reached the safety of the allied lines and the Guards opened their line to allow them to pass through. It was drill manual perfection and all who witnessed it expressed unbounding praise. As John Kincaid wrote:

> The execution of our movement presented a magnificent military spectacle retiring through with the order and precision of a common field day.

And no doubt Major General Craufurd's reputation was restored and even enhanced and the Côa forgiven. This time the commanding officers did drink his health.

Wellington's plan to deny Masséna his last remaining prize in Portugal was only partially successful. All the hard fighting, especially by the light troops at Fuentes, was nullified by the neglect of duty by a subordinate and incompetent officer. Wellington sent written orders to Major General Erskine to block the only escape route from Almeida with his 5th Division. Erskine, about to dine and afterwards play cards, stuck the orders unread in his pocket. Meanwhile Brennier and his Almeida force effected a perfect escape as Erskine got drunk and incapable. The blame was eventually diverted from Erskine to one of lower rank and social position causing disgrace that ruined a man's honour.

Chapter 12

Wellington's Light Infantry and Rifles at Waterloo

The Hundredth Day

The finale of the Napoleonic epoch was played out in the cockpit of Mont St Jean on 18 June 1815, and marked the last bloody act of Bonaparte's appearance on the political stage of Europe. For Napoleon the battle was a win or lose contest with all the combatants locked in a head-on battering to see who might crumple first. Time and space were compacted into a maelstrom of powder, steel and blood, lacking any brilliant military tactical gestures or manoeuvres. Not an action for 'loose files and open order'. Not an action where light infantry could flourish and make use of their special skills. But, as events proved, it was the light regiments and the battalion light companies who, ever adaptable and trained for all eventualities, made massive efforts and helped to seal the victory. Notable was the continuous heroic defence of the Château Hougoumont by the battalion light companies, the flankers of the four Guards battalions, about 400 men. In the grounds were 300 Hanoverian jägers and a battalion of Nassau line troops.

The farm of la Haie Sainte was magnificently defended by Major Baring's 2nd Light Battalion, King's German Legion, a depleted battalion of 376 men who were later supported by two companies from the 1st Light Battalion, KGL, with the remainder of the battalion skirmishing outside the farm area. There were also some troops transferred from the Nassau battalion at Hougoumont. Most were sacrificed in the attempt to hold back the flood of attacking French. They held on until the King's German Legion light troops ran out of their Baker rifle ammunition and were overwhelmed by sheer numbers. There were about forty survivors.

Positioned in the centre of Wellington's front, just left of la Haie Sainte, by the famous sandpit, were the 1/95th Rifles, rested, refitted and with replacements, after spending six years of continuous duties as a key regiment in the Light Division during the Peninsular campaign. They experienced the full onslaught of d'Erlon's attacks and were kept constantly on the move by the battle's momentum, during which they kept up a non-stop skirmishing fire, often in support of the King's German Legion cut off in la Haie Sainte farm.

Light Bobs and Flankers

At the time of Waterloo the new light infantry regiments had been in existence less than twelve years. They had been functioning since 1803, but it was only in 1809 that they were recognized and 'Light Infantry' was added to the regiments' titles. The battalion light companies – the flankers – on the other hand, were first formed in 1758. The elite light regiments were those originally trained under Sir John Moore and made up the famous Light Brigade. The 1/52nd (Oxfordshire) Light Infantry under Colonel Sir John Moore was the first to convert to light infantry in 1803. The 43rd (Monmouthshire) Light Infantry, originally raised in 1741, the senior light regiment in terms of lineage, was not at Waterloo. After serving in the Peninsula as part of the Light Division it was sent to America to take part in the War of 1812. The 1/95th (Rifles), formed in 1800, were trained at Shorncliffe as chasseurs according to the principles contained in the training manual of Colonel Baron de Rottenburg of the 60th. Both rifle regiments, the 60th (Royal American Regiment) and the 95th were light troops, but with special duties, and were armed with rifled flintlocks, the famous Baker rifles. The 5/60th were not at Waterloo: they were stationed in Gibraltar awaiting disbandment so that the men could be returned to a German port. The other 60th battalions were serving in North America. But the 60th was represented at Waterloo by officers either in positions of command or serving on the staff. They were Sir Henry Clinton, Colonel Commandant of the 1/60th Major General Sir James Kempt, Brigade Commander, Lieutenant Colonel E. O. Tripp and four captains acting as ADCs.

All these new light regiments had won their spurs in the Peninsular War together with other light regiments. The 51st (Yorkshire) Light Infantry, Private Wheeler's regiment, were at Waterloo and were positioned to cover an abattis at the rear of Hougoumont. The 71st (Highland) Light Infantry were part of 3 British (Light) Brigade. Both the 51st and 71st were converted to light infantry in 1809, and were trained by Rottenburg. The 68th (Durham) and the 85th (Buckinghamshire) Light Infantry were similarly converted in 1808.

With victory in Spain and the Peninsular campaign finally over and France no longer at war, the 52nd returned to Plymouth on 28 June 1814. After marching from Devon to Hythe Barracks, near Folkestone, the regiment underwent a re-organization over the next six months, making preparations for active service in North America. They left Portsmouth on 20 March 1815 and sailed first to Ireland, entering the Cove of Cork, where, because of contrary winds, they came about and returned to Plymouth on 22 March. By this time news had arrived of the debacle on 8 January at Chalmate, a battle that both sides fought needlessly, two weeks after a peace agreement. They also heard, with little surprise, that the half-expected had happened; clandestinely, Bonaparte, with a 1,000-strong Imperial Guard, had left Elba and landed at Antibes to begin his 'Hundred Days', taking an enormous gamble and risking many more French lives.

Five days later the 52nd was ordered to the Netherlands and arrived at Ostende on 3 April with Lieutenant-Colonel Charles Rowan in command. At this juncture Sir John Colborne was Military Secretary to the Prince of Orange. On the 4th they began their circuitous march to find the French.

This sudden change of direction for the 52nd would have the regiment playing a contributory and significant part in the forthcoming battle at Waterloo at the critical point during Napoleon's final move, the mass attack of the Imperial Guard regiments 'coming on in the same old way'. Part of the failure of the Guards to push home their attack was in no small measure due to their shock repulse by the 52nd Light Infantry, supported by the 71st Light Infantry, although the 52nd's Colonel, Sir John Colborne, recalled more modestly in his letter to Siborne:

> We were all intent in performing our parts, that we are disposed to imagine that the Brigade or Corps with which we were engaged played a most distinguished part, and attribute more importance to the movements under our immediate observation than they deserved.

Colborne's version of 'victory has many fathers and defeat is a lonely orphan' was his public position. Was it modesty, or was it just that he was reluctant to get embroiled in the unseemly wrangling that was being aired by all and sundry in the messes and clubs over claims and counter claims of who or what regiment 'fathered the victory'? It was to his credit that he publicly adopted the same attitude as the Duke who was overheard to say in Paris shortly after the battle, 'Let the battle of Waterloo stand where it does, we are satisfied.' Privately Colborne was bitterly disappointed that the 52nd was not awarded the recognition that it deserved.

In 1815 the then Captain Shaw Kennedy of the 43rd Regiment was ADC to Wellington, attached to the 3rd British Division. Later, on 15 May 1864, as General Kennedy, he stated:

> No man can point out to me any instance, in ancient or modern history, of a single battalion so influencing the result of any great action as the result of the battle of Waterloo was influenced by the attack of the 52nd Regiment on the Imperial Guard.

By selecting drafts of the fittest and the best from the 1st and 2nd Battalions, the 52nd was able to field a full complement of 1,038 men under the overall command of the redoubtable Colonel Sir John Colborne who, like Hardinge and Napier, was one of Sir John Moore's men. Because of its size the battalion was divided into two wings with Lieutenant Colonel Rowan in command of the left wing, and Major William Chalmers the right. The 1/71st under their commanding officer, Lieutenant Colonel T. Reynell, had a strength of 810 officers and men. The six companies of the 2/95th Rifles, under their commanding officer, Lieutenant Colonel Norcott, had twenty-one officers and 550 other ranks, with two companies of the 3/95th with their commanding officer, Brevet-Major W. Eeles, totalling 188 officers and other ranks.

These regiments now formed, under Major General Frederick Adam, 3 British Light Brigade, attached to Lieutenant General Lord Hill's II Corps. They were selected by Wellington as part of his strong reserve on the right of the line, with Hougoumont the anchor point. On 27 May, the 1st Battalion of the 52nd arrived at Lessines together with the whole of Lieutenant General Sir Henry Clinton's Division and Count Estorff's Hanoverian Volunteer Hussars. They remained there until 15 June to cover the Mons sector, anticipating incursions by the French. On the 16th they received the ominous news of the Prussians' defeat at Ligny, followed by orders to march immediately to Mont St Jean.

The division marched off with the 52nd behind their band and no doubt with their morale getting a boost from the stirring martial music. Halfway between Enghein and Soignies they heard the even more ominous sound of the cannonade from Quatre Bras, a distance of nearly twenty-two miles. Braine-le-Comte was reached towards midnight and, just as the order to halt was given, the heavens opened up with a torrential downpour. After two hours' rest, at 2am on the 17th the division was given the order to fall in. Soaked through, they marched to Nivelles and reached there about 7am. After a breakfast halt of four hours they moved off slowly, with British artillery, cavalry and masses of Netherlands troops, towards Waterloo.

At about 5pm at Mont Plaisir the 52nd made their first sighting of the French, light cavalry reconnoitring the allied positions. On reaching Hougoumont the division halted before moving on to rising ground immediately east of Merbe Braine. Wellington intended to stand and fight, and it was in this position that the brigade would face the French on the following day; until then they bivouacked and passed a wretched night suffering the full effects of the violent storm, which some old campaigners thought was usual before the Duke of Wellington's battles.

Most of the brigade had spent a miserable night in the open. Some had tried to find shelter in the nearby woods, all did their best to brave the elements but by morning all were drenched and covered in Brabant mud. Major General Adam must have taken pity on the men, as he gave permission for numbers of them to fall out to form foraging parties. They ransacked a few farm buildings nearby for food and kindling, anything movable that would burn – doors, furniture and shutters. They made fires to dry themselves, their clothes, arms and equipment. They cooked breakfast from what livestock they found at the farm.

That Sunday morning Adam's Brigade was posted in the second line nearly on the Allied right. The 52nd's right was formed by the rest of the 2nd British Division, under Sir Henry Clinton. Also on the right were the Hanoverian Militia brigade under Colonel Hugh Halket, the King's German Legion under Colonel Duplat, the special command of the Brunswick Corps under Colonel Olferman, 4 British Brigade under Colonel Mitchell, which included the 51st and a squadron of the 15th Hussars. On the rising ground to the 52nd's left were twenty guns of the Royal Artillery, which attracted the French gunners' attention, bringing down a destructive fire of shot and shell. Meanwhile Colonel Colborne, anxious to see something of the start of the battle before everything was obscured by smoke, rode with Colonel Rowan to rising ground where he saw a body of French (Polish) Lancers near the crossroads leading to Braine l'Alleud. Were the lancers probing or just 'showing the flag', as they let out a rousing cheer and rode off?

The rest of Clinton's division remained on the left of Adam's brigade but behind them. The five battalions of the Brunswick infantry and their artillery lay on the reverse slope of Adam's main position. The 52nd were in a depression among fields with a very low crop. During these early minutes of the battle, cannon shots were being fired at troops to their front, including the Duke and his staff who were reconnoitring on the ridge. Many shots bounded over, falling mainly among the 2/95th although some landed among the ranks of the 52nd. The regiment suffered its first casualties with an assistant sergeant major and one soldier killed and fifteen wounded.

Prepare to Repel Cavalry

At about 4 o'clock the brigade was ordered by Wellington to move forward to the Nivelles road and form a four-deep line to attack the swarms of French *voltigeurs* who had driven the gunners from the batteries on the crest of the position. The point where the 52nd crossed the first line of the Army was occupied by Brunswickers in squares, front ranks kneeling. These were described by Mercer in his memoirs as very frightened young country boys, 'straight from the plough'. The Brigade formed squares to relieve and take the place of the Brunswick light battalions which had been repeatedly charged by cavalry and cut to pieces by showers of cannon shot. The ground was strewn with their mangled remains. All around was the wreckage of the long line of British guns, silenced by the crushing weight of French shot, the gunners either dead by their guns or gone to seek shelter in the squares.

As the 2/95th crossed the summit of the rise, being nearest it was being shot at by skirmishers from the direction of la Haie Sainte. The 71st took up a position in square joined by companies of the 3/95th near to the easternmost hedge of Hougoumont, about 400 yards to the south. They were in this position only a short time before two guns on rising ground opposite opened fire, causing some losses to those nearest Hougoumont, with the 71st and 3/95th sustaining the heaviest casualties. The other extremity of Adam's brigade was the 2/95th which came under continuous fire from French skirmishers who boldly pushed out of la Haie Sainte almost to the summit of the British position.

Adam's Brigade remained in this position and, because of the constant threat of cavalry, stayed formed in square for about an hour. Because of its size the 52nd formed into two separate squares from the two wings while the 71st formed square 200 yards to its right. Colonel Nicolay of the Staff Corps and several other officers ran into the squares of the 52nd. Very soon there were charges by a large body of cuirassiers who came along the east side of Hougoumont. The right and front faces of the squares of the 52nd opened fire obliquely on the cuirassiers who charged the square of the 71st and 3/95th but were repelled easily.

The Brigade, especially the flank battalions, suffered casualties from a heavy French cannonade during the intervals between the cavalry charges. The 71st and 2/95th suffered heavily, the 52nd but little.

About 6.30 Colonel Hervey, ADC to the Duke of Wellington, dashed up with an order directing the Brigade to retire up the hill. No sooner had Colborne received this order than there came a great noise and clamour from the direction of Hougoumont, as Nassau infantry came running out of the wood as if in flight. It appeared that the château had succumbed and would be abandoned with the flank of the Brigade dangerously exposed. Colborne had the 52nd form columns from squares and wheeled into two lines, the right sub-divisions forming one line and the left sub-division forming the other. With this formation completed they faced about and retired in two lines through the silent British guns.

As they were ascending the rise, a colonel of cuirassiers galloped out of the ranks of the French cavalry, repeatedly halloaing, 'Vive le Roi, vive le Roi'. He made straight for Colonel Colborne, presented himself and said 'Ce coquin Napoleon est la avecles Gardes. Voila l'attaque qui se fait' as he pointed towards la Belle Alliance, at the mass of the Imperial Guard in battalion order squares.

Those on the Allied line could catch, imperceptibly at first, the faint strains of martial music. It was the grenadier band of the Imperial Guard playing 'Let us Watch Over the Empire', and then Gebauer's 'La Marche des Bonnets a Poil'. Mounted in front of the fur-bonneted ranks was the Emperor Napoleon leading a ceremonial advance of the Middle Guard battalions, their eagles held aloft and their drummers beating frantically the call to battle. There were shouts of 'The Guard is going into battle'.

The Imperial Guard – 'The Immortals'

Throughout the day the Imperial Guard, following Napoleon's usual practice had been held back as a final reserve, his ultimate weapon, the last shot in his locker. Their presence in the background, waiting, gave the rest of the army assurance and resolve. The French troops knew that, if desperate measures were called for, the Imperial Guard would be supreme.

But time was against the Emperor. Since 11.20 that morning he had been unable to break the Allied line. The Prussians were now about to burst onto the field and there were only a few hours of good daylight left. It was time for one final decisive blow to crush Wellington's front, face about and crush the Prussians, then on to Brussels. To the French, the Allied line from its centre to the Genappe road appeared to be sparsely covered with infantry. There were gaps, broken guns and signs of decimation. This seemed the weakest sector, the obvious place to attack.

The *grognards* no longer had reasons to grumble. The Young Guard, the élite light infantry consisting of *voltigeur* regiments were, with great effort and loss, holding the Prussian advance guard of Pomeranians and Westphalian Landswehr at Plançenoit. For Napoleon it was the crisis point and he made the decision to order in his final reserve. If the Imperial Guard failed there were no further reserves.

He gave his Middle and Old Guard the task of making the decisive attack, the crushing blow that would win for France the battle, the glory and the final victory. In command of *la Garde Imperiale* was the Deputy Chief of Staff, Lieutenant General Comte Drouet. That evening he issued orders for the *Formation en Ordre de bataille* which stated that the Guard would be drawn up in battalion squares 500 paces from each other on both sides of the Brussels road, between la Belle Alliance and the maison de Coster.

General Petit was commander of the 1st Grenadiers and, according to a document of his that survives, the disposition of the Guards' battalions for the attack seems to agree with almost all other eyewitness accounts, whether French, British or Allied. The general's plan shows that the great column of attack was formed of the 1/3rd Grenadiers and the 4th Grenadiers, the 4th Chasseurs in squares in echelon but in close contact at the beginning of the advance. As they were now in order of column it marched parallel to the Charleroi road until it passed la Haie Sainte. It then changed direction diagonally to its left. Apparently it was not obeying an order but was following the natural tendency of the ground.

Meanwhile the 2/3rd Grenadiers, commanded by Belcourt, stayed in square in front of the road, about half way between la Haie Sainte and la Belle Alliance, which was Napoleon's vantage point. It was here that Colborne saw Napoleon pacing backwards and forwards in front of the 2/2nd Regiment of Grenadiers.

It was this group that the 52nd and the 71st would eventually come up against after they crossed the French line.

When the Light Brigade had formed behind the crest the Duke passed unattended across their front from left to right and, shortly after, returned to beyond their left, which was much more thrown back from the summit. The Duke was making a personal and rapid assessment of his front line before the expected attack. Few troops were visible, due to Wellington's policy of preserving his forces and not letting them suffer from being unnecessarily exposed. In this instance he gave Maitland orders to get his Guards' battalions to lie prone behind the ridge, taking cover from the increasingly heavy bombardment. Wellington then ordered those on the right, the Brunswickers, Adam's Light Brigade to form in line in four ranks, Sir John Colborne thought such a formation with intervals between the files inexpedient and did not comply with the order. He later formed the 52nd into two squares and, as the safest way of complying with the order, placed the left wing of the regiment in the rear of the right wing, closed up.

The Duke's aim was to meet the French with a wall of concentrated volley fire. The four ranks formation was a strong one and good enough to repel cavalry, but not from the flanks. This was only a safeguard as the French cavalry at this stage were 'blown' – a spent force. Those troops and guns that were still operational were given orders to load with canister and some to double load when the French closed and when targets presented themselves. The Duke had covered the right of his front and took up a position near Maitland, all the time watching the advance of the Imperial Guard and the direction they were taking.

Sir John Colborne looked out across the fields towards la Belle Alliance and observed the dense mass of the Guards moving rapidly towards the centre of the Allied position. It was now well past 7pm. And the sun, sometimes obscured by the billowing clouds of gunsmoke, was beginning to set. Colborne took a closer look through his glass and said he saw Napoleon for the first and only time in his life. The Emperor was wearing his grey greatcoat and walking backwards and forwards in front of his position with his hands held behind his back, as the Imperial Guard advanced. Later, when the Guards were repulsed, Napoleon, his generals and aides took cover in the square of the 2/3rd Grenadiers. The artillery of both sides was thundering almost continuously with roaring cannonades.

The first six battalions, about 3,000 men in battalion squares in columns, were the regiments of the Middle Guard, the 3rd and 4th Chasseurs and the 3rd and 4th Grenadiers. Baron Duchard's horse artillery had placed a two-gun team between each battalion. Behind the Middle Guard were about 1,500 men of the Old Guard and behind them came the 2nd Battalions of the 1st and

2nd Chasseurs and the 2nd Grenadiers. At the head of their units rode General Cambronne, adjutant of the 1st Chasseurs, General Roguet, second in command of the Grenadiers, and General Christiani, adjutant of the 2nd Grenadiers.

Trumpets sounded the advance, the Guard marched on, drums beating the frantic drub, drub drubbing of the *pas de charge*. The rhythm of their march was broken by the debris and ravages of battle, the dead, the dying, the broken guns and caissons and the carnage. The smoke thickened, obscuring what lay ahead.

As the Guard neared the rise the Grand Battery fell silent for fear of hitting their own troops. Shouts of 'Vive l'Empereur!' were heard but were soon drowned out as the Allied artillery of nearly fifty guns opened up with a fierce bombardment of shot and shell, soon to change to canister, double-charged for deadly close range destruction.

The dense battalion columns of the Guards were in full march on the plateau of la Haie Sainte and the flank of the columns seemed to form a right angle to the 52nd. Sir John Colborne said to his adjutant, Lieutenant Winterbottom, 'We must bring the regiment up on the flank.' Winterbottom replied, 'We cannot do it, we cannot wheel the regiment.' Colborne's response was, 'Wheel the left company and the others will conform to it.'

At this point the Duke sent Colonel Percy to the 52nd, but as he arrived they were already in motion, with their right flank totally unprotected, moving off in two lines, covered by skirmishers commanded by Lieutenants Anderson and Campbell. It is not certain if the 95th kept up with the 52nd.

The instant the French columns received the fire of the skirmishers they halted. They could see that behind the 52nd the 71st was moving up in support, followed by the whole of Clinton's Division.

The Imperial Guard were now aware that their left flank and their rear were being menaced by a mass of troops. At first they were in some confusion, but then the left companies of the column faced left and began to return a heavy fire on the 52nd. Both Anderson and Campbell were wounded as were many of the men. The right of the battalion also suffered severely, but the 52nd continued on about 300 yards in front of Maitland's Guards and those of Byng's Guards who were not at Hougoumont. Lord Hill, who was observing near Maitland, saw the 52nd move off and noted that the Brigade of Guards were standing like a regiment on parade, but not firing. It is thought that many were out of ammunition by then. The 52nd moved on to within a short distance of the rising ground where it appeared that the Imperial Guard would make a stand.

Colborne, true to the training of light infantry, and in anticipation of an expected order from Wellington, seized the opportunity and acted on his own assessment. He ordered his left-hand company to wheel to the left and formed the rest of the battalion on that one company. Colonel Charles Rowan assisted in the completion of this move.

7.15pm – The Coup de Main

Colonel Colborne had moved the 52nd to place it parallel with the advancing columns of the Guards. As the Imperial Guard advanced they threw out a cloud of skirmishers and, to combat this, Colborne requested the officer commanding two companies of the 95th (no battalion is cited, but it is assumed to be the 3rd) to deploy in front to skirmish. The officer is said to have refused (no explanation is given in Colborne's notes) and so Colborne quickly sent out the right companies of the 52nd. As Colborne recalled he ordered 'a strong company to extend in our front'.

When Major General Sir Frederick Adam rode up to ask Colborne what he was going to do, the latter said that he was going to make the columns feel the 52nd's fire. Adam ordered Colborne to move on and the 71st to follow, and then he rode away wounded. The Light Brigade was left without its commander. Adam recalled in his letter to Siborne that 'it was not judged expedient to receive this attack, but to move forward the Brigade and assail the enemy instead of waiting to be assailed, and orders to that effect were given'. In other words, he had little choice but to let Colborne get on with it.

By this time the 52nd's line was almost parallel to the flank of the Imperial Guard columns. Colborne ordered the extended company of about 100 men, under the command of Lieutenants Anderson and Campbell, to advance as quickly as possible with only battalion support, and fire into the French columns at any distance. The 52nd was formed in two lines of half companies (platoons), the rear line at ten paces distance from the first. After giving three rousing huzzas, they followed the skirmish company, passed along the front of the Brigade of Guards in line and about 500 yards in front of them, almost forming an obtuse angle with them.

Colborne saw that the skirmish attack on the column had caused it to halt and form into line. Facing the 52nd it opened up with a sharp fire on the skirmishers and the advancing battalion. The 2/95th on the left and in the rear of the 52nd had so far not fired, and the 71st and 3/95th were about 150 yards behind on the right and advancing rapidly. Colborne also noticed that Sir Harry Clinton's division was beginning to advance. Colborne stated that he had no doubt that the prompt action of the 52nd and the following general attack by Adam's Brigade and Clinton's division created the first check, and caused the Imperial Guard to halt in its advance.

The 52nd suffered severely from the fire of the Guard, especially the losses suffered by the skirmishers. The right wing lost nearly 150 men during the advance. Ensign Nettles of the colour party was killed just before the advance.

Whilst the left flank of the columns was being attacked by the 52nd and the rest of the Light Brigade, the head of the column or, as some thought, the skirmishers, was feeling the full frontal volleys of the Brigade of Guards who, with the Duke of Wellington's famous command, 'Now Maitland! Now is your time', had risen in four ranks like a wall of scarlet from behind the ridge to the complete surprise of the Imperial Guards.

Wellington unable to resist the opportunity, gave the order 'Make ready! Present! Fire!' The 3rd and 4th Chasseurs, advancing with their generals now on foot, were met at about thirty paces with a resounding volley which instantly killed Lieutenant General Michel of the Chasseurs, Cardinal, Auglet, a further twenty officers and over 400 men. The Guards charged forward and pushed the Chasseurs back on the column behind. The 4th and 2/3rd Chasseurs rallied and returned a devastating fusillade which checked the Guards' charge. They had advanced too soon and were driven back.

The attack by the Middle Guard, intended to be a crushing thrust through Wellington's centre, had faltered. After twenty minutes, sixty officers and 1,200 men had fallen. They paused, stunned by the ferocity of the fire. Hesitant, they began to retreat.

Attempting to change formation in their ascent towards the Allied line, the Imperial Guard columns had become two columns, with a smaller column of about two battalions, probably the 1/3rd Grenadiers and 4th Grenadiers, moving on farther to the east and nearer the Genappe road. This force of about 1,000 men also had the close support of the line infantry of d'Erlon's Corps. They had some success on their right flank against weaker and depleted Allied units. Wellington, aware of the crisis, galloped over to issue direct orders to rally units, especially the Brunswickers who might have crumbled but for Wellington.

At this critical point, Lieutenant General Chasse brought forward six battalions of his Dutch-Belgian Division with fixed bayonets to stiffen the line. He also ordered van der Smissen, in command of Chasse's artillery, to launch the horse artillery into the flanks of the Imperial Guards' columns.

The Dutch-Belgian horse artillery, under the command of captain Krahmer de Binche, galloped furiously in and launched a deadly blast of canister at less than a hundred yards, crippling the flanks of the 1/3rd Grenadiers.

'La Garde Recule!'

The head of the columns was suffering the combined effect of continuous withering fire from all sides, the 52nd and Light Brigade on the left, the Guards Brigade to their immediate front, the rest of the Allied front line and General Chasse's Dutch-Belgian force on their right flank. Halket's Hanoverians were also attacking them in the rear. They were expecting to meet resistance, but not from all quarters. They had marched into the teeth of hell. They paused, stunned by the ferocity of the fire. The vehemence of the repulse was completely unexpected. The ranks contracted. The gaps were too great, too many. Morale drained away.

They began to retreat. Three battalions of the Old Guard attempted to cover the retreat but were engulfed in what was beginning to turn into a rout. The advance of the 52nd with the 71st continued as the Imperial Guard fell back, stunned, incredulous and humiliated.

At this moment, to Colborne's surprise, there were shouts of 'Cavalry', as several squadrons of light dragoons suddenly appeared directly to their front, coming on at a fast gallop. As the cavalry rapidly approached, the two companies on the left halted and fired a volley into them, assuming they were French. The three adjoining companies wheeled back to form square. Colborne recognized the light dragoons to be the 23rd and called out to the adjutant to stop the fire and allow the dragoons to pass between the ranks. Even as the troops opened intervals in the ranks the men were still taking shots at them as they passed. It was an error of recognition and the only mistake the 52nd had made.

At the same time both Colborne's and Colonel Rowan's horses were wounded and they continued on foot. French gun horses were nearby but there was no time to cut the traces. The incident caused a brief halt which lost the momentum of the advance, but it did allow the 71st to catch up on the 52nd's right. The Duke of Wellington, attended by Sir Colin Campbell, rode to the rear of the left of the line near the two companies which had fired. Colborne said to the Duke, 'It is our own cavalry which caused the firing.' The Duke replied with urgency in his voice, 'Well done Colborne! Well done. Go on, go on! They won't stand. Don't give them time to rally.'

The 52nd continued their advance, up to the beginning of the rising ground. The Imperial Guard were gathered in groups, exuding defiance. The state of the ground had caused some break-up of the ranks of the 52nd, with the two right-hand companies in disorder. Colborne, ever watchful for French cavalry, called out to numbers one and two companies to halt and bring up their companies in line. There was growing excitement in the ranks; their blood was rising, they could sense victory and were anxious to go on. Several officers in front, including Major Churchill and Major Chalmers, were cheering and waving their hats.

The 71st came up and formed on the right of the 52nd and Colborne ordered the buglers to sound the advance. They advanced to no more than fifty paces, halted and opened up with a volley, followed by more volleys at decreasing ranges. Then Colborne ordered the 52nd 'to pass the road', and the whole regiment passed through what had been the Grand Battery's line of guns and caissons, passing eighty guns in ten minutes. The Imperial Guard were retreating in three squares in some order, whilst others broke in great confusion. Some continued to fire. Others in desperation threw away their muskets and packs and started to run, with cries of 'Tout est perdu, sauve qui peut!'

All were eventually swallowed up into the streams of fugitives. Fear had taken hold, fear of retribution, fear of the Prussians, and this rabble that had once been the pride of Napoleon's army, fled fast towards the south and away from the wrath of Marshal Blücher.

Postscript

The final defeat of the Imperial Guard was brought about by the total contribution of efforts by all who had immediate and direct involvement. Principally, these were Adam's Brigade with Colborne's prompt use of the 52nd, Clinton's Division, Maitland's Guards, Lieutenant General Chasse's Division, especially his horse artillery, Halket's 3 Hanoverian Brigade, who fired into the rear columns, other units on the centre-right of the line who played their part and, finally, the Prussians who entered the field on the left of the 52nd, and Bülow's artillery that was beginning to pound the French lines.

In the general confusion and clamour, with all the noise and smoke, everyone's vision was restricted to their immediate fronts, and it would have been impossible for any one person to get a clear overall view. So it became questionable when certain participants, who were not involved, and some who were not even there, such as journalists and politicians, began to single out individual regiments for special mention and very disappointing to those whose bravery was ignored. It was probably convenient to seek brevity in an explanation of the victory. It reduced the number of those who 'fathered the victory'. It was tidier and more heroic even to simplify the tactics and present it as a 'Clash of the Titans' (or élite regiments), the Brigade of Guards against the Imperial Guard.

The Duke of Wellington's despatch of Monday 19 June, did not state how the last attack of Napoleon, his last bid for victory, was defeated. No regiments were given any special mention. It was a simple statement written in haste by an exhausted man, probably with a mixture of relief and sadness as his friend was dying of his wounds in the next room.

It read simply:

> About seven in the evening ... the enemy made a desperate effort with cavalry and infantry, supported by artillery, to take our left centre, near the farm of la Haie Sainte, which after a severe contest was defeated, and having observed that the troops retired from the attack in great confusion ... I ... advanced the whole line of infantry, supported by cavalry and artillery, the attack succeeded ... the enemy fled.

In response to a question put by Captain William Crawley Yonge, Colborne's reply was, 'To those who claim for the Guards the credit of repelling this column of attack, we might say as Prince Hal to Falstaff, "Mark how plain a tale shall put you down"'.

The question is, what caused the Middle Guard to fall back with shouts of 'tout est perdu, sauve qui peut'? The Imperial Guard, the 'Immortals', in retreat acted like a bushfire that spread throughout the whole French Army of the North, a panic that turned into a rout. Was there a *coup de grace* and who delivered it? Perhaps the myth was established in the House of Lords on 23 June, five days after the battle, when Earl Bathurst, Secretary of State for War, read the statement:

> Towards the close of day Bonaparte himself, at the head of his Guards, made a desperate charge on the British Guards and the British Guards immediately overthrew the French.

Lord Bathurst must have been briefed by Wellington as individual regiments were not mentioned in Wellington's despatch. Is this a case of Wellington rewriting history with an eye to posterity?

Whatever were Wellington's reasons what is really at stake is the seeming slight to the reputation of Sir John Colborne and the honour of the 52nd Regiment. Both still need to be written in the book; for reasons known to Wellington both were overlooked when later honours were showered in other directions.

The Manoeuvres of General Howe as practised in 1774 at his light infantry camp at Salisbury

(Extracted from Williamson's *Elements of Military Arrangement*)

GENERAL HOWE'S MANOEUVRES FOR THE LIGHT INFANTRY
These manoeuvres are principally calculated for a close or woody country. They are all done from the centre, and the two centre files of battalion, grand, and sub-divisions must be told off for the purpose. They are comprehended in the following table.

From the centre of
{ Battalion
Grand divisions
Sub-divisions
{ To the front
To the rear
To the right
To the left

The different formings are
{ To the front
To the front and right
To the front and left

Wings and platoons might be added in the table, and the same movements might take place from them; but as the above will answer all the purposes that can be intended, to add any more will only serve to increase the trouble and confusion in the telling off. These movements are nothing more than double Indian files from the centre of the battalion or one file from the left of the right wing. When the whole battalion has filed off, the right wing is in one file, and the left wing in the other.

No. 1 BATTALION! FROM THE CENTRE TO THE RIGHT – MARCH
The two centre files march out, and all the others face inward and march to the centre; as soon as they come on the ground on which the centre files stood, each file on the right of the centre turns to the right, and each file on the left of the centre to the left, and march out to the front abreast, covering the two centre files of battalion.

TO THE FRONT, FORM BATTALION

The left centre file stands fast; all the others run up in charging time, and form on the right and form on the right and left of them, dressing by the centre.

No. 2 BATTALION! FROM THE CENTRE TO THE RIGHT – MARCH

The two centre files lead out, and wheel to the right; the others follow the centre files as before, and wheel where they did.

TO THE FRONT, AND TO THE RIGHT, FORM BATTALION

The left centre file stands fast, and the whole left wing runs up by files, and forms on the left of it. The right centre file faces to the right, and the whole right wing runs up by file, and forms on the right of it.

No. 3 BATTALION! FROM THE CENTRE TO THE LEFT – MARCH

The two centre files lead out as before, and, when clear of the front rank of battalion, wheel to the left. The wings file off, as above directed.

TO THE FRONT, AND TO THE LEFT, FORM BATTALION

The right centre file stands fast, and the right wing forms on the right of it, running up by files. The left centre file faces to the left, and the remaining files of the left wing run up, and form on the left of it.

No. 4 BATTALION! FROM THE CENTRE TO THE REAR – MARCH

The centre files go to the right about, and march out to the rear. The wings file off as before and follow them.

TO THE REAR – FORM BATTALION

The battalion is formed as in No. 1

This manoeuvre should seldom or never be practised; not only on account of the danger in forming the battalion with its rear to the enemy, in which situation it is well known by experience that a few shots will discourage men more than a much heavier fire in front, but likewise on account of the length of time required for the whole battalion to file off. As was before observed of columns in retreating, a battalion should file off from the flanks, and the less the columns are, the sooner the manoeuvre be completed; therefore in retiring before an enemy, it should be from right or left of sub-divisions.

When the battalion is to change its front to right or left, it is best done by sub-divisions.

No. 5 SUB-DIVISIONS! FROM THE CENTRE TO THE RIGHT TO THE RIGHT – MARCH

The two centre files of each sub-division lead out, and wheel to the right, and each sub-division acts in the same manner as was described in No. 2 for the whole battalion.

FORM BATTALION

The centre files of the right sub-division halt, and the other files run up and form to the right and left of them. All the other sub-divisions march obliquely to the left, and when the leading files are arrived upon the ground the officers commanding sub-divisions order their respective divisions to form, and dress by the right.

No. 6 SUB-DIVISIONS! FROM THE CENTRE TO THE LEFT – MARCH

This is done in like manner with the above, when the battalion is to change its front to the left.

When a double front is to be formed, it is indifferent whether the movement be made from the centre of the grand or sub-divisions, or from the centre of the battalion. It should be remembered that when the battalion forms to the front and right, the left wing forms to the front, and the right wing to the right; if to the front and left, the right wing forms to the front, and the left wing to the left. That wing which is to form to the flank will be always the first formed, as the rear files of it will have the least ground to go over.

Thus we have taken a view of nearly all the manocuvres now practised by the regiments of infantry; the greater part of which, it must be confessed, are more curious than useful, more calculated to please the eye on the parade ground, than to answer any good purpose in action. Very few manoeuvres will suffice for a battalion, if their utility upon service be the only object considered, and those few judiciously chosen and well performed will do a regiment more credit, even on the parade, than twice the number here collected slatterned over in an imperfect manner. Yet numerous as the particular movements are, if we consider them attentively, we shall find that the general intentions are but few, and that practising a variety of manoeuvres is nothing more than employing a number of different means in order to attain the same end. For the different kinds or species of manoeuvres may be reduced to the following heads:

1 – Moving in file
2 – Moving in column.
3 – Changing front.
4 – Changing order or disposition.
5 – Forming square and oblong.

In treating of the manoeuvres we have insisted the more, as they depend more on principles than any other part of the exercise; and further, as it is incumbent on every officer to study the theory before he attempts to enter upon the practice of them.

The former may be acquired to a tolerable degree in the closet; the latter is to be acquired only in the field.

No rules have been laid down for the time or step with which the different movements are to be made; but none certainly should be done slower than with the common quick step; some, and particularly in forming, should be conducted in charging time. When a battalion, being already in motion, is to perform any manoeuvre, the word March should not be given, unless when meant as an order to take up a quicker step. Thus, if a battalion marching forward in slow time is to retire in quick time from the right of sub-divisions, the word of command may be given.

SUB-DIVISIONS FROM THE RIGHT RETREAT BY FILES – MARCH

On which they march out to the rear with the quick step. Many of the manoeuvres are useful only in particular circumstances of ground and position. Therefore, when regiments are taken out to exercise, it should be confined, as is but frequently the case, to plains and level country; but the scene should be varied to every situation in which they will learn the application as well as the practice of the manoeuvres, and will discern the occasions on which they may be found useful.

Appendix 2

Extracts From *Regulations for the Exercise of Riflemen and Light Infantry and Instructions for Their Conduct in the Field*

Written by Lieutenant Colonel Baron de Rottenburg, Commanding Officer of the Fifth Battalion of the Royal American Regiment

HORSE GUARDS
1 August, 1798

The original of the following work, written by a German officer of distinction, and much military experience, has been perused by His Royal Highness the Commander-in-Chief, and found to contain many excellent rules and observations, adapted to the usual modes of carrying on active service in the field, and much useful instruction to young officers, not familiarized by practice to the arduous duties to be performed in the face of an enterprising enemy: His Royal Highness has therefore been pleased to give directions for it being translated into English, in order that the officers of the army at large, and particularly those who may not have had the advantage of much personal experience in the field, may, by studious attention to the various examples therein stated, and to the useful lessons given for their conduct, imbibe that degree of military skill and information, which will enable them to discharge their duty to the satisfaction of their superiors, and their own honour, on the most trying occasions.

WILLIAM FAWCET
Adjutant General

PART TWO
Of the Service of Light Troops in the Field

During the campaign, light troops are usually cantoned in villages, and are not provided with camp equipage. They may, however, be occasionally required to occupy ground on the flank of a corps in the line of encampment; the men must, in that case, construct huts of earth, or boughs of trees, and will perform all the camp duties, and in every respect comply with the regulations laid down for the discipline of regular infantry.

CHAPTER 1
Of Patroles in General

1. Supposing a patrole to consist of a serjeant and twelve men, the serjeant detaches two men and a corporal in front, and two on each flank, the latter extending themselves to the right and left as far as possible, without losing sight of the main body; but the distance of these skirmishers, both in front and on either flank, must be regulated by local circumstances; in an open and plain country, they may venture to extend themselves further from the main body than in one that is enclosed or hilly. On coming to an enclosure, one man advances into it and examines it closely; the other, remaining behind, keeps upon watch, and takes care to be always ready to support his comrade, in case of his being attacked.

2. On coming to a hill, one man will ascend; the other, remaining at the bottom, will be given to understand, by a signal concerted between them, whether the enemy occupy any of it or not. If an enemy is discovered, both the skirmishers must conceal themselves, and having ascertained as nearly as possible the strength of the enemy, one must endeavour to join the patrole, to give the intelligence; upon which the patrole should retire and, if possible, throw itself into an ambuscade, to observe the enemy's motions. When a flanker sees a detachment of the enemy advancing immediately upon the patrole, and that he is not able *by any other means* to give the alarm of their approach, he must fire, which will be the signal for all the flankers to join the main body, or the signal will be given for assembly, and the patrole with united force will attack the enemy if equal to him in numbers, or will secure its retreat by a firm resistance, if the superior strength of the enemy makes it imprudent to risk an attack.

3. When a patrole marches through enclosed country, or one much inter-sected by hedges, the flankers must be sent on each side of them, in order to examine them thoroughly; in doing which, they must always keep as near as possible in a line with the main body, and resume their proper stations, as soon as they have passed any obstacle which may have drawn them out of their direction. It may sometimes be necessary for flankers to get to the top of trees, for the purpose of reconnoitring, and on no account must they leave any high ground behind them, without first viewing the environs from it.

4. In marching over an open country, and where subjects are seen at a great distance, it will not be necessary to send out skirmishers on the flanks, unless an house or an enclosure is perceived at a distance; in which case they must be detached to examine it thoroughly. By night, or hazy weather, flankers are in all situations indispensably necessary, and must be particularly careful to regulate their movement by that of the main body.

5. Great precaution is requisite when a patrole is under the necessity of passing an hollow way in order to guard against a surprise or being cut off. To avoid this, the patrole should be divided into files, which will follow each other at such a distance that each may able to perceive the two men in front, and the whole patrole will be alarmed, either by their comrades in front being attacked, or by their fire upon the enemy. If there should be turnings or windings in the hollow way, which prevent those in the rear from seeing the file in front of them, the latter must give notice of the presence of an enemy by firing a shot.

6. When a wood presents itself in front of the march, through which the patrole must pass, the flank skirmishers are sent to the skirts of it; they must, however, keep so much within the wood as not to be perceived from without; the main body marches directly through, but if possible by some other road than that which is commonly used. For the security of the patrole when it is a strong one, detachments should be left at the entrance to the wood, to sustain the main body in its march through, and to give the alarm in case of the approach of an enemy. If the wood is of great extent small patroles should be sent in front and on the flanks of the main body; and small intermediate patroles must be sent out, keeping at a distance of 400 or 500 yards from those in front of them, whose object will be to examine all cross roads, there being little apprehension for the safety of the detachments, supposing even the enemy to be in ambuscade in the wood. Three men would be sufficient for these patroles, two of which will advance in line, and keep within sight of each other; the third following them both in view: by this means, should the most advanced patrole be carried off by the enemy, the second and following ones would escape, and the main body would have timely notice of the danger. In returning the patrole should take a different route from that by which it advanced, for the better chance of discovering the enemy; indeed, it must be considered as general rule that no patrole should return by the way it came; nor in case of being attacked, and obliged to retreat, should it ever fall back in a direct line upon the main body. Bye roads always to be preferred to the main route, either in returning from the patroles or in retreating before an enemy; in patroling through a wood, care should be taken not to venture too far, and that the skirmishers

are not at too great a distance from each other, for fear of hazy weather, or the approach of night.

7. Before a patrole ventures into a defile, the two men advanced in front must examine it well, and at the same time flankers must reconnoitre on the right and left of it, where it is probable the enemy lie in ambuscade. In returning, a patrole should if possible avoid a defile it has before passed. When the defile has been passed, a few men may be left at the extremity of it, to give the alarm by a shot, in case a detachment of the enemy should attempt to cut off the patrole; these men will eventually disconcert the enemy's plans, who may naturally conceive them to be the head of a detachment passing the defile, as a support to the patrole.

8. When a patrole is to reconnoitre a village, the directions that have already been given for its conduct during the march must be strictly adhered to. Whether the patrole is a strong one or not, it must halt at a few hundred paces from the village, assemble all the skirmishers, and lie concealed; a few men must then be sent towards the village, and must endeavour to seize one of its inhabitants, and conduct him to the officer commanding the patrole, in order that he may be examined respecting the presence of the enemy. If upon diligent inquiry it is found that the enemy are in the village, the patrole must make its retreat; the deposition of one person should not however be depended upon; the men who have been sent in the village must endeavour if possible, to take another person, who must be separately examined, to see whether his report coincides with the former one. If after all inquiry it appears that the enemy are not in the village, some men must be sent into it, and small parties to the right and left to examine its environs, and all the avenues must at the same time be occupied. The men who were sent into the village must immediately repair to the mayor or chief magistrate of the place, and make him accompany them to search all the houses, stables, barns and all other places where the enemy might be concealed.

If they find all safe, the men must return to the main body, and make their report.

After this, should the commander of the patrole wish still to be himself convinced of the truth of the report, he may go in person into the village, accompanied by a few men, for prudence would suggest the impropriety of taking the whole patrole, as, notwithstanding the former search, it is still possible the enemy may be in ambuscade, and only watching the opportunity of the whole detachment being in the village, to attack it to advantage. When a non-commissioned officer commands a patrole, before he leaves the village he has been directed to examine, he should require a certificate of his having been there. When a patrole is to reconnoitre a village by night, the whole must assemble at some distance in front of it, as in patrolling by day, and the environs must be examined; but the men who are sent into the village must, in this instance, be directed to creep gently along the fronts of the houses, and particularly along the front of public houses, looking at the same time in at the windows, and endeavouring to distinguish whether any of the enemy are within. Should this be found impracticable, they must conceal themselves, and wait the opportunity of some inhabitant passing, whom it will be their object to carry off to the commanding officer of the patrole with as little noise as possible, and without raising any alarm. If it should appear to be certain, from the report that the prisoner makes, and from other intelligence, that the enemy are not in the village, the same directions must be followed as have been already laid down for the day patrole; but should the enemy be in the village, the patrole must retire; an attempt should be made to carry off one of his vedettes, in order to gain more certain accounts. Whatever has been said with respect to villages, is applicable also to any place or town.

9. When skirmishers give notice of the approach of the enemy, the patrole should endeavour to conceal itself, the object of a patrole being to reconnoitre a country, and to get intelligence of the enemy, their movements &c; all engagement should be avoided, and, unless absolutely compelled to fight, a patrole should always endeavour to get away undiscovered. If a patrole allows itself to be unnecessarily drawn into affair with one of the enemy's, it must have an equal risk of being captured, and the service it was to have performed remains unaccomplished, so that the army of detachment, from whence the patroles were sent out, may wait in vain for the intelligence that was expected from it. If a patrole should be unavoidably engaged in an affair, the officer commanding it will send immediate notice by two trusty men to the corps from which he was detached, and at the same time a written report of whatever information he may have been able to obtain, which he should always have ready in case of such an event. When a patrole is to be sent out, every sort of instruction for its conduct during the march should be communicated to the men. The greatest attention in the officer commanding a patrole will be requisite to watch the conduct of his men; they must be attentive, obedient, and vigilant, from the moment of their departure till their return; and, under pain of the severest punishment, they must be forbidden to go into any public-house during the march; they should therefore be supplied with their complete ration of provisions. A patrole should always endeavour to conceal its march; therefore woods and enclosures are to be preferred in its progress through a country. Bridges should be avoided, for fear of ambuscade or of being cut off. If, however, a bridge must of necessity be passed, a few men should be posted at it, to give the alarm to the patrole on the approach of the enemy. In this case it will be advertised of

the danger by a shot; by which means it may gain time to re-pass the bridge, and at least avoid being cut off. Should everything remain quiet, at the expiration of a certain time, previously determined, the men who were left at the bridge will follow, and join the patrole.

If the patrole is forced to pass places, where, notwithstanding every precaution, there is still a probability of being cut off, small posts should be left at such places, or the patrole should be divided into a number of small detachments, advance by different routes, and some place should be appointed for a rendezvous of the whole. When a patrole finds itself *unexpectedly* in presence of an enemy, if of equal force it should attack; but should the enemy's numbers be very superior, and there remain a possibility of getting away undiscovered, the patrole must disperse, and each man save himself as he can. In such a case, and when, in apprehension of danger, the patrole is advancing in small detachments, one in front of the other, as soon as those in the rear are made aware of the enemy being so superior, they must immediately retreat, without waiting for the detachments in their front. It is the duty of a commanding officer of a patrole to point out to each man all the dangers to be expected, the manner in which he is to conduct himself in retiring singly, the roads that are open to him in such a case, the places at which the patrole may rendezvous, and (should that be impracticable) the position of the detachment or army, to which he must endeavour to make his escape. The above instructions it is absolutely necessary to impress strongly on the minds of the men, in order that each man may know how he is to save himself under the above mentioned events.

As the greatest prejudice may arise from a patrole having committed the most trifling error, and as, on the contrary, the greatest advantage may be derived to an army from the good conduct of one, all the above instructions, and as many more as may be thought useful, should be *explained to the men in the clearest terms* previous to the marching off, and during the march of the patrole.

Appendix 3

Titles of the Regiment

1755   62nd (Royal American) Foot

1757   *Renumbered* 60th (Royal American) Foot

1824   60th (Duke of York's Rifle Corps)

1830   60th or The King's Royal Rifle Corps

1881   The King's Royal Rifle Corps (four battalions)

1958   *Redesignated* 2nd Green Jackets (The King's Royal Rifle Corps)

1966   *Redesignated* 2nd Battalion, The Royal Green Jackets (The King's Royal Rifle Corps)

1968   *Redesignated* 2nd Battalion, The Royal Green Jackets

2007   The Royal Green Jackets amalgamated with the Devonshire and Dorset Light Infantry, The Royal Gloucestershire, Wiltshire and Berkshire Light Infantry and The Light Infantry to form The Rifles.

Bibliography

Anderson, Fred, *Crucible of War*, (Alfred. A. Knopf, New York; Faber and Faber, London.)

Atkinson, C. T., *Foreign Regiments in the British Army 1793–1815* (Cambridge University Press, Cambridge.)

Blackmore, Howard, *British Military Firearms 1650–1850* (Herbert Jenkins, London.)

Baker, Ezekiel, *Remarks on Rifle Guns* (Kessinger Publishing, Montana.)

Bailey, De Witt, *Small Arms of the British in America* (Mowbray Publishers Inc. Lincoln, Rhode Island.)

Beamish North, Ludlow, *History of the King's German Legion Vol. II* (Naval and Military Press, Uckfield.)

Bryant, Arthur, *Jackets of Green* (William Collins, Sons and Co. Ltd, Glasgow.)

Berleth, Richard, *Bloody Mowhawk* (Blackdome Press Corp, New York.)

Caldwell, and Cooper, *Rifles at Waterloo* (Bugle Horn Publications, Leicester.)

Chandler, David, *On the Napoleonic Wars* (Greenhill Books, London.)

——, *Waterloo – The Hundred Days* (Osprey Publishing, Oxford.)

Cope, William Henry, *The History of the Rifle Brigade, The Prince Consort's Own: Formerly the 95th* (New York, General Books Publications.)

Craufurd, A. H., *Craufurd and His Light Division* (Ken Trotman, Cambridge.)

Chartrand, Rene, *Fuentes de Onoro 1811: Wellington's Liberation of Portugal (Campaign)* (Osprey Publishing, Oxford.)

Cooke, John H., *With the Light Division: The Experiences of an Officer of the 43rd Light Infantry in the Peninsula and South of France During the Napoleonic Wars* (Leonaur Limited.)

Crocker, Thomas E., *Braddock's March* (Westholme, Pennsylvania.)

Day, Roger, *The Life of Sir John Moore: Not a Drum Was Heard* (Pen & Sword Books Ltd, Barnsley.)

Dobbs, Captain, *Recollections of an Old 52nd Man* (Spellmount, Tunbridge Wells.)

Darlington, Mary C. (ed), *History of Colonel Henri Bouquet* (Ayer Co. Publishers Inc., Salem.)

Fuller, Colonel J. F. C., *Sir John Moore's System of Training* (Hutchinson, London.)

——, *British Light Infantry in the Eighteenth Century*, (Hutchinson, London.)

Fletcher, Ian, *Craufurd's Light Division* (Spellmount, Tunbridge Wells.)

Foy, General Maximilien, *History of the War in the Peninsular, Under Napoleon* (Nabu Press, Charlston.)

Guy, A. J., *The Road to Waterloo 1793–1815* (National Army Museum, London.)

Gates, David, *The British Light Infantry Arm 1790–1815* (Batsford Ltd, London.)

Goodhart, Philip, *The Royal Americans* (Wilton 65, Windsor.)

Gould, Robert, *Mercenaries in the Napoleonic Wars* (Tom Donovan Publishing, London.)

Glover Michael, *The Peninsular War 1807–1814* (Penguin, London.)

Green, William, *When Duty Calls Me: Experiences of William Green of Lutterworth in the Napoleonic Wars* (Synjon Books, West Wickham.)

Gibbes-Rigaud, Maj Gen, *Celer et Audax History of the 5th Battalion 60th Regiment* (Ken Trotman, Cambridge.)

——, *History of the King's Royal Rifle Corps Vol. II*, (Gale and Polden, Aldershot.)

Haythornthwaite, Philip, *Napoleonic Imperial Guardsman* (Osprey Publishing, Oxford.)

——, *The Armies of Wellington* (Arms & Armour, London.)

——, *Napoleonic Source Book* (Weidenfeld & Nicolson, London.)

Howard, Donald D., *Napoleon and Iberia – The twin Sieges of Ciudad Rodrigo and Almeida 1810* (Greenhill Books, London.)

Hibbert, Christopher, *A Soldier of the 71st* (Windrush Press, Oxford.)

Hamilton-Williams, David, *Waterloo – New Perspectives* (Caxton Editions, London.)

Hathaway, Eileen, *A True Soldier Gentleman – Memoirs of Lt Cooke, 43rd Regiment 1791–1813* (Shinglepicker Publications, Swanage.)

Kincaid, John, *Random Shots of a Rifleman* (Spellmount, Staplehurst.)

Lachouque, Henri, *The Anatomy of Glory: Napoleon and His Guard* (Greenhill Books, London.)

——, *Waterloo* (Arms and Armour, London.)

Leeke, William, *The History of Lord Seaton's Regiment: Volume I* (Hatchard and Co., London.)

——, *The History of Lord Seaton's Regiment: Volume II* (Hatchard and Co., London.)

Liddel-Hart, Basil, *The Letters of Private Wheeler* (Cedric Chivers Ltd, Bath.)

Leach, Lt Col J., *Rough Sketches of the life of an Old Soldier* (Ken Trotman, Cambridge.)

Lawson, Cecil, *Uniforms of the British Army* (Kaye & Ward, London.)

Levinge, Sir Richard, A., *Historical Records of the Forty-third Regiment, Monmouthshire Light Division* (W. Clowes and Sons, London.)

Moorsom M., *History of the 52nd Regiment 1755–1816* (Worley, Tyne & Wear.)

Mercer, Cavalie Alexander, *Journal of the Waterloo Campaign 1815* (Da Capo Press, Massachusetts.)

Moore-Smith, George, *The life of Sir John Colborne, Field Marshal Lord Seaton* (John Murray, London.)

Marston, Daniel, *The French-Indian War 1754–1760* (Routledge, London.)

McLynn, Frank, *1759: The Year Britain Became Master of the World* (Jonathan Cape, London.)

Napier, Sir William F., *History of the War in the Peninsula and the South of France* (John Murray & Thomas and William Boone, London.)

Nafziger, George, *Imperial Bayonets Tactics of the Napoleonic Battery, Battalion and Brigade as Found in Contemporary Regulations* (Greenhill, London.)

Nosworthy, Brent, *Battle Tactics of Napoleon and his Enemies* (Constable, London.)

Newbolt, Sir Henry, *The History of the Oxfordshire and Bucks Light Infantry the old 43rd and 52nd Regiments* (Naval and Military Press Ltd, Uckfield.)

Ompteda, Baron, *In the King's German Legion: Memoirs of Baron Ompteda, Colonel in the King's German Legion During the Napoleonic Wars* (Nabu Press, Charlston.)

Oman, Sir Charles (1993) *Wellington's Army 1809–1814* (Greenhill, London.)

——, *A History of the Peninsular War 1807–1809: From the Treaty of Fontainebleau to the Battle of Corunna* (Greenhill, London.)

Page, Julia (ed), *Intelligence Officer in the Peninsula: Letters and Diaries of Major the Hon. Edward Charles Cocks* (Spellmount, Tunbridge Wells.)

Parkman, Francis, *Montcalm and Wolfe: The French and Indian War* (Da Capo Press, New York.)

Reid, Stuart, *Wolfe – The Career of General James Wolfe from Culloden to Quebec* (Sarpedon, New York.)

Siborne, Herbert Taylor, *The Waterloo Letters: Accounts of the Battle by British Officers for Its Foremost Historian* (Greenhill, London.)

Simmons, Maj Gen Verner Willoughby (ed), *A British Rifleman – The Journal and Correspondence of Major George Simmons, Rifle Brigade, during the Peninsular war and the campaign of Waterloo* (Naval and Military Press Ltd, Uckfield.)

Spring, Mathew, *With Zest and Bayonets Only: The British Army on Campaign in North America, 1775–1783* (University of Oklahoma Press, Norman.)

Starkey, Armstrong, *European and Native American Warfare 1675–1815* (University of Oklahoma Press, Norman.)

Stuart, Kenneth, *Defenders of the Frontier: Colonel Henry Bouquet and the Officers and Men of the Royal American Regiment, 1763–1764* (Heritage Books, Maryland.)

Weller, Jac, *Wellington at Waterloo* (Greenhill, London.)

——, *Wellington in the Peninsular* (Greenhill, London.)

Verner, Willoughby, *The History and Campaigns of the Rifle Brigade 1800–1813* (Naval and Military Press Ltd, Uckfield.)

Index